D1174426

Maurice Cranston

Political Dialogues

Maurice Cranston

Political Dialogues

British Broadcasting Corporation

Published by the
British Broadcasting Corporation
35 Marylebone High Street
London W.1

SBN: 563 07428 0

First published 1968

© Maurice Cranston 1968

Printed in Great Britain by Richard Clay
(The Chaucer Press), Ltd., Bungay, Suffolk

Contents

The Broadcasts

A Dialogue on the State was first broadcast in the BBC Third Programme on 19 May 1957. Cast: Savonarola, Carleton Hobbs; Machiavelli, Hugh Burdon.

A Dialogue on Toleration was first broadcast in the BBC Third Programme on 19 October 1953. Cast: John Locke, Felix Aylmer; Lord Shaftesbury, Robert Eddison.

A Dialogue on Progress was first broadcast in the BBC Third Programme on 30 March 1966. Cast: Denis Diderot, Marius Goring; Jean-Jacques Rousseau, Robert Eddison.

A Dialogue on Morality was first broadcast in the BBC Third Programme on 16 September 1967. Cast: Voltaire, Max Adrian; David Hume, Moultrie Kelsall.

A Dialogue on Revolution was first broadcast in the BBC Third Programme on 3 January 1962. Cast: Edmund Burke, Godfrey Quigley; Thomas Paine, Andrew Cruickshank; Mary Wollstonecraft, Margaretta Scott.

A Dialogue on Anarchism was first broadcast in the BBC Third Programme on 3 October 1962. Cast: Marx, Marius Goring; Bakunin, Meier Tzelniker.

A Dialogue on Liberty was first broadcast in the BBC Third Programme on 6 September 1959. Cast: John Stuart Mill, Felix Aylmer; James Fitzjames Stephen, Richard Hurndall.

A Dialogue on Democracy was first broadcast in the BBC Third Programme on 24 February 1961. Cast: Sir Henry Maine, Felix Aylmer; Matthew Arnold, Stephen Murray; John Morley, Allan McClelland.

The production of all the dialogues was by Douglas Cleverdon.

Introduction

The dialogues which appear in this book were all originally written for broadcasting. The wireless, or 'sound radio', lends itself readily to this literary *genre*, for the ear, which tires of hearing a single voice for any length of time, feasts on variety. And when the ear demands a change of sound, the mind demands a change of standpoint; a relay of voices uttering successive parts of a single discourse would be worse than a monologue. What the listener can best appreciate is a conversation, a discussion, a debate, provided the speeches are not too long, or an argument, if it is a measured one and not a battle of passions; a 'battle of wits', perhaps, if the military metaphor is not misleading; at any rate, a dialectical exchange of antithetical opinions and perspectives.

The dialogue is also a form of writing which has been favoured by philosophers. Plato, for example, and Hume and Berkeley exploited the form with notable success. Assuredly these three are not mere technical philosophers, but men of letters, each commanding a distinctive style of his own; and yet the secret of their success may lie in the very nature of the subject. Plato said that philosophy is a kind of dialogue of the soul with itself. And those modern philosophers who see philosophy as the province of 'dialectical reason' can hardly be said to disagree with him. So the dialogue form seems to be a natural manner in which philosophical ideas can be articulated and explored.

However, the various philosophers and ideologists who are brought together in the dialogues which are printed in this book did not choose to present their thoughts in this manner. These dialogues are 'imaginary' ones in the sense that they are constructions for which I, as author, am alone responsible. But these constructions are not mere fabrications. They are built on the real beliefs and words of the men who figure in them. Several are conversations that may well have taken place, in the sense that the participants did really meet and talk about the subjects that they are heard discussing here; but one or two of the dialogues, such as that between Voltaire and David Hume, who corresponded but never actually met, are more purely conjectural.

The materials I have used in preparing these dialogues include the unpublished letters and notebooks as well as the published works of the men concerned. I have drawn on primary sources, especially in the case of Locke and Rousseau, whose manuscripts (Locke's in Oxford and elsewhere, Rousseau's in Neuchâtel and Geneva) I have had occasion to consult in connexion with other researches. The easiest to write was the 'Dialogue on Liberty' between John Stuart Mill and James Fitzjames Stephen, because each of these men compressed his thoughts on freedom into one single book, Stephen's being in large part a direct reply to Mill's. The most difficult to write were the 'Dialogue on Progress' between Diderot and Rousseau, and the 'Dialogue on Morality' between Voltaire and Hume: the thoughts of all these men on the chosen subjects being scattered in many different writings, and often elliptically expressed—particularly in works intended for publication. The letters and notebooks of these, and of others, have helped me to get behind the often veiled and disguised public utterances and a little nearer to the true sentiments of the philosophers concerned.

I think that I have most enjoyed writing those dialogues in which I have been able to exercise, and perhaps exploit, the translator's privilege of rearranging the sequence of another man's words. Although I have tried to reproduce wherever possible the *ipsissima verba* of the English-speaking theorists who take part in these dialogues, I have had, from time to time, to break down long sentences intended for the reader's eye into shorter sentences more readily intelligible to the listener's ear. In the case of Voltaire, Rousseau, Diderot, Machiavelli and Savonarola, I have been able to turn a literary language into a *langue parlée* in the process of translating it. Hence, rearranging their words, I have felt more freedom, and less constraint, than I have in clipping or editing the solemn periods of a John Locke or an Edmund Burke.

The eight dialogues in this book are all on political problems—or, more exactly, on problems in political theory: liberty, progress, toleration, the state, revolution, democracy, morality and civic virtue. These are matters which have been central to theorizing about the state since Plato's time and even earlier: they are the problems which are, so to speak, continuously topical. For the purpose of this book I have arranged the dialogues in a temporal sequence, beginning with the conversation between Savonarola and Machiavelli at the end of the fifteenth century and ending with that between Matthew Arnold and Sir

Henry Maine at the end of the nineteenth century. My own impression, in reading them through, is that the dialogues from the earlier centuries have more vitality and freshness than those from the nineteenth century. I think this is perhaps because ideology began at that stage in our history to trespass more and more into the field of philosophy. Burke, for example, as compared to Hume, emerges as a distinctly ideological type of conservative; while Paine, in a modest way, and Marx, in an ambitious way, are quintessential *idéologues*, seeking to change the world rather than to understand it.

These dialogues have been written over a period of some fifteen years, and during that time I have accumulated a great debt to the BBC producer who was responsible for putting them on the air: Douglas Cleverdon, bibliophile and scholar, who first conceived the idea of the dialogues, and who helped me at every stage of their preparation. I am happy to have this opportunity of expressing my gratitude to him.

M.C.

The London School of Economics, July, 1967

Savonarola and Machiavelli

A dialogue on the State

Girolamo Savonarola and Niccolò Machiavelli were contemporaries in fifteenth-century Florence. When Savonarola, friar and
prior of St Mark's, was the dominant political figure in the
Florentine republic, Machiavelli, who was seventeen years his
junior, was only beginning his career in the Florentine Civil
Service. Machiavelli, the impoverished son of an ancient Tuscan
family, was never of the friar's party, and rose to be a Secretary
of State only after Savonarola's fall. Once he had despised
Savonarola. When he first heard him preach, Machiavelli wrote
scornful reports of the sermons in letters to his friends. But later he
came to speak and write of him, if sometimes critically, always
with great respect. Whether Savonarola and Machiavelli met and
talked in the last months of the friar's life is a matter of conjecture;
but if such an interview happened, one must imagine it taking
place in 1498 in the prison cell where Savonarola, having offended
the Pope and forfeited his political power to his enemies, was
awaiting execution.

Savonarola: There is no need for ceremony, Signor Machiavelli, I have never
set any store by it. And it has a somewhat ironical edge now that I
am where I am.

Machiavelli: But Fra Girolamo, I ask your consent for this interview because it
has no purpose but to satisfy my own curiosity. I have not come as
an official of the state. I am here as a student of history, of politics,
of what the ancient writers called the Art of Legislation.

Savonarola: I am no authority on the ancient writers, if by that you mean the
pagan writers. I have always thought it more important to study
the Holy Scriptures.

Machiavelli: But you are an authority on statecraft itself, Fra Girolamo.

Savonarola: I have never meddled in politics. I am a humble Dominican friar.
People say I was ambitious, that I wanted a Cardinal's hat. Believe
me, if I had desired such a thing, I should not be wearing this
tattered robe. No, the only crimson hat I have ever desired, is the
crimson hat Christ wore, a hat reddened with a martyr's blood.

Machiavelli: I should not think of accusing you of 'meddling' with politics,

Fra Girolamo. And I well know that you never sought either secular office or clerical preferment. But if you were never, in the narrowest sense, a statesman yourself, you have been a teacher of statesmen; others acted, but it was your policy that they executed. And as I have described myself as a student, you will understand why I should seek the conversation of a teacher.

Savonarola: What do you think I can teach you now that I am rejected, defeated, and condemned to death?

Machiavelli: You might teach me the lesson of political failure as well as of political success. For the historian, that would be all the more instructive.

Savonarola: And what about the civil servant?

Machiavelli: I am, as yet, a very insignificant civil servant.

Savonarola: 'As yet'? So you have hopes for the future?

Machiavelli: Is not the service of the public and the state the highest goal a man can have?

Savonarola: No. The service of God is the highest goal. The service of the state is an honourable thing, admittedly. But a desire to serve the public is too often a cloak for the desire to accumulate power.

Machiavelli: Let us talk about the accumulation of power, then. Even though my own ambitions are those of an administrator rather than a politician, I have no wish to dress them up in the garments of morality.

Savonarola: We cannot talk of power unless we talk of morality. Whether power is good or bad depends on the character of the state which uses it.

Machiavelli: No state, I am sure, is perfect. I believe no state ever will be. Perhaps one reason why you, Fra Girolamo, have suffered a setback . . .

Savonarola: Do not mince your words. I have suffered something more than a setback. Very soon I shall be hanged, and my body burned.

Machiavelli: What I meant was that one reason why things have turned out as they have, may be that you tried to make Florence perfect.

Savonarola: I have never believed that Florence, or any other republic, could be made perfect. I hoped that our republic could be changed, bettered, reformed, lifted out of the slough of vice and selfishness and paganism into which it had sunk under the government of the Medici. But I have never believed that Florence could be made into a heaven on earth.

Machiavelli: Not a heaven on earth, admittedly. For the constitution of heaven is presumably monarchical rather than republican.

Savonarola: I am not sure how flippantly you are speaking, but what you say is quite true. Indeed, I have always regarded a republican constitution as the best practicable one and not as the most perfect one. In the perfect state we should have the absolute rule of an absolutely good man. It is because no man is absolutely good that I reject the principle of absolute rule in favour of a more democratic system.

Machiavelli: There I entirely agree. The best case for republican government—for democracy, liberty, and so forth—is not based on the perfectibility of man but on his imperfectibility. Princes and oligarchs are far more corruptible than the masses. The republican or democratic system reduces corruption by distributing power more widely and facilitating peaceful change. I do not think one can hope to get rid of all corruption. The advantage of the republican system is that it keeps it to a minimum. Besides, is not liberty inherently desirable?

Savonarola: Not necessarily. I myself encouraged the love of liberty in the Florentine people, but only in order that they should use it well. I tried to show them that the freedom which is worth having is the freedom to do what is right, not the freedom to follow one's own desires. I should want no one to love liberty for its own sake. The Christian loves nothing for its own sake but Christ.

Machiavelli: So you, Fra Girolamo, are in favour of liberty and democracy only because they are conducive to a religious end?

Savonarola: Yes.

Machiavelli: That is not how I think. I see the end as political, the means religious. I am in favour of religion because it can be conducive to liberty. But not all religions are such.

Savonarola: Manifestly not.

Machiavelli: By no means all religions are conducive to sound republican government. For example, your own religion is not.

Savonarola: Are you speaking of the Christian religion?

Machiavelli: Yes. Christianity is one of the least satisfactory religions. First of all, it is not conducive to virtue. For the proof of that one has to look no farther than the present head of Christendom, Roderigo Borgia, Pope Alexander VI.

Savonarola: It would be strange if I were to defend the morality of the present Pontiff in view of all I have said in public about his monstrous viciousness. But you must not judge the Church by those who rule it, and disgrace it.

Machiavelli: Vice is not confined to the princes of the Church. It is rife throughout Italy, as you yourself have often said. I grant that in some religious communities and orders, there is none of the same corruption. But Italy as a whole has become a depraved and irreligious nation because Christianity has failed in the first task of any religion, which is to teach and uphold virtue.

Savonarola: I do not deny that the Church has become in many ways a positive hindrance to righteousness. That has been the great sorrow and shame of my life. But the fact remains that she is the Church, the true and only Church.

Machiavelli: There is another thing to be said against it. Christianity is the greatest single hindrance to the unity of Italy. For the Pope is too weak to unite Italy under his own leadership, but strong enough to prevent its being united by anyone else.

Savonarola: It is perhaps the will of God that the unity of Italy should not be accomplished as soon as we might like. We must be patient.

Machiavelli: Patient? I think you have gone to the heart of the matter there. The strongest objection to Christianity is that it teaches the wrong virtues. It glorifies humble and contemplative men. It instils contempt for worldly things, and exalts the principle of abnegation. All this is inimical to liberty, because you cannot maintain a free state unless its citizens are brave and patriotic, proud of themselves and their republic.

Savonarola: Christianity teaches us that humility can overcome pride. It teaches us to believe in the triumph of the cross.

Machiavelli: There is no evidence in history to show that humility overcomes pride. On the contrary, humility is always taken for pusillanimity by one's friends, who desert one; and for weakness by one's enemies, who treat it as an invitation to attack one. No, Fra Girolamo, the case against Christianity is overwhelming. How much better was the religion of ancient Rome. For there was a religion which bred character in the citizens, and upheld the state; a religion which instilled a proper *virtù*—not your self-destructive other-worldliness—but courage and strength and public spirit.

Savonarola: How much *better*, do you ask? Your question is so astonishing that I can hardly grasp it. All I can say to you is that it is not a question of history, of this or that example you may find in history; but of truth. The Christian religion is the true religion. The religion of ancient Rome was a false religion.

Machiavelli: What is the true religion but the religion which leads the people to *virtù*? The Roman religion did so. The Christian religion does not.

Savonarola: The Roman religion was a brutish cult of idolatry and lust and cruelty. It was an evil religion as well as a false one.

Machiavelli: How can you prove it was false? Or prove that the Christian religion is true? Many have denied it.

Savonarola: The truth of Christianity does not rest on the credence of the sinful. It is one of the terrible features of sin that it blinds men's eyes to truth. Our religion rests both on reason and on revelation; on logical proofs which are clear to the well-ordered mind, and on the revelations which God has vouchsafed to the faithful.

Machiavelli: You will have no difficulty in convincing me with rational proofs. But if I have read Aquinas aright, those rational proofs are merely proofs of God's existence; and I have never denied that God exists. What they don't prove is that God is the sort of God that Christians say he is, or that his will is what they think it is.

Savonarola: That is why revelation is needed.

Machiavelli: But most of us do not receive revelation, Fra Girolamo. We are not privileged, as you have been, to hold converse with God. You, after all, are a prophet.

Savonarola: I am no prophet. I say to you what I said to my judges when they accused me of being a false prophet: 'I am no prophet. I have never claimed to be a prophet.'

Machiavelli: But you have prophesied and prophesied correctly. Everyone knows that you foretold the coming of Charles VIII of France to Italy in 1493. Indeed, one might even say that that was the beginning of your ascendancy in Florence. For people had never dreamed of the danger before you warned them, and when it came, exactly as you had predicted, they naturally turned to you to lead them.

Savonarola: A man may sometimes speak prophetically and yet not be a prophet. You will remember—or you would remember if you had read the Holy Bible—that Amos and Micah and Zechariah and even John the Baptist denied that they were prophets. And when I denied—on the rack—that I was a prophet, I was repudiating nothing that I had ever claimed.

Machiavelli: Rightly or wrongly, people thought of you as a prophet. They believed you had the power to perform miracles. I imagine that it is why there was such a popular reaction when nothing happened on the occasion of the ordeal by fire.

Savonarola: That unhappy incident was due, alas, to the zeal of my friends. But let me explain what happened. Domenico da Pescia, a friar of my own order, unwisely provoked a dispute with certain Franciscans. The Franciscans proposed that one of their number should walk through a blazing fire together with Domenico.

The ordeal was designed to test the power of my faith to protect the person of my brother. Despite misgivings, I consented, but only after careful thought and prayer. Then, when the fires were lit and all was ready, the Franciscans refused Domenico's demand to take the Host through the fire with him, and he refused to go without it. That, and that alone, was why the ordeal did not take place.

Machiavelli: Even so, you would not deny that the multitude came to the market-place, hoping to see you work a miracle; and when they were disappointed they turned against you. Though let me hasten to tell you that I myself would not be influenced by such things. I do not believe in miracles.

Savonarola: Neither do I believe in man's miracles. The only miracles I recognize are those which are the work of God.

Machiavelli: Surely if they are the work of God they are not miracles? There would be nothing miraculous in the all-powerful Creator of the universe making some variation in the order of the universe. An irregular universe is no more wonderful than a regular one—indeed it would be rather less wonderful in my opinion. Of course it would be miraculous if a *man* could alter the course of nature. But it would not be miraculous that its omnipotent Maker should alter its course. People are, I agree, amazed at what they call God's miracles, but they are amazed only because they are thinking, ignorantly, of God as being, like themselves, limited in his powers.

Savonarola: If you deny all miracles, then you are compelled to admit a far greater miracle. Think of the prodigious effects created by Christ in the world. If he could have done all that, without a miracle, would it not be all the more astonishing? For his works have infinitely surpassed the power of all false gods. Think how many men have been pleased to die for him.

Machiavelli: It is no service to make men pleased to die, unless at the same time you make them pleased to fight for the sake of their country.

Savonarola: You speak as a true votary of the pagan cults.

Machiavelli: No political society can survive in this world unless its citizens are ready to destroy its enemies. It is easy enough to set up a free and republican commonwealth. The difficulty is to keep one alive. Five years ago, the vast majority of the people of this city were ready to accept you, Fra Girolamo, as the Pericles of Florence. For a time they did. But think how soon they changed.

Savonarola: The multitude is fickle.

Machiavelli: But you must have known that before. Why did you not guard against it? Do you not think now that you should have dealt with your opponents more severely?

Savonarola: On the contrary, I ask myself if I was not too severe.

Machiavelli: I admit you urged the people to seize Piero de' Medici and cut off his head. But afterwards you pleaded for reconciliation with his supporters.

Savonarola: That is the lesson of Christ: that we should love our enemies.

Machiavelli: It is not the lesson of history. The lesson of history seems to me more and more clear. After a revolution one must destroy the enemies of the revolution. Otherwise they will live on in your republic, like the men in the wooden horse in Troy, waiting for the moment to destroy it. The republic of Rome was stronger than the city state of Athens because the Romans did not make the mistake the Athenians made of tolerating the enemy within. A prince cannot live safely in a principality while those who have been despoiled of it are alive; neither can the people of a free republic be secure unless they kill 'the sons of Brutus'.

Savonarola: What if 'the sons of Brutus' are very numerous?

Machiavelli: It will be all the more necessary to kill them.

Savonarola: Such wholesale bloodshed is contrary to the will of God. Christian ethics allows men to kill armed and hostile soldiers in a just war, and to execute criminals condemned to death by properly appointed judges. But it does not allow the cold-blooded assassination of political opponents.

Machiavelli: Piero de' Medici was neither an armed soldier nor a criminal tried by law. If it was right to cut off his head, I do not see how it would be wrong to cut off several hundred heads like his. Do numbers make the principle different?

Savonarola: Between a single tyrant whose guilt was abundantly evident, and a great number of men whose guilt is only potential, there is a great difference, Signor Machiavelli. However, I will agree that what you recommend is wholly in keeping with the cruel and barbarous morality of the ancient Roman religion.

Machiavelli: I admit there was ferocity in the Roman religion. Bloody sacrifices served the useful purpose of inspiring men with military virtues. Yet I do not think that there was more cruelty in their religion than there is in Christianity. Both believe in the torments of hell. But the torments are far less terrible in the Roman religion than they are in yours, which makes them perpetual.

Savonarola: There is nothing irrational in the idea of perpetual punishment. Just as human justice separates criminals from the community by imprisonment or exile or death, divine justice rejects them for ever from heaven.

Machiavelli: The duration of human punishment is not eternal. And it varies according to the magnitude of the crimes. It would not be justice if it did not do so.

Savonarola: Divine punishment is not so much for a sin committed in time, but for the infinite revolt of the sinner's will. God has offered men through Christ the entire remission of sins, but if they reject salvation they must live in unending expiation of their guilt.

Machiavelli: In hell's fires?

Savonarola: Yes, in fires that will never go out. And remember that the bodies of the damned will not be consumed. The fires of hell will torment, but not destroy the flesh. The agony will be everlasting.

Machiavelli: Fra Girolamo, you condemned as barbarous my proposal that the enemies of a new republic should be killed; and I admit it is a harsh policy. Yet it entails for its victims no more than the momentary agony of the executioner's axe, or, at worse, fires which would dispatch the creature from its suffering in a matter of minutes. Yet you believe it is just that such suffering should be inflicted on people not momentarily, but eternally. I do not see how you can accuse me of cruelty.

Savonarola: God's justice is omniscient. No man will go to hell who does not richly deserve that awful punishment.

Machiavelli: But I myself have heard you preach on the subject of original sin. If I am not mistaken you said that men would be punished not only for their own sins but also for the sins of their fathers and forefathers.

Savonarola: There is nothing strange in that. When our first father was given free will, given the choice between good and evil, and chose evil, he deprived his posterity of original rectitude. This privation of original rectitude on the part of the first man is a sin for all humanity, seeing that by their participation in human nature, all men are counted as one single man, of whom Adam was the head, and all other men the members.

Machiavelli: Surely we can only justly punish a man for what he has chosen to do. No living man has chosen to be the son of Adam or to participate in human nature. How can it be right that another man should go to hell because Adam chose evil?

Savonarola: No man will go to hell simply because Adam chose evil. A man will go to hell because he has himself turned away from God and refused salvation. That is why it is not only just that he should be punished, but why we should rejoice in his sufferings. It is a glorious thing that the wicked should burn in hell for ever.

Machiavelli: Its glory eludes me.

Savonarola: At any rate you will find in God's punishment of sinners no justification for your policy of killing 'the sons of Brutus'.

Machiavelli: I sought no such justification. That policy would be sanctioned by its results. It is the end which justifies the means.

Savonarola: It does not do so if the means are wrong. Even if you could bring about a good result by doing a sinful deed it would still be a sinful deed, and therefore wrong.

Machiavelli: You have said that war is permissible, and you will admit that in war we have to kill and injure our fellow men. These would be sinful deeds if done for other ends. So if they are allowed in war, it can only be because the end redeems them.

Savonarola: I said that *just* war is permissible.

Machiavelli: What is a just war? A war fought for good ends. When you say it is right to kill in such a war, you admit the principle that the end justifies the means.

Savonarola: The end does not justify sinful means.

Machiavelli: If I killed a man to seize his property you would rightly say it was sinful. But if I killed a man in battle in order to defend my country you would say it was not sinful. What is the difference between those deeds but the ends they are designed to achieve?

Savonarola: They are different actions. The first is a case of murder. The second is not.

Machiavelli: Was it not Aristotle who said murder is wrong by definition? There can be no question of whether murder is right or wrong because the word 'murder' means 'wrongful killing'. But 'killing' is not necessarily culpable by definition. So one *can* ask whether killing is right or wrong. I say it is not wrong if it is a necessary condition of the survival of the republic. Killing in battle is one such necessary condition. Killing 'the sons of Brutus' is another.

Savonarola: You may preserve the republic. But what of the life to come? Your policy of ruthless slaughter might conceivably prosper in this world for a time, but it would be punished in the next. You would meet that dreadful retribution of which we have already spoken.

Machiavelli: You speak of 'ruthless slaughter' as if I gloried in it, as you tell me the Christian rejoices in the sufferings of the damned. I do nothing of the kind. I hate the idea of inflicting pain. But I think it is sometimes imperative; and I think it best that one should face that fact.

There is a tendency in Florence for men to shut their eyes to disagreeable things; or to call them by different names, which make them seem agreeable. You remember how they changed the name of the Council of Ten for War to the Council of Ten for Peace and Liberty.

Savonarola: It was I who proposed that reform. It was intended to be more than a change of name; it was intended to register a change of spirit and of principles.

Machiavelli: But it did not register a change of function. The Council of Ten was still responsible for War, not Peace, it was still in fact in the process of fighting a war. I dislike that sort of hypocrisy. It leads people to deceive themselves, and that is always harmful. Though, of course, it is sometimes an excellent thing to deceive others. Fraud, in general, is infinitely better than force.

Savonarola: Again you astonish me. Fraud is always sinful.

Machiavelli: So you would rather be murdered than swindled?

Savonarola: It is not a question of what I should choose to suffer, but which I should choose to do.

Machiavelli: And you think force is better than fraud, Fra Girolamo?

Savonarola: The question is a misleading one. As you yourself recalled just now, Aristotle pointed out that some actions are by definition culpable. Fraud is like murder in that respect. But force, on the other hand, is not necessarily culpable. Force used on behalf of lawful and moral authority is wholly permissible. Force used with malice is wrong, it might sometimes be even worse than fraud. The question turns on the principle for which force is invoked. We know that even God employs force sometimes. But it is inconceivable that God should use fraud.

Machiavelli: I was thinking only of men. Fraud is much more serviceable than force to a man who wants to rise in the world, and what is true of individuals is true of states. A republic at the outset of its career is too weak to rely on force alone; hence the importance of fraud. Rome did not forget to use it. Look how she deceived her Latin neighbours into servitude by offering them spurious treaties of alliance.

Savonarola: I would not agree that fraud is even a shrewd policy, quite apart from the matter of its wickedness. It may be that a statesman might bring off an occasional successful stroke by means of fraud, but he could not do so more than once, because, having been found out, his word would no longer be trusted. Nothing is so injurious to success as a reputation for acting deceitfully.

Machiavelli: Of course deceit is worse than useless if it does not deceive. The statesman should never be found out, or gain the sort of reputation you speak of.

Savonarola: Such a reputation is easily gained. The Latin allies of Rome soon discovered that they had been deceived.

Machiavelli: But by then it was too late for them to do anything about it.

Savonarola: That is a very cynical remark.

Machiavelli: I speak in favour of fraud, not because I like fraud, but because I dislike force, and fraud is the alternative to force. Fraud is better in the sense that it causes less physical suffering; and better in the sense that it often works more effectively. Indeed, one might ask: what would diplomacy be without an element of fraud?

Savonarola: I dare say there is in fact some simulation and dissimulation in diplomacy. But remember, even Aquinas said there were circumstances in which equivocation was permissible.

Machiavelli: Simulation? Dissimulation? Equivocation? I prefer, as I said, plainer words. I would rather call it fraud.

Savonarola: But it is not always fraud. It is not always wrong to conceal the whole truth. Still, I agree that the distinction is a delicate one. And I certainly think one should never risk one's prosperity in the world to come for sake of prosperity in this world.

Machiavelli: Fraud is justified, like force, by the value of the end it achieves.

Savonarola: Again you speak of ends. And what is the real end of man?

Machiavelli: I do not know. You would say salvation, I imagine. Shall I say happiness?

Savonarola: Then I will say happiness too. But what is true happiness? Surely that happiness in which there is no admixture of pain and sorrow: to be in a condition in which nothing further is desired. But in this life no one can be so satisfied as to desire nothing. We cannot have in this life the happiness we all yearn for. That is why we must look to the life beyond death. The gift of salvation Christ offers is not something to be bought at the cost of true happiness. On the contrary it is only by accepting that gift that we can find true happiness.

Machiavelli: You yourself, Fra Girolamo, have said it can only be bought at the price of pleasure.

Savonarola: Bought at the price of sensual pleasure, yes. That is why I told the people of this city to close their theatres and brothels, to stop gambling and dancing. They did it, but they did not do it willingly. They had grown too attached to the pleasures—and their vices. 'Drive out the paederasts as well as the prostitutes' I told them. 'Drive them out of the city on pain of death.'

Machiavelli: What about the bonfires? Didn't you send the children from house to house at carnival time to collect all the things that gave people pleasure so that you could burn the lot in the market-place?

Savonarola: Yes, we burned all their vanities: dice, cards, backgammon boards, the adornments of women—their powder and paints and false hair; and licentious books and songs, and musical instruments, pipes, lutes, harps.

Machiavelli: Harps even. And yet we are told that harps will be heard in paradise.

Savonarola: Some people have thus envisaged it.

Machiavelli: Then presumably the harp is not a source of sinful pleasure.

Savonarola: In this life, such music may take people's minds off more important things. Nothing is good in this life but the contemplation of Christ.

Machiavelli: I would admit that might be the only good thing for priests and monks to do; and sometimes one wishes they would confine themselves to doing it. But you can hardly claim that the same vocation is for the laity as well, for then the special mission of the clergy would cease to have any meaning. You began by excluding sensual or sinful pleasures and finished by banishing the pleasures of this life entirely, including even the pleasures of the mind: poetry, music, art.

Savonarola: But did not Plato himself—Plato whom everyone in Florence now exalts to the skies—did not he declare that it was necessary to expel all poets and artists from the republic? Did he not speak against music and drama; and declare that the only books which should be tolerated were those which led man to righteousness?

Machiavelli: Yet it is said that Plato was a poet himself, and you, Fra Girolamo, I am told, have written verses.

Savonarola: I have never been minded to condemn the art of verse as such, but only the abuse of it by those who are honoured as poets. Such men are honoured because they are judged by the elegance of their metre and rhyme. But those qualities have no real value. For what is the value of a painted and decorated ship if she does not ride the waves and carry her passengers to port? What use is it if one tickles the ears of the listener and forgets his immortal soul? The only true poetry is that which brings men to Christ; and that is the only poetry that is fit to preserve.

Machiavelli: The ancient poets had not heard of Christ.

Savonarola: Then their poetry is not worth reading. When all is said and done, the greatest poetry is to be found in the Holy Scriptures where we see the beauty of wisdom and the majesty of Providence. Instead of feeding men's minds with a mass of words, the Bible imbues them with the knowledge of reality, shows them the essence of things, and gives marvellous nourishment to the spirit.

Machiavelli: It seems to me that you would rob us of all that makes life full and rich, and turn us into a race of Bible-reading monks and nuns.

Savonarola: If you really believe your own principle that the end justifies the means you would agree with what I say. For if the path is hard, the objective is priceless. It is nothing less than perfection.

Machiavelli: But you have yourself admitted that perfection is unattainable.

Savonarola: In this life, yes.

Machiavelli: And I do not believe that the means you advocate would achieve the end you propose. You might take away men's culture by legislation—their music and art and literature, even their civility. That would not be impossible. But you could not take away their sensuality by legislation. You did not remove the lust from men's hearts by burning Boccaccio; or remove the vanity from women by destroying their jewels and finery.

Savonarola: Have you forgotten the example of ancient Rome? You have said that that should be our model. And did not Rome have sumptuary laws? Did not the Lex Oppia restrict the extravagance of women's dress? And the Lex Julia de Adulteriis punish adultery by law? And what of the Lex Didia and the Lex Licinia?

Machiavelli: The lesson of those laws is to be found precisely in their failure. They were introduced at a time when there was a need for political reform in Rome. But instead of reforming their institutions, the Roman rulers tried to reform the citizens instead. In truth, the institutions were the source of corruption; and the laws you mention were introduced step by step as the people became more corrupt. But the laws did not arrest their moral decay. Still less did they make the people good.

Savonarola: The reform of institutions and the reform of men's morals must go hand in hand. That is the lesson of my own failure in Florence. We changed the institutions easily. It was not difficult to copy the constitution of Venice. It proved far harder to change people's hearts. God knows, I tried to. I told our people that if they succeeded in purifying their lives and spirits, in thinking always of the common good and forgetting their private interests, they would have achieved a greater glory than all the cities of antiquity.

Machiavelli: We must not expect to learn too much from history. History can teach us how to achieve a given objective: it cannot provide the objective for us. For example, although I think republican government far better than monarchy, nevertheless, if I were asked how a prince should conduct his principality, I could answer him simply with reference to history. I could show him how necessary it is to be respected at home and to be dreaded abroad; and how a prince could achieve that hold over people's minds. All those questions history answers because they lie within the realms of means. But when we move into the realm of ends, history is silent.

Savonarola: Then I have persuaded you that there is something higher?

Machiavelli: I have never pretended that history can tell us what to want; it can only tell us how to get what we want. It happens that you and I want different things. Your objective is happiness in the world to come; mine is happiness in this world.

Savonarola: There is no necessary antithesis between present happiness and happiness to come.

Machiavelli: In theory then, the same form of government might be conducive to both our ends. We are, in any case, agreed that it should be republican. But I think the agreement goes no further. For your republic is theocratic, free only in the sense that people are free to do what they ought to do—namely to fit themselves by unremitting self-denial for paradise. In my republic people would be free to do what they wanted to do, providing they did not break the law.

Savonarola: Free to follow their desires, however base?

Machiavelli: A republic would not last long if its citizens were men of base desires. A republic will only work if men are fit for freedom: that is if they have civic virtue or *virtù*. It is necessary that the members of a political community should want to live together, honour one another and respect each other's rights; that they should love their country and its institutions; that they should obey the law, and not seek always to evade it.

Savonarola: How often do you expect to have those conditions met?

Machiavelli: Not often. Liberty is a very compelling idea, but very few societies know how to preserve it. If people are not accustomed to freedom, and are suddenly liberated by a revolution, they are like wild animals which have been kept in captivity and then released. They have forgotten how to live on their own, and they become the victim of the first man who tries to chain them up again.

Savonarola: I have always thought that the condition of liberty was that people should transcend their selfish interests and desires, and will only that which is for the good of all.

Machiavelli: That is true, but I do not believe we can eliminate conflicts altogether, or even that it is desirable to do so. In every republic there are two different dispositions, that of the possessing class and that of the populace; and it seems to me that all legislation favourable to liberty is brought about by the clash between those two classes. The populace may be ignorant, but it is not stupid; it is capable of knowing where the shoe pinches. A populace which is conscious of its class interests will demand democratic institutions which are favourable to liberty if they are not abused. On the other hand, an intelligent possessing class will correct any excess of democracy. It will be conservative in tendency, and set up an alternative party to prevent the dictatorship by the popular party.

Savonarola: I do not feel that harmony can come out of conflict.

Machiavelli: But balance can come out of it; and the defence of liberty is a matter of equilibrium. One needs a perpetual safeguard against the abuse of authority. Alternative political parties, which are the outcome of social conflict, are an excellent safeguard: for then each party is in fear of losing its power to the other; and neither dares to go too far.

Savonarola: When the government of Florence was reformed after the fall of the Medici, there was great distress in this city side by side with great wealth. You know what our policy was. We put a stop to private usury by law, and set up a state bank which lent money at moderate rates. I begged the rich to give up their fortunes, because I do not believe, as you do, that the struggle for sectional interest is conducive to the health of society. Unfortunately the Church itself is too rich; so although Christ himself was poor, it is difficult for a Christian priest to teach poverty; and if he speaks of it, no one understands.

Machiavelli: I admit that some form of equality is a necessary condition of freedom. I do not mean equality of rich and poor, but equality of political rights. Given an hereditary nobility with their castles and vast domains, then you cannot have a republican government.

Savonarola: Up to a point I agree with you, but remember that even in Venice, whose constitution served as the model for so many of our own reforms, there are the two classes of gentlemen and commoners.

Machiavelli: But in Venice gentlemen are gentlemen in name rather than in fact. The name 'gentleman' is a title of social standing, not an indication of constitutional privilege. The 'gentlemen' of Venice are the property owning class. They are not a real aristocracy, men of the kind you will find in plenty in the baronial castles of Lombardy and the Romagna and the Papal States. Fortunately there are no such castles in Tuscany, and no such feudal caste, so that republican government is a real possibility in Florence and Sienna and Lucca—and the smaller places, too. If such great noblemen did exist, we should have to kill them to preserve our republican liberties.

Savonarola: Such men are 'sons of Brutus', too?

Machiavelli: In effect, yes. But I do not pretend that the transition from a corrupt feudal society to a free patriotic republic can be brought about simply by eliminating the feudal nobility. There is almost bound to be an intervening stage of autocracy. Think of Moses, Lycurgus, Solon, and other founders of kingdoms and republics. They could not have done what they did do if they had not been, for a time, alone in their authority.

Savonarola: Yet you hinted just now that I had been too much alone in the authority—or at any rate the influence—I exercised here in Florence.

Machiavelli: That was not my criticism. A short-term autocracy—and the essential thing is that it should be short—can be conducive to the long-term liberty of a newly founded state. My criticism of your power was not that it was too great, but that you demanded too much of the people.

Savonarola: I demanded only that they should let their lives be ruled by God.

Machiavelli: But religion is not the whole of life, any more than politics is the whole of life. You cut out philosophy, poetry, art, music, learning; all the ornaments of civilized living.

Savonarola: What are such things worth, if one has them, and loses salvation?

Machiavelli: They are the glory of humanity.

Savonarola: You might almost be describing the Florentine ideal of the time of Lorenzo de' Medici. There were plenty of ornaments of civilized living then. In fact the ornaments became the end in themselves. Why, men would not even read the Bible because it was not classical enough. They were afraid it would spoil their literary style. You have mentioned precisely what was wrong with Florence under Lorenzo de' Medici. Men lived for the glory of humanity instead of the glory of God.

Machiavelli: I should have said that what was wrong with Florence under Lorenzo de' Medici was Lorenzo de' Medici. Then we had humanism without liberty.

Savonarola: You must know that Lorenzo on his deathbed sought absolution from me. I offered it on three conditions. He accepted two. The third was that he should restore liberty to Florence. He declined. That is why he died without absolution. What he refused to give, Florence took from his son.

Machiavelli: If only you had been content with liberty, Fra Girolamo, you might still be preaching in the *duomo* or St Mark's. Looking back on it all, do you not now think it would have been better to have saved a few souls slowly rather than to have tried to turn the whole city into a community of saints overnight?

Savonarola: Not a community of saints; only a community of Christians. You cannot go on accusing me of preaching the perfectibility of man; for I have spoken time and again about the inherent sinfulness of man. Even so, it would be a great mistake to think that because perfection is impossible, one should resign oneself to evil.

Machiavelli: Surely if it can never be eliminated, one must resign oneself to its existence.

Savonarola: No, if we adopt that attitude, evil will be magnified. We must always be at war with it. Though it is not enough to fight evil. Salvation, after all, has been offered us. And if we accept salvation, if we know we are saved . . .

Machiavelli: How can anybody know he is saved? He might believe he was saved, but I don't see how his belief could be tested and verified, and established as knowledge.

Savonarola: Salvation brings its own inner conviction.

Machiavelli: Many false beliefs, unfortunately, carry their own inner conviction. The intensity of a belief is no proof of its truth.

Savonarola: There is a knowledge that is God-given. That is why it should be possible to build a truly Christian republic: for if each man knew that his future life was assured, he would gladly bear the discipline which is necessary on earth to fit him for heaven. It is when men think that this is the only life which counts, that they become bad citizens, for in trying to grasp as much as they can while there is still time, they become enemies, living in perpetual competition or a state of war, one against the other.

Machiavelli: There is surely a vast difference between competition and war. War within a society would obviously be disastrous, since the original purpose of government is to put a stop to the state of war which would exist between men if they lived in a condition of anarchy. Competition within a society, on the other hand, is highly beneficial. It stirs men to better themselves. Seeking to be richer, braver, more learned and civilized, and generally more to be admired than his neighbours, each man raises not only himself but the whole level of the community.

Savonarola: You are describing a society in which every man is for himself.

Machiavelli: It is natural that every man should be for himself. We have to teach men to love their country as well as themselves: sometimes even more than themselves. But there is still a great deal of room for self-love: and it is a good thing there is, for we could certainly never remove it entirely.

Savonarola: The love of God can overcome self-love. In the society I visualize, a Christian society, there would be co-operation instead of competition, because everyone would love his neighbour as himself. Pride, acquisitiveness, the desire to possess, would be removed. Men would be truly brothers, each thinking only of the general good; taking what he needed from the common pool and giving back what was in his power to give. No man would wish to be richer or more powerful than his neighbour.

Machiavelli: Nor even more righteous?

Savonarola: There would be no vying for God's favour. Everyone would desire his neighbour to be as righteous as he.

Machiavelli: I should call that a distinctly pharisaical desire.

Savonarola: One should not be too afraid to be thought a pharisee. It struck me when I first came to Florence that even good men were half ashamed of their righteousness. That was one result, I suppose, of the ideal of civility which grew up under the Medici—that deplorable ideal which exalts manners above morals.

Machiavelli: But one must not go too far in the other direction. Manners may not be more important than morals, but they are still extremely important.

Savonarola: They are not important to God.

Machiavelli: But what could be more ceremonious than the rituals of the Church? What are they but forms of civility towards God?

Savonarola: That is a fair point. There is far too much ceremony in the Church. There was a time when the vessels of the Church were wooden, while the souls of the priests were of gold. Now the vessels are golden, and the souls of the priests are of wood. Too often worse than wood. The priests have withdrawn from God. They spend their nights with harlots and their days chattering in choirs.

Machiavelli: I shall not disagree with you there. I do not, as you do, hold chastity among the highest virtues. But I agree that the want of it is unseemly in a priest.

Savonarola: Licentiousness is unseemly in any man. Think of the evil which has been wrought in Italy by lascivious princes and statesmen.

Machiavelli: I have heard it said that a lascivious prince helps the cause of liberty, on the grounds that a prince who is taken up with his private pleasures will not bother about politics. But this is an illusion. Nothing palls so quickly as the pleasures of the flesh. Lascivious princes grow bored, and interfere intermittently and disastrously with the government of their principalities. So I would agree with you, Fra Girolamo, that luxury and excessive self-indulgence in a prince, or any other ruler, is a harmful thing. I think, with Aristotle, that moderation is essential.

Savonarola: Moderation will save no man's soul. Absolute belief in the truth of the Christian dogmas is the first essential: together, of course, with absolute purity of living.

Machiavelli: I notice you put faith before works.

Savonarola: I do so because it is more necessary to salvation. A man could be saved by faith alone; he could not be saved by works alone.

Machiavelli: That seems to me another reason for resisting your religion. What men do is far more important to society than what they believe. It is their behaviour that counts, not what goes on in their heads. Besides, I very much wonder whether even the priests of the Church have an absolute belief in the truth of its dogmas.

Savonarola: You could hardly be more critical of the priests of our Church than I am myself, Signor Machiavelli. The Church needs to be purified.

Machiavelli: Or a new Church built in its place?

Savonarola: There can be no other Church. You might build temples in honour of your pagan deities, or any other false god, but there is only one Church, the church established in Rome by St Peter.

Machiavelli: But if the Church of St Peter cannot satisfy the religious needs of Italy then there will have to be such other temples. And as the Church of St Peter appears to be decaying, can one not predict that such other temples will be built?

Savonarola: I shrink from the thought.

Machiavelli: And yet you have looked into the future, and not shrunk from the vision of Italy destroyed.

Savonarola: That was a warning vision. It was not a prediction. Though it may yet happen. I have foreseen my own death—dare I say my own martyrdom?—many times. And that is now assuredly upon me.

Machiavelli: You face death bravely, Fra Girolamo.

Savonarola: Why should I be afraid for myself seeing that I have the promise of eternal life? I am more afraid for my judges, for Florence, for Italy. My death is a triumph for the wicked: and those who survive will be the ones to suffer. The worst of all forms of government is the absolute rule of absolutely bad men, just as the best is the absolute rule of the absolutely good. Unfortunately, if there is no absolutely good man on earth, there *are* absolutely evil men.

Machiavelli: I should say that there are very few absolutely evil men. Perhaps men would prosper more if they were absolutely evil. As it is they generally try to steer a middle course between being good and being bad; and often they throw away the profits of their bad deeds by trying afterwards to be good. You see, Fra Girolamo, I do not look on politics, as you do, as a struggle for righteousness and an ideal commonwealth against the tyranny of the wholly evil. I see it as a struggle for liberty against the tyranny of the partially evil; and I want political institutions which will ward off that evil rather than institutions designed to generate positive goodness. I know nothing about the life to come; whether there is or is not one. But this life on earth is something we can learn about, provided that we go about it in the proper way. The way to learn about this life is to study history; not to find what we want to find, but to find out what is there, to find out what causes produce what effects, or rather, what tends to be the regular consequence of certain kinds of actions and policies. This will show us what men are like, what life is like, and what the future will probably be like. It shows us how to achieve our ends.

Savonarola: But, as you have said, it does not give us our ends.

Machiavelli: We choose our own ends and, when there is liberty, we can pursue them. If we know history, we can pursue them wisely.

Savonarola: It is more important that we should choose them wisely. In other words, that we should choose the ends which God, in his infinite wisdom, has designed for us. You speak, Signor Machiavelli, of the value of learning; you would make history, philosophy, science your guide. But that was not what Christ believed. He taught us to be as little children. Oh, the philosophers have praised God, I know; but not as children have praised him. Philosophers praise God according to the light of the world; children praise him according to the light of heaven. What is the good of science, if we lose our simplicity of heart? Sophistication of the mind quite as much as riches can hinder a man from entering the kingdom of heaven. You are a scholar, Signor Machiavelli. And what has your learning brought into your life but the demon of scepticism and doubt? I will not call you an atheist; you are not one. You are a pagan. Pagans who have never heard of Christ will be spared perdition. But not the pagan who has heard, and refused to listen.

Machiavelli: I am no more a scholar than you are, Fra Girolamo. I am a different kind of scholar, that is all.

Savonarola: You have forgotten to guard simplicity.

Machiavelli: If simplicity means the lack of knowledge, one could not acquire knowledge and at the same time retain simplicity.

Savonarola: It is a quality of the heart. It is something I cherish; and something you despise. But that is not the greatest difference between us. The crucial truth, Signor Machiavelli, is that you do not love God. So you can never really understand—with all your history and science, you will never appreciate what I believe.

Machiavelli: And you, Fra Girolamo; you do not love this world, or this life; so perhaps, in the same way, you could never appreciate what I believe. Perhaps we are both destined to be misunderstood.

John Locke and Lord Shaftesbury

A dialogue on Toleration

In the summer of 1704, John Locke received his last visitors at
the country house in Essex where he lived as a paying guest. He
was aged seventy-two, and had not many more months to live.
He was in poor health, suffering from asthma, which he thought
was consumption; and retirement did not suit him. Unlike the
philosophers of classical antiquity, Locke was not by nature a
contemplative. He was a man of action. By turns he had been a
doctor, diplomatist, a civil servant, an economist and a pamphle-
teer. In the later years of his life he had thrown himself whole-
heartedly into politics and public administration. In many ways
Locke was a typical Englishman; but he was also a remarkably
modern thinker for his time. He believed in Christianity because
he held that the teaching of the Bible was essentially reasonable.
It consisted of no more than the simple proposition 'That Christ
is the Messiah'. The wars of religion which had tormented
England and Europe for so many years arose, Locke thought,
from an unreflective and passionate attachment to religious
dogmas which were no part of true Christianity whatever. If
only people would calm themselves, if they would learn to separate the truths from the myths in the Scriptures, if they would
follow their own reason instead of listening to priests, then they
might be able to do what Christ told them to do—love one
another. Towards the end of his life Locke was depressed by a
revival of the persecuting spirit among his own countrymen.
But he was comforted in his retirement by visits from a few young
men who were his pupils. One of these was Anthony Ashley
Cooper, third Earl of Shaftesbury, author of *Characteristics of
Men*. Locke had been a close friend and adviser of his grandfather,
the first Lord Shaftesbury; and he had supervised the grandson's
education from the beginning. Young Shaftesbury at the time of
his last visit to the philosopher was aged thirty-four and had not
yet published any of the books in which he was to put forward
theories sharply opposed to those of Locke; and the two men still
met as master and pupil. Shaftesbury had been spending a year in
Holland for the sake of his health. After all this time in the com-

pany of liberal Dutchmen, he was ill-prepared for the atmosphere of political reaction he found on his return to the England of Queen Anne.

Shaftesbury: No, Mr Locke, I had not expected such a revival of intolerance.

Locke: Intolerance, my Lord Shaftesbury, is never far beneath the surface.

Shaftesbury: It was obvious that the accession of Queen Anne would fortify the extremists in the Church of England; but I had not looked for such a sharp renewal of the attack on Nonconformists. There was also, I am told, a Bill before the House of Commons this year to restore the censorship of the Press.

Locke: There was: but thanks to the efforts of our friends, it was rejected.

Shaftesbury: And there have been fresh attacks on you from clerical quarters, Mr Locke.

Locke: Fresh, my lord, but not severe. A man who has been in danger of his life acquires a certain stoicism, I will not call it courage, before the intemperance of the English clergy.

Shaftesbury: They are against you, I hear, even in Oxford.

Locke: You say 'even' as if to imply that persecution is less to be expected in that place than elsewhere. Experience, my lord, breeds different expectations. I am, as you know, an Oxford man. For nearly thirty years I enjoyed a Studentship at Christ Church, but as soon as I was connected with your grandfather I was spied on by my colleagues and my movements reported to the Court; and the College was very quick to expel me when Charles the Second demanded that as one of 'Lord Shaftesbury's men', I should lose my place.

Shaftesbury: And now, after all these years, they have suppressed your books.

Locke: I did not realize that was generally known.

Shaftesbury: I was told that the Heads of Colleges considered that the reading of your *Essay Concerning Human Understanding* was undermining Aristotle and the philosophy of the Schools; and they suppressed your books because they feared there would soon be no scholastic philosophy left in Oxford.

Locke: That is so; and how I wish their fears were justified. I regret nothing more than the time I had to waste in my first few years at Oxford in frivolous scholastic disputations. I should be very pleased to think that the reading of what I have written might turn the minds of young men today to more fruitful inquiries.

Shaftesbury: I am sure it would, if the books had not been burned.

Locke: *Banned*, my Lord Shaftesbury, not burned. Indeed, I have had a letter from Bodley's librarian at Oxford, from Dr Hudson, asking *if* I would, as an Oxford man, make a gift to the Bodleian Library of those very books the heads of colleges have suppressed.

Shaftesbury: That sounds in the circumstances, Mr Locke, an impertinent request.

Locke: And yet I imagine that the demand for my books is greater now in Oxford than it has ever been. What is more certain to prompt a man, and especially a young man, to read a book, than to say he must not read it? To burn books is wrong. To ban books and not burn them is merely stupid. So I have made the gift to Dr Hudson. He says that if I send a few more books he will inscribe my name in the honourable roll of donors.

Shaftesbury: I understand you have also been attacked in print.

Locke: In which print?

Shaftesbury: By Mr Proast. I hear that after twelve years' silence he has written another pamphlet against you.

Locke: Mr Proast?

Shaftesbury: The Chaplain, I believe, of All Souls. He seems to be the author of the new reply to the *Letters of Toleration*.

Locke: But why, my lord, do you say he has written against *me*?

Shaftesbury: Surely, Mr Locke, you *are* the author of the *Letters of Toleration*?

Locke: I cannot think why you should suspect it.

Shaftesbury: Mr Furly told me when I stayed with him in Rotterdam.

Locke: Mr Furly should hold his peace. Those Dutch tongues wag too freely. When I was a political refugee in Holland and depended for my life on the discretion of my hosts, I can assure you I felt far from safe.

Shaftesbury: I have read Mr Proast's pamphlet. His argument seems to be that the government of a Christian country has the sacred duty of upholding the true religion, even by force.

Locke: And how do we know the established religion is the true religion? The Catholic faith is established in France, the Reformed in Geneva, the Mahometan in Turkey. They are all established, but since their dogmas are at variance with one another, they cannot all be true.

Shaftesbury: But you are a member of the Church of England, sir, and that suggests you think, as I do, that the established religion of this country is the true one.

Locke: I think it embraces truth.

Shaftesbury: Then ought not the government to uphold it, even by force?

Locke: No, my lord, a government does not exist to uphold religion.

Shaftesbury: Some governments claim that they do.

Locke: Alas, my lord, it is the habit of rulers to claim more responsibilities than are properly theirs, in order to claim more power than is properly theirs. But I was thinking of government, of civil society, as an *institution*. It is worth asking why men created civil societies in the first place, and appointed governors to rule them.

Shaftesbury: I should say because life in a state of natural anarchy was too hazardous.

Locke: And yet the state of nature had its own advantages. Men were free from many of the evils which beset us today. There were no emperors and Popes, no soldiers, no spies, no censorship and no taxation. On the other hand, there were disadvantages. Every man had to defend his own life and possessions, because there was no higher power to defend them for him. There was no system of positive law, so that every man was necessarily a judge in his own cause. And the answer to our question; why did men create government? is simply; to provide security and justice. Each surrendered the right to uphold and enforce the law as he chose in return for the advantages of having an impartial judge to maintain the same law over all. Men have a natural right to life, liberty and property, and they established governments on earth in order to formalize and secure their rights. They did not establish governments in order to save their souls.

Shaftesbury: But surely, Mr Locke, the salvation of souls is a noble task.

Locke: It is, but that does not mean it is a proper task for governments to undertake. The healing of the sick is a noble task, but it does not follow it is a proper task for untrained men to assume. The salvation of souls is nothing to do with governments. It is the business of a church.

Shaftesbury: Yet a government has force at its command, which a church has not. Our Church of England has much to recommend it. It is free from the horrid superstitions, the monstrous enthusiasms and wild fanaticism which are found in so many Christian denominations. Its established rites are decent, chaste and dignified. The principle of charity is more marked than it is in any other Protestant or Catholic church. It teaches us to lead a good and virtuous life, to serve our country and mankind, and to observe its modest ceremonies. Does that not answer the highest character of religion?

Locke: My lord, our Church of England has these merits you name, but only in so far as the moderate party has power within it. That power may not endure. It has already been diminished, as you yourself have seen.

Shaftesbury: Mr Locke, I am only putting this to you as it has been put to me; a question of principle. If we were satisfied that the Church of England would remain as it should be, ought we not then to allow the government to sustain the authority of the Church, even by force?

Locke: My Lord Shaftesbury, do you believe a man's soul can be saved by the sword? You may bring a man to his knees, you may bring a prayer from his lips; so much you can do with a sword, but you cannot bring a prayer from his heart or alter his inmost thoughts.

Shaftesbury: Then why do so many rulers do it? Why does the Catholic King of France, who is certainly not a fool, impose his religion by force?

Locke: Perhaps he is content with appearances.

Shaftesbury: I think you underestimate the effectiveness of force, Mr Locke. I agree that you cannot alter one man's inmost thoughts by the sword, but you can use force to impose preachers and teachers on a nation, and thereby indirectly alter by force the inmost thoughts of many people.

Locke: You might propagate false religions by such methods, but not the true religion. For one thing, the truth does not need to be driven into men's minds by force. God has given them reason with which to recognize it.

Shaftesbury: But it seems commonly agreed that we should use force—that is to say, the coercive arm of the realm—to save people from temptation.

Locke: I do not believe the devil can be so easily thwarted.

Shaftesbury: But there are so many examples. How many public authorities have not closed brothels, and taverns, and theatres? What is such action but force? And what is its aim but the diminution of temptation? It seems to me a very short step from saving people from temptation in this way to saving their souls by more positive legislation.

Locke: A short step, you say, my Lord? I should say it was, on the contrary, a leap—a leap from one kind of action to another. The suppression of brothels and certain sorts of tavern is a justifiable policy; I am by no means opposed to it. But it is justifiable because brothels and the like are disorderly and noxious institutions; they threaten the tranquillity and welfare of society. We do not close them to save anyone from temptation. If anyone is tempted by what is offered at a bawdy house, he will be no less tempted if such places are closed; for the devil will then appear to him in the guise of an orange-seller or a chambermaid.

Shaftesbury: But, you, Mr Locke, were an undergraduate at Oxford at the time of Oliver Cromwell, when all the taverns and places of amusement were closed; surely it was easier for the undergraduates to apply their minds to work and prayer in those years, than it became in the time of Charles II, when there were three hundred alehouses in Oxford. That is to say, it was easier to be virtuous because there were fewer temptations in your time—the Commonwealth had suppressed them.

Locke: I shall not answer that my contemporaries had to look farther for their pleasures, and therefore took more time doing so; but I will remind you that I was not only an undergraduate in the Oxford of the Commonwealth, but also a college tutor in the Oxford of the Restoration. It was not my impression that righteousness prevailed at the one time, and vice at the other. I cannot pretend that I noticed a great difference.

Shaftesbury: But, Mr Locke, you have advised parents, in your work on education, to keep their sons away from public schools in order to save them from moral corruption.

Locke: My Lord Shaftesbury, how can I persuade you that there is no more dangerous analogy than that which is so often drawn between the family and the nation. What is fitting in the relationship between his father and his children is by no means appropriate to the relationship between a government and the citizen. The simple reason for this is that citizens are not children. There is also an important difference between the administration of a university and the administration of a kingdom. When I went to Oxford I was already twenty years of age; but many undergraduates are thirteen, fourteen, fifteen, years of age when they matriculate. They cannot be given the liberties of men, because they are not men.

Shaftesbury: It seems to me, Mr Locke, that there is a very great similitude between a university and a kingdom. A college makes itself a Christian college by insisting on daily attendance at chapel, the reading of Grace before meat, the wearing of surplices and so forth compulsory. A kingdom can make itself a Christian one by similar compulsion.

Locke: A college can expel a non-conformer; the nation cannot.

Shaftesbury: It can inflict other penalties.

Locke: You mean, it can persecute them.

Shaftesbury: If you call it persecution, when it is done for a godly purpose.

Locke: My Lord Shaftesbury, I have lived for seventy-two years. I have witnessed persecution in England and France and Holland. I have witnessed the persecution of Catholics and Calvinists and Church of England men. I can assure you they have all the same excuse for their intolerance. They have a godly purpose; they are doing the divine will. It is one of the persistent delusions of the tyrant that he is prompted by God. And yet when I open the Gospels, as I now do daily, I find they declare that the true disciples of Christ must suffer persecution; but I can never find that the Church of Christ should persecute others by fire and sword to make them embrace her faith.

Shaftesbury: I have noticed, Mr Locke, that the *Letters of Toleration* seem chiefly designed to make Christians more tolerant towards other Christians.

Locke: That may be because Christians are most intolerant towards other Christians.

Shaftesbury: What about Mahometans and Jews? Should we tolerate them?

Locke: We pray daily for their conversion, and I think it our duty to do so. But it will, I fear, hardly be believed that we pray in earnest if we exclude them from the ordinary and probable means of conversion, either by driving them from us, or persecuting them when they are among us.

Shaftesbury: Do you think we should tolerate those sects which carry eccentricity to the frontiers of lunacy? I am thinking of such congregations as those which might wish to sacrifice human infants or lustfully pollute themselves in promiscuous uncleanness.

Locke: Of course we should not tolerate in religious assemblies that which is not lawful in the ordinary course of life. The reason why we could not tolerate the ritual sacrifice of infants is that we cannot tolerate the civil murder of infants. On the other hand, I see no objection to the ritual sacrifice of calves, so long as the congregation which sacrificed a calf owned it.

Shaftesbury: Presumably we should also extend toleration to atheists.

Locke: No, my lord, we should not. Political and social relations depend on trust. And you cannot trust an atheist; for a man who does not believe in the existence of God cannot take an oath on the Scriptures; so we cannot rely on his word.

Shaftesbury: You say that *a priori*, Mr Locke. In your justly celebrated *Essay* you maintain that all knowledge of fact is derived from experience. Surely it would be better to observe the conduct of atheists to find out if they *are* untrustworthy? They might prove to be as reliable as believing men. Somebody might say *a priori* that every Christian is virtuous. But he would not say it on the basis of experience. On the contrary, many of the greatest evil-livers are the most conscientious men in the outward observances of the Christian faith.

Locke: Notably in the outward observances of the Church of England. I imagine that is partly because the laws of this realm provide so many inducements to be a churchman and at the same time close so much—the universities, the professions and the public offices—to Nonconformists.

Shaftesbury: Then you would suggest, Mr Locke, that the Church of England should offer no inducements to membership. I mean other than the prospect of salvation?

Locke: I fear it would be a very small Church of England if it offered no inducements to membership other than the prospect of salvation. What I object to is the use of the civil power to force men to conform. I will be frank with you. I *did* write the *Letters for Toleration*, many years ago: the first in Holland, the second when I returned to London, and the third here, in Sir Francis Masham's house. The third, I am afraid, grew to such prodigious dimensions that very few readers can have reached the end of it. It seems to have taken Mr Proast twelve years to do so. So now I have on my hands, when I am dying . . .

Shaftesbury: But, Mr Locke . . .

Locke: Yes—remember I am a physician, a Bachelor of Medicine of Oxford, although that university, among its other kindnesses, refused me the degree of Doctor—and I know what I am saying. You find me, a dying man, with a fourth *Letter for Toleration* on his hands.

Shaftesbury: There is certainly a present need for such a letter, Mr Locke. In Holland no less than in England. Mr Furly told me the Calvinist magistrates there have become worse than the Roman Catholic Church in persecuting heretics.

Locke: Mr Furly has written as much to me. Mr William Penn, another Quaker, used to say the Church of England was worse than the Roman Catholic Church. But the first Lord Shaftesbury never made that mistake. And no one understood the principles of toleration better than he.

Shaftesbury: I have always supposed, Mr Locke, that my grandfather acquired his thoughts on the subject from you. Of course I was an infant in the years of his power, and hardly thirteen when he died. I heard more, as a boy at Winchester, of his failures and disgrace than I heard of his triumphs. But I remember him as a scholarly man who realized he had in you, Mr Locke, a great philosopher in his own house.

Locke In the years I lived in your grandfather's house, I was of course very close to him. We shared many thoughts on several subjects, and since I learned from him, he may well have learned from me. But your grandfather was a champion of toleration when my views were quite otherwise. I wonder if you remember his record in Parliament in the years that followed the restoration of Charles II? It was a Parliament with very strong feelings against Dissenters. Your grandfather was the first to stand up for their liberties. He resisted the Corporation Act which compelled all holders of municipal offices to take the sacraments: he resisted the Act of Uniformity which made all clergymen accept episcopal ordination, and the Conventicle Act, which forbade Dissenter's meetings of more than five persons. He resisted the Five Mile Act, and all the other measures which were intended to make pariahs of the Nonconformist Christians.

Shaftesbury: I am proud that he did so.

Locke: But I, my lord, cannot claim the honour of implanting those principles in your grandfather's breast. On the contrary, in the first year or two of the Stuart Restoration, I disapproved of toleration.

Shaftesbury: But you, Mr Locke, were not a Member of Parliament.

Locke: True, I was still an Oxford tutor. And yet I had thoughts on those matters. I even went so far as to write a pamphlet, and prepared it for publication, though in the end it was never printed. I have a copy of it still among my papers. It might surprise you to read it. It was a reply, I remember, to one by Mr Edward Bagshawe, who had argued that the government has no right to impose the forms of public worship. I held, against him, that the government must necessarily have an absolute and arbitrary power over its subjects.

Shaftesbury: Then you agreed with Mr Thomas Hobbes' *Leviathan*?

Locke: I came to my own conclusions. You must remember the year was 1661. I was then a man of twenty-nine, and I had seen nothing but civil strife all my life. When I was a boy of ten in Somerset my father went away to fight with the Parliamentary Army. When I was sixteen, a boy at Westminster School, King Charles the First was beheaded nearby at Whitehall. We prayed for him in school, because our Master was a Royalist. At twenty I went to Oxford, and there I enjoyed the rule of the Puritan saints for eight years.

Believe me, when the King returned, I wanted nothing more than to give him unlimited power. I was impatient of the name of 'liberty' because the people who had proclaimed it had destroyed it.

Shaftesbury: Had you met my grandfather then?

Locke: I met Lord Ashley, as he then was, in 1667. By that time I had changed my views. Those early Restoration Parliaments were so intolerant that I soon lost my early fears of anarchy, and like many others I began to see that Mr Edward Bagshawe was right after all: he, poor man, died on bail from Newgate before the tide of opinion turned. So in justice to your grandfather, you must not suppose he was indebted for his thoughts to *me*. God knows, he has been sufficiently ill-used.

Shaftesbury: 'A name to all succeeding ages cursed
For close designs and crooked counsel fit
Sagacious, bold, and turbulent of wit,
Restless, unfixed in principles and place
In power unpleased, impatient of disgrace;
A fiery soul, which, working out its way
Fretted the pigmy body to decay.'

Locke: Unfortunately, Mr Dryden did not speak for himself alone. Your grandfather had many enemies.

Shaftesbury: Is that not, perhaps, strange? Tolerant people do not usually have many enemies.

Locke: Your grandfather's enemies were Papists.

Shaftesbury: And of course he would never tolerate Papists.

Locke: I should never have wished him to.

Shaftesbury: I cannot help thinking, Mr Locke, that it is very illogical to uphold the liberties of Protestant Dissenters in the name of religious toleration and yet to deny the same liberties to Roman Catholics.

Locke: Your reasoning, my lord, is reminiscent of King Charles the Second's.

Shaftesbury: Charles the Second was in many ways a tolerant man.

Locke: He was an indulgent man.

Shaftesbury: Is there much difference between toleration and indulgence?

Locke: A great difference. Toleration is a mark of strength; indulgence is a mark of weakness.

Shaftesbury: I agree that self-indulgence is. But surely, Mr Locke, indulgence towards others is the same as toleration.

Locke: No, my lord, it is by no means the same. We are indulgent towards the things and the people we like. To be tolerant means to put up with the things and the people we do not like.

Shaftesbury: (*Laughing*) I am exceedingly tolerant of the things and the people I like.

Locke: Your words seem to refute me, my lord, but your laughter confirms my point.

Shaftesbury: My remark was intended as a pleasantry.

Locke: Precisely. And what made a pleasantry? Nothing other than the play on words, the misuse, in fact, of the word 'toleration'. Sir Francis Masham has a friend who is given to the same pleasantry. Having helped himself unasked to Sir Francis Masham's Canary-wine, he always praises what he has 'accepted'. I confess the remark never fails to amuse me.

Shaftesbury: Perhaps it would fail to amuse you if the Canary-wine were yours and not Sir Francis Masham's.

Locke: It would still be a comical remark, and it is comical because it is incorrect to speak of 'accepting' what one is not offered.

Shaftesbury: And equally comical because equally incorrect to speak of 'tolerating' what one likes?

Locke: Yes, my lord. In all circumstances I must beg you to remember the strict use and usage of words. There would be no such word as 'toleration' if men disliked nothing.

Shaftesbury: Supposing a man is completely indifferent? Is he not then a model of tolerance?

Locke: The indifferent man has no occasion to be tolerant since the indifferent man, by definition, has no particular dislike.

Shaftesbury: But in your *Letters for Toleration* people are called upon not only to tolerate what they dislike but what they disapprove of.

Locke: I have used the word 'dislike' very broadly, to include 'disapproval' and even 'fear of'. That is the most difficult thing of all, to tolerate what we fear.

Shaftesbury: I suppose that is because fear is the most intense emotion.

Locke: It is, but it is none the more rational for that. There is a manifest connexion between being rational and being tolerant.

Shaftesbury: And you would suggest, Mr Locke, that being tolerant is neither being indulgent nor being indifferent?

Locke: The three words have different meanings, my lord. That is a fact about the English language. It is not a matter of what I would suggest.

Shaftesbury: Mr Locke, men are judged by their deeds and not their words. Let me put a question to you. A painful question for both of us. When people hear the name of Shaftesbury do they think at once of toleration, and all the splendid speeches my grandfather made in its favour? Or do they remember what actually happened when he was a man of power in this realm, and think instead of persecution? Do they remember those men, the great men like Stafford and Plunket, the humble men like Staley and Coleman, who were sentenced to death, and the hundreds who were put in prison, thanks to the efforts of my grandfather to put an end to Popery?

Locke: There was evidence of treasonable plots.

Shaftesbury: The evidence of Titus Oates?

Locke: Titus Oates was, of course, a liar. We know better now than to listen to men like him. But, my Lord Shaftesbury, we live now in times of relative security. We owe that security to the events of 1688 which placed our late King William on the throne. Before that Revolution, England was neither tranquil nor safe. France had become an ambitious and predatory nation. How much so, I observed myself in the years I lived in France. The King of France had agents everywhere, and his agents in England and Ireland were the communicants of the Roman Catholic Church. It was a patriotic duty to watch them and curb them.

Shaftesbury: But was it even a wise policy? My grandfather tormented his enemies on the pretext of a Popish Plot, and a few years later his enemies tormented him on the pretext of a Protestant Plot. Possibly, if he had been more tolerant of Catholics, he would not have had to die, as he did, in a Dutch exile, and you too, Mr Locke, might not have had to follow him there.

Locke: The reverse was temporary; I never despaired of our ultimate success.

Shaftesbury: So you think the persecution of Catholics was both logical and prudent?

Locke: My Lord Shaftesbury, I wonder if you wholly understand my attitude, which was also your grandfather's attitude? I have never said the Catholic has not precisely the same right as every one else to worship as he pleases. I have never wished to punish men for believing in the Real Presence or the authenticity of sacred relics or the infallibility of the Pope, even though I think such beliefs unworthy of men's intelligence. I have never wished to prohibit their religious ceremonies. Let them celebrate as many masses as they please. I have no objection to their mummeries. But the activities of Papists do not stop short at religious observations. Papists engage in political conspiracy—political conspiracy on behalf of a foreign power. Their Pope is a foreigner, and temporal rulers who share their religion—principally the Kings of France and Spain—naturally claim their support. If any sect of Protestant Dissenters had analogous relations with a foreign power, I think we should, on the same grounds, deny freedom to them. It is not a question of religious toleration, but of political toleration.

Shaftesbury: Then, Mr Locke, you would recommend religious toleration but not political toleration. That seems to me a very Jesuitical distinction.

Locke: My Lord, you distress me. I do, indeed, recommend political toleration. The difference is that whereas religious toleration may, and I think should, be unlimited, political toleration cannot be. In the creation of civil society some liberties are necessarily forfeited, and it is the essential purpose of government to exercise force. Since you have discovered that I am the author of the *Two Treatises of Government*, published fifteen years ago, you know it is my belief that subjects should continue to enjoy in civil society the greatest possible freedom and that governments should exercise the least possible force. Even so, the toleration must stop at a certain point.

Shaftesbury: At what point?

Locke: Ah, that is the whole problem of liberty. At what point would you suppose, my lord?

Shaftesbury: No government, I imagine, can tolerate murderers and thieves.

Locke: There you have two excellent examples. But we must try to formulate a principle. I think we have to go back to a subject we have already touched upon: the original purposes of government which we saw as the preservation of life, liberty and property. The murderers and thieves you mention cannot be tolerated precisely because they violate a man's natural rights. And there we can locate the point at which toleration must end: the point at which any man's natural rights are invaded or imperilled.

Shaftesbury: I am not sure that I follow you entirely, Mr Locke. I can see that governments exist to defend the rights to life and property. But how can you say they exist to defend the right to liberty, when liberty is relinquished in the act which brings them into being. Can men be both ruled and free from rulers?

Locke: Certainly, *some* liberty was lost when men left the state of nature to live in civil societies. But we must remember that while liberty is *in principle* unlimited in a state of natural anarchy, in practice it must however be severely limited by the perils of lawless life. In a civil society a man's liberty must stop short at the point where it jeopardizes the liberty of another, but given this not unreasonable limitation to his liberty, a man has far better prospect of enjoying it than he had in a state of nature, when his joy in unlimited freedom was likely to be terminated at any moment by a sudden bloody death.

Shaftesbury: So you would say that freedom, like toleration, cannot be absolute?

Locke: The degree of freedom enjoyed by citizens corresponds to the degree of toleration exhibited by governments. I favour the highest possible measure of both that is compatible with the safety of the commonwealth.

Shaftesbury: But how much *is* compatible with the safety of the commonwealth? You mentioned Mr Hobbes.

Locke: No, my lord. It was you who mentioned Mr Hobbes.

Shaftesbury: It is not that I agree with Mr Hobbes. Far from it. I detest his *Leviathan*. But I think it more worthy of refutation than the *Patriarcha* of Sir Thomas Filmer, on which you, Mr Locke, have spent so much of your fire.

Locke: I cannot remember whether I have read the *Leviathan*. It may well be a better book than *Patriarcha*. I did not attempt to refute *Patriarcha* because it was a good book, but because it was an influential book, because its policy is that of the court party in our national politics. *Patriarcha* is, so to speak, a party manifesto. As for Mr Hobbes, whatever he says, he speaks for no one but himself.

Shaftesbury: But you know what it is he says?

Locke: Refresh my memory. You appear to have become an authority on the subject. Give me, my lord, the benefit of your knowledge.

Shaftesbury: Mr Hobbes believed that any division of sovereignty, any tolerance of any opposition to the established power would jeopardize the security of the commonwealth.

Locke: If that was Mr Hobbes's belief he was unfortunately not alone in holding it.

Shaftesbury: He held it because he thought that man is naturally rapacious, and that once the restraints of an absolute sovereign were removed, we should relapse into an appalling state of anarchy and chaos.

Locke: That seems to me a most mistaken view. I do not think that man is naturally perfect. But I do not think rulers any less imperfect than the common man; indeed I shall submit to you, my lord, nobleman that you are, that the rulers of the world appear to me to be, as a body, *more* imperfect than the men they rule; so I think it is no defence against the sinfulness of us all to give absolute authority to one of the less virtuous minorities among us.

Shaftesbury: Mr Hobbes did not say that rulers were any better than subjects. He said that bad government is better than no government at all.

Locke: And do you think it is, my lord?

Shaftesbury: Since we have no record of what life was like before governments were instituted, it is very difficult to say.

Locke: But no doubt you have read the writings of travellers who have sailed to those remote regions of the earth where government is unknown, where men still live in a state of nature. They tell us that such men are, for the most part, happy and contented; not, as Mr Hobbes suggested, brutish and rapacious. You will certainly not persuade me that they were worse off than men living under an evil sovereign in what we please to call a civilized condition.

Shaftesbury: So that if you were asked, Mr Locke, why you advocate toleration and freedom, you would say: scepticism concerning rulers and faith in mankind as a whole.

Locke: I would rather say: scepticism concerning temporal institutions and faith in God's creations. Government is a temporal institution; men are created by God, and created, the Scriptures assure us, in God's own image.

Shaftesbury: Some people say that government is a divine institution, or at least that kingship is.

Locke: Many people say so; and I can think of nothing more obviously false. Nowhere in the Scriptures is there any account of God having instituted civil societies or placed monarchs on their thrones.

Shaftesbury: Are you forgetting the Jews?

Locke: God *chose* the Jews as his people; he did not institute their sovereign. Still less did he institute the sovereignty of the House of Stuart.

Shaftesbury: Who did institute the sovereignty of the House of Stuart?

Locke: The English and Scots people, my lord, and from their consent alone the House of Stuart derives its right to rule us. A king's right to rule is a trust, and where that trust is violated, as it was violated by King James the Second, his right to rule is forfeited, and it becomes the people's duty to remove him.

Shaftesbury: But, Mr Locke, you are maintaining a very paradoxical position; a ruler, you say, must be tolerant towards his subjects; but subjects need not be tolerant towards their ruler.

Locke: My Lord Shaftesbury, I do assuredly believe that subjects must be

tolerant towards their ruler; all I am saying is that there are limits
to what subjects need tolerate, just as I previously said that there
are limits to what a sovereign should tolerate.

Shaftesbury: You said that a sovereign should not tolerate breaches of the law
by the citizens.

Locke: Now I am saying that citizens need not tolerate breaches of the
law by the sovereign. There is no paradox in that. The law must
be above both ruler and ruled, and if either party breaks it, the
other may act. The right of resistance belongs to the people just
as the right of inflicting punishment belongs to the sovereign.

Shaftesbury: I cannot help thinking that the right of resistance is a dangerous
thing for men to possess.

Locke: Of course it is, my Lord Shaftesbury; but remember also, men are
not children.

Shaftesbury: I suppose it is because you believe that men are, for the most part,
reasonable and well disposed, that you are willing to trust them
with liberty.

Locke: Yes.

Shaftesbury: In other words, it is because you think men are naturally good.

Locke: If you prefer such words.

Shaftesbury: There is also the Christian doctrine of the Fall of Man. If we
reflect on that, and think of the corruptness, instead of the goodness of men, does it not lessen our zeal for their liberty, and make
us consider instead the necessity of discipline or strong government?

Locke: The Fall of Man would be an argument for strong government if
it had happened that the rulers of this world did not participate in
the Fall. If you suppose they did not, my lord, I shall venture to
question your knowledge of Christian theology.

Shaftesbury: I wished simply to suggest that we cannot build our politics on the
assumption that man is naturally virtuous, and on the contrary
that Christian theology teaches us to acknowledge his natural
wickedness. If there were no wickedness in men, I imagine there
need be no such institution as government. Could we say that
government is a means for diminishing the harm that human
wickedness can do?

Locke: We could indeed. I believe I have already said so in my *Second
Treatise of Government*, but it does not follow that the stronger the
government the less harm human wickedness could do; quinine is
a means for diminishing the harm that fevers can do to the body,
and it certainly does not follow that the more quinine you take,

the less harm the fevers will do to your body. Reason prescribes the use of so much quinine and no more; reason also prescribes the vesting of so much power in governments and no more.

Shaftesbury: You talk of law, Mr Locke, and what is law but what the ruler makes? So how can a ruler be 'under the law'? He can always make a new law to fit his action if any action of his is contrary to an old law.

Locke: There is a law of God above the law of princes; a law of Nature above the law of commonwealth.

Shaftesbury: How do you know what that law is?

Locke: The law of Nature is perceptible to the eye of reason.

Shaftesbury: The 'eye of reason' is a metaphor, Mr Locke. In your *Essay on Human Understanding* you show how all knowledge is derived from experience, which is, of course, sensory observation. But you deal in that book only with the outer senses such as seeing and hearing. Surely if there is moral knowledge also, then there must be a corresponding faculty within us—a moral sense— through which we can perceive moral laws—those laws which are higher than the edicts of princes.

Locke: We have no need to invoke a moral sense my lord; we can simply speak of conscience.

Shaftesbury: 'Conscience' seems somehow too common a word.

Locke: No word is too common, if by 'common' you mean universally known and understood. We should avoid words that are exotic, lest, from imposing our own meaning on them, we pass to the belief that we are using them correctly; and our discourse, though comprehensible to ourselves, becomes incomprehensible to others. Remember, people dislike admitting that any discourse is incomprehensible to them. Unless they are philosophers, they pretend to understand what they do not understand.

Shaftesbury: And if they are philosophers, they pretend *not* to understand what they do understand.

Locke: *Our* sort of philosopher perhaps, my lord; we must not conclude that the age of oracular philosophy has ended.

Shaftesbury: I remember, Mr Locke, you once proposed to write a treatise on moral philosophy to set beside what you had already written on the philosophy of knowledge. Did you ever write it?

Locke: Never. I pondered carefully, and came to the conclusion that there was no need for a treatise on moral philosophy. There is already an incomparable one.

Shaftesbury: And which is that?

Locke: The New Testament, my Lord Shaftesbury. The New Testament read in the light of reason and common sense.

Shaftesbury: Or moral sense.

Locke: Which I presume you to suppose, like common sense, to reside in each one of us?

Shaftesbury: The difficulty is that different men have different moral promptings. What one man feels is right, another feels is wrong. Nor is the New Testament an unequivocal guide. For two men of contrary convictions can each find Biblical authority for their attitudes. As for the light of common reason, if that illumination is universally distributed, no one can claim to have more of it than anyone else.

Locke: Assuredly differences occur, and this occurrence provides yet another argument for toleration. If there is no knowing which of two equally sincere, but contrary, moral views is correct, then it is only right that we should allow the free expression of both.

Shaftesbury: Mr Locke, the problem does not stop short at expression: there is also the question of action. For example, the Quakers refuse, in the light of their moral convictions, to bear arms, while most of us think it a duty to bear arms for the defence of the realm, to say nothing of our own persons.

Locke: The point at which toleration ends is always the same, my lord; it ends when the action in question imperils the safety of the commonwealth. If a Quaker goes unarmed in time of peace, and is assaulted by robbers—as I have been assaulted from time to time in Epping Forest—he has only himself to answer to if he loses his purse or his life. The government cannot compel a man to defend himself. But if the nation were invaded, we might well have to compel every man to take up arms to help defend us all.

Shaftesbury: If the Quaker claimed in such circumstances that the moral law was above the law of governments, he would only be saying what you have said.

Locke: I fear he would say it inopportunely.

Shaftesbury: And yet on your premises, logically.

Locke: My lord, I do not think it logical to press to the service of extreme persuasions, precepts which are intended as a general guide. There is always an exception to any rule of conduct: and it is the mark of the moderate mind that it recognizes such exceptions. The ten commandments enjoin us not to lie or kill and so forth; yet we can easily imagine circumstances in which it would *not* be wrong to lie or kill; but being *exceptional* circumstances, they do not invalidate the *general* necessity of obedience to the ten commandments.

Shaftesbury: So in spite of your distaste for Aristotle, Mr Locke, you would agree with him that moderation is the golden rule.

Locke: If Aristotle thought so, yes; any rational mind must, I should think, perceive it; and if men's minds were not blinded by false philosophy and prejudice, there would surely be no disagreement on it.

Shaftesbury: In the case of a private individual, tolerance and moderation go together. I suppose it is also true of governments and churches; the more moderate their beliefs the more tolerant their politics.

Locke: Tolerance is more important in governments and churches than in private individuals.

Shaftesbury: Yet what is a virtue in a public body must also be a virtue in a private person.

Locke: I did not say it was not a virtue in a private person, my lord. I said it was a *less important* virtue. That is because public institutions are powerful, whereas most individuals are weak. The intolerance of the powerless does relatively little harm.

Shaftesbury: But you would agree, Mr Locke, that tolerance and moderation go together?

Locke: I think no one would deny it. Intolerance, as we have seen, may spring from several motives. Sometimes it is prompted by vanity, as in the case of a ruler who cannot suffer to have his wisdom questioned. Sometimes it is prompted by anxiety, as in the case of a tyrant who is tormented by the thought of his victims seizing power and exacting retribution. But there are also men whose intolerance stems from the illusion of omniscience and righteousness, and such is the case with Roman Catholics. I once enjoyed the acquaintance of a learned Jesuit, and he would say to me 'Toleration is a pleasant word, but it is wrong to tolerate error'.

Shaftesbury: What did he mean by error?

Locke: For one thing, my beliefs; but in truth all beliefs that were at variance with his own. He had an absolute confidence in the truth of his excessively comprehensive philosophy. You are quite right to say that toleration goes with moderate opinions. The less people claim to know, and the less rigidly they hold their convictions, the more tolerant they will be. Certainty is a great enemy of toleration. I do not mean that a man should have no definite persuasions. I only wish men to achieve sufficient understanding to entertain the possibility that they may, after all, be wrong. Toleration comes with the awareness of how limited our knowledge is.

Shaftesbury: Nevertheless, we must admit that intolerance sometimes springs from good intentions. The Jesuit priest who thought it wrong to tolerate error is not in the same class as the tyrant who will brook no opposition.

Locke: My lord, I can assure you from experience that it is small comfort to a man who is persecuted to know that his persecutors believe their motives to be good. There is something to be said for the Borgias. I am sure they were no less infallible than their successors as Vicars of Rome; and what is more, they did not deceive themselves with the belief that they were instruments of righteousness.

Shaftesbury: I was about to suggest that intolerance is still intolerance whether the intentions are good or bad.

Locke: Good intentions are often mixed with bad ones. Tell me, my lord, what do you think the most striking violation of the principles of toleration we can observe in recent history?

Shaftesbury: I think I should say the revocation of the Edict of Nantes.

Locke: You could not find a better example of what I have in mind. I think we could say that the revocation of the Edict of Nantes was prompted both by religious motives, by the desire to save the people of France from the scandalous heresy of Protestant faith; and also by a political motive, by the desire of the King of France to enlarge his authority, and to restrict the liberty of his subjects. But what happens in such circumstances? The temporal ends are accomplished. The spiritual ones are not. The restoration of the Edict of Nantes strengthened the authority of the King of France, but it did not purify the Catholic religion. The work of God cannot be done by such means; the work of God is done by persuasion and prayer; it is not done by coercion.

Shaftesbury: Mr Locke, we have agreed that the truth does not need to be imposed by force. We have agreed that force should only be used by governments so far as it is needed to defend the realm and to secure liberty and property of citizens. We have also agreed that the profession of unorthodox beliefs, no matter how absurd, ought to be tolerated, because the profession of such beliefs constitutes no danger to society and because the freedom of each of us depends on the freedom of all. I have agreed with you that Catholics forfeit their right to toleration in so far as they transfer their allegiance from the English crown to a foreign potentate. But you do not seem to have accepted my suggestion that tolerance is a quality of the mind or character, like patience or fortitude, and that the way to further a policy of toleration in politics is to cultivate this quality of tolerance in private persons.

Locke: My lord, you will easily convince me that the most enduring foundation for a policy of toleration in the nation is this quality of tolerance in individual citizens. I allow myself to believe that the spread of knowledge and decline of superstition will do much to effect that end. But we must not make the policy of toleration appear a counsel of perfection, an ideal goal, which, by reason of its ideal nature, can never be achieved. The policy of toleration is not the sum of all forbearance, strength, humanity and wisdom; it is something much more commonplace and near at hand. To speak out for toleration is simply to say to the rulers of this world: 'Leave us alone, let us speak, let us print, let us preach, meet and worship as we please. It is no part of your business as civil rulers to interfere with these activities. Do the duties with which you were entrusted when our forefathers brought governments into being; and do no more.'

Shaftesbury: I am pleased to hear you put it in those terms. For I must confess, Mr Locke, that I have been troubled by one thought. I see and approve the policy of toleration, but I know in my heart that I am not a tolerant man.

Locke: You must not let that hinder you, my lord. Your grandfather, in his personal life, was not a tolerant man.

Shaftesbury: That, Mr Locke, I am old enough to have noticed.

Locke: I will mention another thing. I, in my personal life, am not a tolerant man. But please do not tell me, my Lord Shaftesbury, that you are old enough to have noticed that as well.

Diderot and Rousseau

A dialogue on Progress

In his celebrated *Confessions*, Jean-Jacques Rousseau claims to have had a revelation on the road to Vincennes, when he was going to visit his friend Denis Diderot, imprisoned there for offending orthodoxy by his freethinking writings. Rousseau came upon an advertisement for an essay prize on the question of whether the advancement of science and the arts had helped to purify or corrupt morals. The thought came to him, he said, as a great emotional shock, that progress had in fact corrupted morals. At Vincennes, Diderot urged Rousseau to develop this thought in an essay, and compete. Diderot was a born journalist—his monument is the great French *Encyclopédie*, which he edited—and he predicted that an opinion as unfashionable as Rousseau's would startle the judges and win the prize. He was proved right; Rousseau won.

But what did Diderot, or indeed Rousseau himself in his maturity, really think about progress? In the following dialogue I have tried to construct an imaginary conversation between the two philosophers as it might have taken place in the twilight of their friendship, in the year 1757, when Rousseau was forty-five and Diderot forty-four.

In the broadest terms, Diderot believed in progress and Rousseau did not. Diderot, a typical bourgeois intellectual of the French Enlightenment, believed, with Lord Bacon, that science could save us. The way it should do so was first through the abolition of superstition, otherwise religion, and secondly through the organization of knowledge (hence the *Encyclopédie*). Rousseau, a true child of Calvin's Geneva, preferred natural ignorance to cultivated scepticism. Society, he believed, could either improve man or worsen him. All advanced societies corrupted men; salvation lay in simple ones. The intellectual differences between Rousseau and Diderot were perhaps linked with temperamental differences. When they found that they really disagreed, their friendship ended.

Diderot: What a pleasure it is, for a change, to see you here in Paris, my dear Citizen.

comme

Rousseau: So you are in that mood, are you, Diderot? I am not sure that I can bear much mockery.

Diderot: What mockery?

Rousseau: 'My dear Citizen.'

Diderot: But is that not how your name appears in your publications: 'Jean-Jacques Rousseau, Citizen of Geneva'?

Rousseau: And you are described in your official papers as 'Denis Diderot, Bourgeois of Paris'. Am I to address you as 'Bourgeois'?

Diderot: It would be a less flattering greeting.

Rousseau: Then you will grant that we Genevans have that advantage over you French. We are a nation of citizens; you are a nation of bourgeois.

Diderot: In a city without royalty or nobility, your citizen and your bourgeois must be the same man. If Geneva ever progresses from Swiss rusticity towards more sophisticated forms of social hierarchy . . .

Rousseau: You dare speak to me of *that* as progress?

Diderot: For lack, perhaps, of a better word.

Rousseau: I have sometimes doubted your friendship, Diderot, but I have never doubted that you understood my thoughts.

Diderot: I merely wished to suggest that your native city, though advanced in some respects, might be less advanced in others.

Rousseau: I sometimes think you try to wound me.

Diderot: My nature is much too cheerful to seek any such morbid satisfaction.

Rousseau: What about that play of yours—*Le Fils Naturel*? But, no, I don't wish to think about it.

Diderot: Well, I know you were affected by it.

Rousseau: Affected? That is an odd way of describing what I felt when I read those words of yours: 'The good man lives in society; only the bad man lives alone.' Do you think I did not see that those words were directed at *me*; and, what is worse, that every other reader would see that they were?

Diderot: We all know you have quit polite society, my dear friend, and apart from those two housekeepers of yours, Madame Le Vasseur and her daughter, I suppose you do live alone; but that is not what I was thinking of when I put those words into the mouth of one of my characters. I intended simply to suggest that man needs some form of civil society—you have often said as much yourself.

Rousseau: I live alone because I have to—to earn my bread, to write, to think. People know me as a solitary man. When I first had some success in Paris I was shy of polite society because I had not been brought up to it. I felt a false shame about what you speak of as Swiss rusticity, and I fled from the *salons*.

Diderot: You also fled from the King when he was in a mind to bestow a pension on you.

Rousseau: The more I tried to escape the more they pursued me; when it became known that I refused invitations, I acquired a scarcity value, and women vied to entertain me. I have had to struggle ever since for solitude. It's a human need. So how can I forget those words of yours, Diderot; 'Only the bad man lives alone'.

Diderot: You should read them in their context.

Rousseau: I prefer not to read them at all. But I have found something in the Scriptures, in the Book of Ecclesiastes: 'Hast thou drawn thy sword against thy friend? Be comforted: all may be as it was before. Hast thou assailed him with angry words? Thou mayst yet be reconciled.'

Diderot: I am afraid that play of mine has been unfortunate in many ways. I suppose you know that I have been accused of plagiarism; the gossip all over Paris is that *Le Fils Naturel* is a copy of Goldoni's *Il Vero Amico*.

Rousseau: Yes, I heard the gossip, and I read Goldoni. I know there is no truth in the rumours. *Il Vero Amico*—The True Friend. I said to myself 'I am the true friend of Denis Diderot; he has injured me, but I will not have him unjustly accused. If I keep away from him, people will think I believe he is guilty. So I shall go to visit him in Paris, to demonstrate my feelings.'

Diderot: I am very grateful. Though I would have gladly come to Montmorency, as I have often done before, despite the cab being damned expensive.

Rousseau: You are fortunate you can afford a cab. When I used to visit you at Vincennes, I had to come on foot, walking—do you remember? —six miles each way through the worst of the summer heat.

Diderot: Inside a prison, one is not much troubled by the summer heat. But I was greatly touched by your visits, of course.

Rousseau: My health hasn't been the same since that summer. It was a turning-point. Since then, my bladder has never ceased to torment me.

Diderot: I had forgotten about your bladder, but I remember that it was a turning-point for you. That summer marked the beginning of your fame.

Rousseau: That is true, too. It was eight years ago, my thirty-eighth year. I shall never forget how I paused under a tree on my way to visit you, opened a copy of the *Mercure de France*, and found the announcement of that essay competition arranged by the Academy of Dijon.

Diderot: 'Whether the progress of science and the arts has done more to corrupt or purify morals.'

Rousseau: Yes, when I read that question, and realized what the answer was, I saw another universe and became another man.

Diderot: You were certainly very disturbed when you appeared at Vincennes. But I can't remember that you had actually made up your mind to uphold the view that progress *had* corrupted morals. I urged you to do so, of course. You were afraid it would displease an academy of learning to be told that the advancement of knowledge had undermined morality. But I remember telling you that if you wanted to win the prize you should say something different and original.

Rousseau: But I had seen the truth, Diderot. What did I care for the prize? I never expected to win it. What mattered was that I had realized for the first time that civilization does not improve men but makes them worse.

Diderot: It's a half truth; but it's a half truth that is worth saying because it affords an entertaining paradox.

Rousseau: You may think like a philosopher, Diderot, but you speak like a journalist.

Diderot: I *am* a journalist. I should like to be a dramatist, the Molière of the eighteenth century. But, as you have seen, I am not lucky in the theatre. My success has been the *Encyclopédie*. If I am remembered at all, it will be as editor of that.

Rousseau: I have never really understood the real aim of the *Encyclopédie*.

Diderot: But you have written parts of it, and some of the best parts, if you will allow me to say so.

Rousseau: I mean your final aim.

Diderot: To enlarge knowledge.

Rousseau: By diminishing faith? To turn the reader into a man who knows everything and believes nothing?

Diderot: Like the philosopher Locke, we have to clear away some of the rubbish that lies in the path of knowledge.

Rousseau: I admit you are wholly in line with the trend of modern culture, which is to carry man forward from natural ignorance towards unnatural scepticism.

Diderot: If the inspiration for the *Encyclopédie* comes from anywhere it comes from Francis Bacon, the Lord Chancellor of England, and you have more than once written of him, my dear friend, as the greatest modern thinker. How can you call Bacon great if you deny the first principles of his teaching, which is that all real knowledge is scientific and that the development of science might immeasurably improve the life of men on earth?

Rousseau: I admire Bacon's theories of morals and law, but you know I don't accept his doctrine of progress. How could the further advancement of science improve men's lives, when it has already done so much to worsen them.

Diderot: There is much wrong with our modern culture, I agree, and Bacon thought so, too. Didn't he say that modern philosophers knew even less than the ancient Greeks? But that is because our culture has been dominated by religion. Learning, for centuries, has been the study of metaphysics; knowledge has languished because religion, which is based on superstition, is hostile to science.

Rousseau: It is right to be hostile. Science has grown up with men's vices. Indeed every science you can name has its roots in some moral defect. Arithmetic springs from avarice, physics from idle curiosity, mechanics from ambition. And this evil origin appears again in their purposes. If men were not unjust, what use would they have for jurisprudence? And what would become of history, if there were no wars or conspiracies or tyrants?

Diderot: The value of science is clearly explained by Bacon: it is not simply a matter of satisfying curiosity about the mysteries of nature, but of learning to master nature for the advantage of humanity, to diminish the poverty of man's life on earth by creating a new abundance.

Rousseau: Abundance? But that is to make things worse. Luxury is an evil in itself, and it has always been recognized by the wisest men as an especially corrupting evil. Frugality is necessary to a good and upright life in an individual, and for a strong and healthy state. Luxury undermines nations as it undermines men. You have only to compare the fortunes of Sybaris with those of Sparta. A handful of peasants defeated the Sybarites: the Spartans became the terror of Asia.

Diderot: 'Luxury' is your word. I did not use it, and neither did Bacon. The hope he entertained was to end the servitude of man to hunger and disease. This is not a question of luxury, though I dare say the first man who wore clogs may have seemed a voluptuary to the rest who walked barefoot. I have no wish to see another Sybaris. But I might like to see another Athens.

Rousseau: Athens was no better than Sybaris. It made itself the seat of politeness and taste, a city of poets and orators, its buildings as elegant
as its literature. A perfect model of culture, my dear Diderot; but
also a model of vice and corruption.

Diderot: What about the philosophers of Athens? What about Socrates and
Plato?

Rousseau: Yes, there were some wise men in Athens who withstood the
general torrent and preserved their integrity even in the company
of poets. But what was their situation? Socrates was condemned
and made to drink hemlock. Plato was a bitter critic of Athenian
values; he said specifically that poets and artists must be banished
from a just republic and that what you call scientific knowledge is
not knowledge at all.

Diderot: But, my dear friend, Athens would not have been remembered if
it had had no literature, no arts, no science, no historians, no
orators. The grandeur and the glory of Athens, the reason why we
speak of it today lies wholly in its culture.

Rousseau: Is it so important to be remembered? To be celebrated? Surely it
is more important to be virtuous and happy, like the Spartans.
Let us imagine you, my dear Diderot, making a speech in a
market-place of Sparta: 'Open your eyes citizens,' you would say.
'Do you realize that your whole lives are devoted to duty, to the
exercise of courage and the defence of liberty? You are forgetting
the supreme need to entertain posterity; you are writing no
poetry, carving no statues, devising no systems of philosophy that
will capture the attention of generations to come. Spartans, give
up this way of life that makes you virtuous and happy, and adopt
one that will make you famous, like the Athenians.' Well,
Diderot, can you imagine anything more absurd?

Diderot: I cannot imagine anything more false. There is no reason to think
that Sparta was any happier than Athens. Success in arms is no
measure of joy. It might even be fair to conclude that those who
like war most must be those who like life least.

Rousseau: You will agree that the Spartans were virtuous?

Diderot: They were not; they were conspicuously wicked. Consider how
they treated their helots. They condemned them to hard labour,
left them no rights of property, kept them outside the protection
of the law, strode among them, lash in hand, striking at everyone
irrespective of sex and age. And from time to time they killed off
a number of them. No, my dear Rousseau, the Spartans were a
cruel as well as a frugal people.

Rousseau: If you won't accept the lesson of Greece, look at Rome. As soon as Rome came to be filled with scholars and orators, military discipline was neglected, agriculture was despised, and society was split up into rival factions. A love of good living took the place of the love of duty, and the greatest Romans themselves declared that since learned men had appeared among them, honest men had been in eclipse. Before that time, the Romans were satisfied with the practice of virtue; as soon as they began to study theories of virtue they were undone.

Diderot: It was only their learning that made the Romans better than the Goths and Vandals.

Rousseau: They were no better; and in time they became worse. What would the great soul of Fabricius have felt if he had come back to life in the later years of Rome; 'What,' he would have asked, 'has become of those thatched roofs and rustic hearths that were once the dwelling-place of temperance and manliness? What fatal splendour has succeeded to the ancient Roman simplicity? What is the meaning of all these statues and marble buildings? What are all these effeminate manners? You, the lords of the earth have made yourselves the slaves of the frivolous nations you are supposed to have subdued.'

Diderot: And what are those words, my dear friend, if they are not oratory? Yet you use it to attack oratory, just as you use philosophy to attack philosophy, and learning to attack learning.

Rousseau: Certainly, philosophy must help to cure the evil it has caused. A culture, once it has lost its simplicity, must be criticized in its own language.

Diderot: Criticized, yes; and no one is more critical than I, of the civilization of France as we know it today. But you, my dear Rousseau, you do not criticize. You attack. Your posture, like that of your beloved Spartans, is warlike.

Rousseau: It is right to be militant against evil.

Diderot: But it is not constructive. The rational answer to a defective culture, is a better one; your answer is no culture at all.

Rousseau: You misrepresent me; my answer is a simple, natural culture.

Diderot: You would have us become a nation of soldiers and woodcutters.

Rousseau: Why not? That would be better than being a nation of jewellers and pastrycooks.

Diderot: If you deny that progress improves morals, you cannot deny that it improves manners. It makes men more gentle.

Rousseau: Gentleness is not always a merit; it may turn into softness or weakness. Virtue is not gentle; it must know how to be severe against vice and how to punish crime.

Diderot: But virtue is not a running battle. Virtue means knowing how to behave well. Culture teaches men civility.

Rousseau: But what is that civility but a form of play-acting? Civilized man knows how to cover his true feelings with false appearances. He knows how to *seem* virtuous without being virtuous.

Diderot: But it is also part of a civilized upbringing to learn how to penetrate such appearances, to read what lies behind them.

Rousseau: Are you saying that the relations between civilized men are bluff and counter-bluff? I readily believe you; and the more advanced the society, the more elaborate the bluff. In Paris, society has reached a stage where nobody ever says what he really thinks. Except myself, of course.

Diderot: But you have already begun to make sincerity fashionable, my dear Rousseau. Nowadays at the theatre, women show they are shocked at the slightest impropriety. They would not have done so in the time of Molière.

Rousseau: That is because they have in fact become less modest. The greater the outward show they make, the more corrupt they are within.

Diderot: But you, my dear friend, have taught such ladies to weep quite genuine tears, to embrace their children and fondle their dogs. Women of fashion used once to admire restraint; you have taught them to show their emotions.

Rousseau: I detest the world of fashion.

Diderot: But that world does not detest you. Have you forgotten the efforts that you and I once made to recommend the Italian opera to the favour of polite society? You even wrote operas in the Italian style yourself. That scarcely suggests hostility, or even indifference, towards the world of fashion.

Rousseau: Indeed, one may use art to attack art, as I have already said. But the whole theatre is a poisonous institution. And that is another reason why I can't forgive you for printing that article in the *Encyclopédie* proposing that a theatre should be built in Geneva.

Diderot: It might seem a desirable amenity.

Rousseau: An amenity for whom? For Monsieur de Voltaire, who hasn't the courage to live in Paris, but lurks like a fox on the frontier of Geneva? I can well believe that that miserable buffoon is bored by country life, and would like to have a theatre to go to.

Diderot: Voltaire did not write the article. You know it was written by D'Alembert.

Rousseau: Voltaire told him what to say. What does D'Alembert know about Geneva? You should have invited a more qualified contributor.

Diderot: I am not responsible for the article. If I had invited anyone, I should have invited you. But D'Alembert, as you know, is a co-editor with me of the *Encyclopédie*. He does little of the work, but he has authority to write what he pleases. I do not like the article on Geneva, and I wish it had not been printed; but I am bound to tell you that my dislike of it has nothing to do with the proposal for a theatre in Geneva; I think that an excellent idea.

Rousseau: You would be willing to see the whole republic of Geneva corrupted so that Voltaire may have his treats?

Diderot: I do not think the theatre corrupts. On the contrary I look on it as a school of morality. It was such for the ancient Greeks; it was such in France during the reign of Louis Quatorze. I believe it might become one again.

Rousseau: How can you call the Greek theatre a school of morality? For what do we learn from Oedipus and Phaedra but that man is not free and that heaven punishes people for crimes it makes them commit? Is that morality?

Diderot: The aim of the ancient theatre was to purge the passions by a form of catharsis.

Rousseau: I fail to see how anything can purge the passions by exciting them. What the stage does, in fact, is to purge men of passions they never feel and to stir up the passions that they do feel.

Diderot: Tragedy shows how the wicked suffer.

Rousseau: It also shows how the wicked enjoy themselves before they suffer. The public remembers the joys and forgets the punishment, which never really touches them.

Diderot: Tragedy also calls forth human sympathy.

Rousseau: Pity is a sterile and fleeting emotion.

Diderot: I meant sympathy in the sense of a deeper awareness of the predicament of even the greatest men.

Rousseau: The tragic theatre is unduly interested in great men, great names, great crimes.

Diderot: That may be true of the classic theatre. The modern theatre is trying to create a more domestic form of tragedy.

Rousseau: The modern theatre is even worse. It deals with love, which the Greeks, at least, had the discrimination to omit.

Diderot: Modern plays show the suffering that love brings.

Rousseau: If love is depicted on the stage as it really is, it is bound to captivate, to seduce the spectator. The misfortunes of love make it all the more appealing. People begin by admiring honest love, as a result of what they see in the stage, and they end by giving themselves to illicit love.

Diderot: If you disapprove of tragedy, you will surely agree that comedy can be a school of morals.

Rousseau: I will not agree. Comedy works by means of ridicule. And ridicule is the best friend, the favourite arm, of vice.

Diderot: I am thinking of the best comedy.

Rousseau: And so am I. I am thinking of Molière. And what happens in nearly all Molière's plays? Fools are made to be the victims of scoundrels.

Diderot: But that is what happens in the real world. Molière's plays mirror truth.

Rousseau: But Molière more than half approves of the defeat of fools by scoundrels. The applause goes to the cleverest, the most adroit characters. It does not go to the virtuous. In *Le Misanthrope*, for instance, the perfectly worthy Alceste is made a figure of fun. Indeed, the lesson of all Molière's plays is the same; that in order to be an honest man, it is enough to avoid being an absolute rogue.

Diderot: I think there may be something in what you say, my friend. Molière's plays are out-of-date. They reflect the values of the seventeenth century. I think we need a new drama that is true to the experience of our own age. There is something absurd nowadays about the very title of *Le Bourgeois Gentilhomme*. In Molière's time, it was unthinkable that anyone could be both a bourgeois and a nobleman. But it is not at all unthinkable today. Half the house of peers in England consists of ennobled bourgeois. What has happened there is beginning to happen here.

Rousseau: I can see that a bourgeois audience will not relish ridicule.

Diderot: It is not only a question of that. Modern domestic and bourgeois life has its own dignity and its own values, which need to be represented on the stage. That is what my own plays are intended to do. You may have noticed that in *Le Fils Naturel*—if your eyes were not too riveted on what you felt to be an offensive line. One of my characters makes a plea for commerce, on the ground that it is the only occupation where great fortunes correspond to the effort and industry and the hazards that bring them into being. If the theatre is to be a school of morality, it must reflect enlightened views of justice.

Rousseau: Is that an improvement? At least Molière's plays speak of virtue and honour; yours speak only of trade and money, like our modern politicians. But, in fact, whatever plays you wrote, my dear Diderot, you could never make the theatre a school of morality, for the simple reason that the theatre is a place of entertainment, which means that the dramatist must flatter the fixed tastes, customs and prejudices of his audience. When he addresses such passions as pride, cupidity, lust, his public will be inwardly excited; when he appeals to noble principles, they will be only outwardly stirred. Each will proclaim his own merit by applauding the better, but each in his heart will feast on the worse. Your whole proposal is impossible. Only reason can overcome the passions; and reason has no effect whatever on the stage.

Diderot: If you suppose that only reason can overcome passions you must look again at your own writings, my dear Rousseau. Besides, the dramatist does not instruct with words alone. The pit of the theatre is the only place where the tears of the good man mingle with those of the vicious one. The wicked man becomes incensed against the very injustices that he himself has caused, and grows indignant against his own character. He leaves the theatre sickened by evil, which would not be the case if he was scolded by a judge or reproached by an orator. He is improved because he has learned to know himself better. The Greeks regarded the theatre as a sacred place, and it is no coincidence that the earliest drama of modern Europe was a religious drama.

Rousseau: I do not deny that the plays that were once performed in Christian churches may well have done good. All things that belong to a simple culture are innocent. It is the development, the advance of these things, that turns them from an aid to virtue into a hindrance. Culture goes wrong when it loses its contact with nature.

Diderot: In a sense, I agree with you. But where are we to find a society that has kept its contact with nature?

Rousseau: I remember seeing in my youth on a mountainside near Lake Neuchâtel . . .

Diderot: I fancied it would be something Swiss.

Rousseau: . . . a whole mountainside covered with small wooden houses, each standing at the centre of the piece of land on which it depended. Each was about the same size: a community of equal families. And there they were, happy peasants, unburdened by taxes and tithes, supporting themselves by their own work, and all skilled in a great variety of tasks. There was no cabinet maker, locksmith, glazier or carpenter among them; they all built, and maintained, their own houses. And their lives were not only devoted to work. They could all play the flute and dance and sing the songs that had been handed down to them by their forefathers. Their taste was good, too; the things they made with their hands were simple but pleasing, and so was their music. Such people have no need for poets or pedants or philosophers or dramatists. They only need to be shielded from corrupting contact with your more advanced societies.

Diderot: You may be surprised, my dear Rousseau, if I tell you I think that may be true. I do not feel the charm of your Swiss life. I grew up, as you know, in Langres, which is not so very far from the Jura mountains, and I have heard the mournful note of the Alpenhorn and felt the cold touch of snow; but there are other societies that I have read about which seem to me to have been so good, happy and natural, that contact with our own was ruinous.

Rousseau: Then I have convinced you?

Diderot: No, it is Bougainville who has convinced me. I have been reading his *Voyages* and thinking about Tahiti. How happy those islanders were, living, as so few men do, where nature was bountiful, where the sun was always warm and sea breezes soft, and the naked bodies of human beings were as beautiful as pagan gods. What a disaster it was for them when our French mariners brought modern Christian culture to their shores. The Tahitians were innocent and happy. They lived by instinct. They had no political institutions or private property, no sense of 'mine' and 'thine'. Their wives and their daughters were common to them all. The word 'incest' had no place in their language. The very idea of crime was unknown to them. Our sailors introduced them to the concepts of sin, greed, chastity and jealousy; possession led to rivalry; rivalry to bloodshed, and the blood that was not shed was poisoned by diseases imported from our European brothels.

Rousseau: The community you depict seems more like a creation of imagination than of history, but I am glad to find that we agree, at least, in preferring the simple to the sophisticated.

Diderot: But our agreement is, I fancy, qualified. We are at one in regretting that simple societies have lost their innocence and in thinking that our French culture has grown corrupt with age. But you, my dear Rousseau, yearn for simplicity again. I recognize that we cannot recover the innocence of youth, even if we in Europe ever had it. We must correct what we have, and not pine for what cannot be ours.

Rousseau: If you wish to correct, you must see what is wrong.

Diderot: I do see what is wrong, and you, I am sorry to say, dear friend, do not. The reason why our European civilization is worse than the Tahitian was, is not that Europe has more knowledge, science and arts; the reason is that Europe has worse moral values and worse religious beliefs. The Church has been teaching the people of Europe for so many centuries that happiness lies in the after-life, that most Europeans simply do not know how to be happy here on earth. That is why the first problem we have to solve is that of removing religion.

Rousseau: The Church may need reform, but you cannot remove religion altogether. It answers a great social and human need.

Diderot: I never know what your religious views are, Rousseau, except that you are a Catholic in Savoy and a Calvinist in Geneva.

Rousseau: That is a matter of politics. I am like King George III, who is an Anglican in England, a Presbyterian in Scotland and a Lutheran in Hanover. Every state must have its established cult; it is the right of the sovereign to choose it and the duty of the subject to accept it.

Diderot: You appear not to mind whether the established cult is true or false.

Rousseau: A civic religion performs a social function, by inculcating patriotic sentiment, and harnessing spiritual aspiration to the interests of the state. That is the question that matters: does it answer the social need that civic religion is required to answer?

Diderot: I cannot regard truth as irrelevant. But that may be because I was, as you know, intended for the ministry when I was young. I heard a lot about truth. Only I heard it in turn from Jansenists and Jesuits, and I must have been most impressed by the criticisms that each addressed to the other. For I soon ceased to believe in either version of the Catholic faith. Indeed I rejected all religious dogmas save the simple belief in the existence of God. Then I, in time, ceased to think that it mattered whether one believed in the existence of God or not.

Rousseau: Yes, I know you have become a total sceptic.

Diderot: I do not believe there is such a thing as a total sceptic. It is simply that I think we ought to have good grounds for anything we accept as true. Even Pascal says of the existence of God, that nobody knows either what he is or that he is. But I am not an atheist among atheists, my dear Rousseau; when I am with unbelievers, I think of all the reasons for God's existence; when I am with believers, I think of all the reasons against it.

Rousseau: Then you will hardly deny, my dear friend, that you are endowed with the spirit of contradiction.

Diderot: Contradiction, or at least disagreement, is the embellishment and spice of conversation.

Rousseau: Only if you talk for the sake of talking.

Diderot: An excellent reason for talking. What is talking but thinking aloud? I hope you have not yet reached the stage of supposing that thinking itself is harmful.

Rousseau: I have always disliked the spirit of contradiction.

Diderot: It seems to me to be an advantage in a mind to be able to see both sides of a question. After all, there are at least two sides to every subject, except in logic and mathematics.

Rousseau: There are undoubtedly two aspects to the question of religion. Two religions, if you like. There is private religion, which is wholly an inward thing, a matter between a man and his maker. Then there is civic religion, with its temples and priesthood and outward ceremonials. This is a social institution, and rightly controlled by the state.

Diderot: I cannot see that religion is at all important.

Rousseau: Religion is important because it teaches men to act well.

Diderot: Very few religions teach men to act well. Our priests say that atheists are wicked, but all the atheists I have known have been most scrupulous and upright men, while the history of the Church is stained with blood.

Rousseau: Doubtless some sceptical philosophers may be honest men, but how can you expect the ordinary people to be moral without a religious sanction?

Diderot: If a religious sanction is what makes them act as well as they do, then their conduct is not moral. Good actions are those that are done because they are good. The virtuous man is animated by a love of virtue. If he acts from fear of hell, or in the expectation of divine reward, then he acts from cowardice in the one case and from greed in the other. Both are bad motives; and actions done from wrong motives are not good actions.

Rousseau: It's plain enough, Diderot, that you have been educated for the priesthood. You have had so much training in the theory of religion that you are incapable of understanding what religion really is. An illiterate peasant in Corsica has a better notion of God than any of your professors of theology at the Sorbonne; and that is because God lives in men's hearts and not in their minds.

Diderot: I do not deny it; and I have no wish to rob the Corsican peasant of his myths; I only wish to remove the professors of theology and replace them with professors of natural science and mechanics.

Rousseau: Do you think mechanics will succeed where religion has failed?

Diderot: It will. For mechanics can build canals, and take water to barren land, and make wheat grow where nothing grew before, and feed men who had previously gone hungry. Mechanics can do miracles far greater than anything the saints are believed to do.

Rousseau: I do not know how any man can live without faith. I could not do so. I have passed many years in the company of sceptics like yourself, but my faith has never been shaken. I am deeply attached to you, as you know, my dear Diderot, but I could never stand your atheism. I admit I don't know how to refute it with rational arguments. But that only means that where religion is concerned I prefer nature to reason. I believe in God, and God would not be just if my soul were not immortal.

Diderot: So you honestly believe in the life after death?

Rousseau: Yes.

Diderot: Do you believe in the eternal punishment of the damned, that many souls are going to burn in hell for ever?

Rousseau: No: but I believe there are many souls that will never enjoy eternal happiness, I am inclined to think that the souls of the wicked are annihilated at death, and that a continued consciousness may itself be the reward of the virtuous. But it is enough for me, now that I am approaching the end of my life, to know that I can hope for a better existence in the world to come.

Diderot: But you are scarcely older than I; you cannot be more than forty-five, my dear Rousseau; how can you say you are approaching the end?

Rousseau: I do not think I have long to live. I have suffered too much. But my faith in the world to come has helped me to bear my sufferings in this world more easily.

Diderot: It is not for me to question the value of your consolations. If a man feels better after taking the physician's medicine, there is no profit in telling him that the bottle contains only coloured water. All I would want to say is that if we could make life in this world better for mankind as a whole, few people would seek comfort in stories of a world to come.

Rousseau: And you really believe, my dear Diderot, that you can make life better for mankind simply by enlarging knowledge?

Diderot: You may remember what I wrote in the first volume of the Encyclopédie: 'Our aim is to gather all knowledge together, so that our descendants, being better instructed, may become at the same time happier and more virtuous, and that we may not die without having deserved well of the human race.' That, my dear friend, is the only immortality I aspire to.

Rousseau: I can think of no surer way of plunging into error than by making such an effort to know *everything*. If people had not claimed to know that the world stood still, they would not have persecuted Galileo for saying that it moved. If the title of 'philosopher' was claimed only by true philosophers, your *Encyclopédie* would never have been persecuted. It is not ignorance which is to blame for the ills of mankind; but error. What hurts us is not what we do not know, but what we think mistakenly that we do know.

Diderot: You may be right; and you certainly have the advantage, as a self-educated man, of not having had your mind filled as mine was filled at the *lycée* and the university, with elaborate systems of error. But I think error can be cured. Just as we have Bacon's method of accumulating knowledge by observation, so we have Descartes' method of testing knowledge by the process of systematic doubt.

Rousseau: I agree that both Descartes and Bacon were men of genius. But the world might well have been a better place if neither of them had written a word. They are the two chief makers of your modern philosophy; and, whereas in the time of St Thomas Aquinas (a happier period in human history) philosophy was the handmaiden of faith, your modern philosophy has tried to take the place of faith by making a false promise of knowledge. The decline of Greece began when Greek religion was changed into metaphysics; and we are now witnessing a similar decline of Europe.

Diderot: We are not witnessing a decline. The decline took place many centuries ago with the passing of classical antiquity. We are witnessing a revival, something that began in Italy in the thirteenth century, and which passed to us in France when the Church suppressed it there. I am an optimist, my friend. Even if the Church succeeds in doing in France what it has already done in Italy, science will go forward in England, a great and progressive kingdom, where, after all their passionate religious conflicts, the people have finally realized that religion does not really matter, and the bishops wisely devote their lives to hunting and port wine. English freedom flourishes where religious zeal is cool.

Rousseau: There is little freedom in England—or under any other monarchy.

Diderot: I hear the voice of the Citizen again. But it must be said that republican city-states like Geneva have little to teach us French.
We are a large nation. And you have said yourself, my friend,
that a large nation needs a monarch.

Rousseau: I have certainly said that only a small one can be a democratic
republic.

Diderot: A monarchy has certain advantages. For power is concentrated in
a single man, and once you have enlightened him, then his power
can be used to further enlightened schemes, to set up royal
academies, laboratories, colleges, and learned societies to advance
the work of science.

Rousseau: Enlightened despotism is as bad as any other despotism.

Diderot: But better than an unenlightened democracy. The trouble with
your Swiss forms of government is that everything stagnates. All
the best authorities from Tacitus onwards have held that legislation by assemblies of all the citizens is not only a Germanic but
also a very primitive institution. Your Swiss cantons have remained democratic for the simple reason that they have never
moved forward in politics or in anything else. The lives of those
mountain folk have scarcely changed since the time of Tacitus.
But France has entered the modern world—the world of explora-
tion and manufacturing, and engineering and science. Quaint
survivals from the distant past, like the Swiss democratic cantons,
are no models for the modern state.

Rousseau: Naturally Swiss democracy is conservative. For you in France,
liberty is something that men dream of having in the future,
something that even Montesquieu was foolish enough to think
you might gain by copying the political institutions of England.
But the Swiss have no occasion to yearn for freedom; they have
had it for centuries, and their only problem is to keep it. It is a
change, and the seductive charm of progressive thought, that the
Swiss must beware of, if they are to stay free men.

Diderot: Then the English are better placed. They enjoy both freedom and
progress.

Rousseau: The English do not know what freedom is. You speak of Tacitus;
you might also mention a more illustrious Roman name, Cicero,
He said that liberty had more than one ingredient. The lesser part
of freedom was being allowed to do whatever you liked so long as
it was lawful. But the greater part of freedom was to play an active
part in the political life of the republic. The English may have the
lesser kind of freedom, in that they are not tormented by the

censorship of the Press and so forth, as you are in France, but they have not the least experience of what Cicero called the greater part of freedom, which is a positive participation in government.

Diderot: The English people have a vote in elections for parliament, and we know how much they keep their king subordinate to parliament.

Rousseau: What is the significance of that? An Englishman, or rather an English property-owner, is entitled from time to time to choose the least repellent candidate from a list of two or more political adventurers or placemen. If that is representation, Englishmen can choose their representatives; and if that is freedom, Englishmen are free for two or three weeks every three or four years at the time of a general election.

Diderot: Since you are so very critical of the way that ancient Rome developed, you can hardly blame the English for choosing another path.

Rousseau: I do not blame them; I simply say they have no experience of freedom or equality.

Diderot: Is there equality in your Swiss democracies? There is clearly none of the one kind of equality that Plato believed in, the equality of men and women. As in oriental and many primitive societies, Swiss women are kept in domestic servitude.

Rousseau: Swiss women are appreciated for what they are. The Swiss admire modest women, as the ancients did. In Paris the only women who are admired are those who create a sensation, make a noise, and bear the most ostentatious appearance. A mountain woman blushes if she meets a man. A city woman in France would be ashamed to blush. Modesty is thought to be something provincial and ill-bred.

Diderot: Well, I will agree that our French women are very different from the Swiss. And perhaps they bring us to our knees too often. But you can hardly say that you believe in liberty, and deny liberty to women.

Rousseau: A woman should have liberty but not licence. The ancients had very strict ideas about how women should behave. They felt that a house without a mistress was a body without a soul, and that a woman outside the home was deprived of her greatest lustre and ornament. In public, a woman was simply out of place. The Romans felt this as the Greeks did. But then, with the invasions of barbarian armies, all these standards were forgotten. The barbarians brought with them the values of an army camp, in which the soldiers dream of carrying off a woman and the women dream of being carried off by a handsome knight. This was the origin of all those ideas of romance and gallantry which have shaped the modern French image of a woman. Your woman of Paris owes nothing to the model of a Roman matron; she is directly descended from the camp-followers of the northern hordes.

Diderot: I think it is because she is educated, that the modern city woman expects equality with men.

Rousseau: I do not doubt it, and that is another argument against so-called education. Nature has made women different from men, so that they may complement each other. Of course I favour equality as a political and legal principle, but that does not mean we should ignore natural differences. We must follow nature, not defy it.

Diderot: Many differences between the sexes are artificial, not natural.

Rousseau: The latter are the more important. In France, your fashionable women are so eager to do everything that men do, that chastity itself is no longer prized.

Diderot: Why should chastity be prized? You say we should follow nature, and not defy it. The law of nature prompts men to unite with the opposite sex. And the purpose is obvious: to secure the propagation of the species which is nature's end. There is something profoundly unnatural about those man-made laws which impose celibacy on the clergy and chastity on the laity.

Rousseau: I have no wish to defend celibacy, but chastity is a manifest virtue, and all societies except the most corrupt have cherished it. And it is right that they should, for chastity rests on a triumph of reason over the passions, or of the higher feelings over brutish instincts.

Diderot: It is not for me to say what unites you to Thérèse le Vasseur, but I protest that what drives me into the arms of my beloved Sophie is not a brutish instinct.

Rousseau: No doubt you revel in your concupiscence.

Diderot: But, my dear friend, the Spartans that you admire so much had their catamites. Why should we not have our mistresses? Or will you suggest that a boy is a more natural partner than a woman?

Rousseau: You should save your obscene suggestions for your novels, Diderot. If you are to repeat the success of *Les Bijoux Indiscrets*, you must not waste your impurities on me.

Diderot: You appear to be shocked. Remember what you were saying about women who looked shocked at the theatre.

Rousseau: I merely criticized displays of a spurious sensibility. My own is quite genuine. I admit that I am easily shocked. I am sure you will tell me that it shows a lamentable want of urbanity.

Diderot: I shall only say that you are shocked by the wrong things. We are all shocked sometimes. I was shocked when you told me you had put your children in an orphanage.

Rousseau: I did it in their own interest. They were illegitimate. I know myself. I know their mother; in a sense I regard her as my wife. But neither she nor I can provide the environment in which a child could flourish. If they were known to be my children, they would suffer from the consequences of my own notoriety. As it is, being orphans, with no idea who their parents are, they start life with even chances. Plato, you will remember, proposed that the children of the philosophers should be brought up communally, without knowing who their fathers were.

Diderot: But Plato was speaking of an ideal republic. We must adjust ourselves to the world as it is.

Rousseau: I will never trim my sails to the wind.

Diderot: My dear Rousseau, if you elevate your whims into moral maxims, you may logically claim that your deeds are dictated by scruples. If conscience means anything, it must mean more than that. When I wrote that line in *Le Fils Naturel*, that 'the good man lives in society', I was not speaking lightly. I think Aristotle was right; that man is naturally social; and that what makes man social are certain natural impulses that attach him to other people. The sexual impulse is a natural force that impels us to seek the companionship of women; the paternal impulse is a natural force that prompts us to cherish and protect our offspring. Nature did not design us to live as hermits, but to live in mutual dependence, one upon another.

Rousseau: You are mistaken. Society is not based on nature, but on agreement, or covenant—the social contract.

Diderot: The theory of a social contract is unhistorical. I do not believe that men once lived in a condition of anarchy, and then contracted together to form civil societies. I think that what happened was simply a form of progress. From the earliest natural groupings around the family, men advanced towards more complicated relationships with their neighbours, the tribes passing by degrees into kingdoms, and the kingdoms into nations. There may be an element of contract or covenant in the later and more elaborate systems; the earliest ones are based on nature.

Rousseau: The difference between a state of natural anarchy and a civil society is not one of degree; it is one of kind. In the one there is only force; in the other there is law. So it is no good talking of a gradual progress. The institution of civil society itself entails a radical conversion, or transformation of mankind. Take away law, which civil society introduces, and man is a base and brutish creature; but once man lives under law, he is changed into a moral, intelligent being, and for the first time, into something truly human.

Diderot: So you think it is the introduction of law which transforms a naturally brutish man into a fully human one? But what is that but another way of saying that culture, as opposed to nature, makes men good? And does not that fly in the face of everything you have so far said against culture and in praise of nature?

Rousseau: Nature has two aspects, and culture has as well. Nature puts some instincts into men which drag him down to the level of the beasts, but it also puts other aspirations into him, which impel him towards the perfection of humanity. That is to say that man is a divided creature. Culture can help him in his struggle to perfection; or it can hinder him. It either lifts him up or drags him down. It never leaves him untouched. The cultures of the modern world are almost all bad ones; and as they are not making man better, inevitably they are making him worse.

Diderot: That second, higher nature that you believe in, Rousseau, is not real nature, but a kind of ideal nature; not the source of man's self-love or his social feelings, but something which answers your passion for abstractions. No wonder you are religious, my friend. No wonder you love God. It is because you do not love man. You do not allow your natural impulses to prompt you to congress with a pleasing woman; you do not allow natural impulse to unite you in domestic harmony with the children of your own loins. But you are none the less a man of impulse. Only, instead of all those drives within you finding their natural expression, they are changed into a militant zeal for virtue, rectitude, chastity, sincerity and civic justice—and an equally impassioned antipathy to pleasure, art, civility, scholarship, and all the material adornments of terrestrial life. You are right to remind us that you are Citizen of Geneva. Not that I think the Citizen's title so splendid, or that your republic bears much resemblance to that of ancient Rome; but you are true Genevan, Rousseau, in the sense that you are a veritable, quintessential Calvinist.

Rousseau: That is nonsense; the truest Calvinists have always been among my greatest persecutors.

Diderot: I am not thinking of theological details. I am thinking of your temperament and cast of mind. There is a certain line of Christian moralists—St Augustine, Savonarola, Calvin—to which you, my dear Rousseau, undoubtedly belong. They, like you, have dreamed of a Christian Sparta, republics of virtue kept virtuous by strict and cruel control of private as well as of public life. These moralists have done little to further the progress of humanity; in fact, they have done great harm. And what must be said of them might also be said of you, my friend. To build up such passion and intensity behind an abstract conception of perfection, which is both unnatural and unrealizable, is not to increase the amount of virtue in the world, but greatly to increase the violence. Is that what you wish to bequeath posterity?

Rousseau: It appears to be *you* who are becoming impassioned now, my dear Diderot. But I shall not attempt to soothe you. I shall only quote the rest of the verse I cited just now from the Book of Ecclesiastes. For it did not end with the words: 'Thou mayst yet be reconciled.' Angry words can be remedied: 'But' the verse adds, 'the taunt, the contemptuous reproach, the secret betrayed, the covert attack—all these mean a friend lost.'

Diderot: You mean you will not be persuaded.

Rousseau: I mean I will not even stay to listen.

Voltaire and David Hume

A dialogue on Morality

For many years Voltaire and David Hume entertained the hope, and even the expectation, that they might one day meet. They never did so. In August 1776 David Hume, who was seventeen years younger than Voltaire, died in Edinburgh at the age of sixty-five. The conversation that follows is an imaginary one, conceived as taking place in Voltaire's house at Ferney, near Geneva, when both men were approaching the end of their lives.

Voltaire: Monsieur Hume, at last . . .

Hume: Monsieur de Voltaire, how many years have I not awaited this pleasure?

Voltaire: May I greet you, as I always think of you, as my own Saint David?

Hume: I am honoured, though I had never imagined that you cared for saints.

Voltaire: Apart from yourself, I do not. You may notice that the chapel I have erected here at Ferney has no patron saint whatever.

Hume: That must bewilder the faithful.

Voltaire: It is intended to. I tell them it is the only church in France dedicated to God alone.

Hume: A most pious intention.

Voltaire: Yes, they cannot well object to a chapel being dedicated to God, can they?

Hume: They should be grateful enough to see any chapel at all erected by Voltaire. The clergy of Scotland will never have the satisfaction of seeing a chapel built by David Hume.

Voltaire: You live in a free country, my friend. You can afford to disclose your opinions.

Hume: You would be surprised perhaps to know how much I have suffered for doing so, careful as I have been in what I have published. For example, I was once denied a chair at Edinburgh University on the grounds of supposed atheist views.

Voltaire: All universities are ridiculous. It is no place for a philosopher. But you must have been of good repute in the eyes of the authorities or they would not have made you British Ambassador in Paris.

Hume: Only *chargé d'affaires.*

Voltaire: Nevertheless, an important public office. No, my friend, you Englishmen and Scotchmen have no idea what persecution means. Why, here in France there is neither freedom of speech nor freedom of action. A man is not allowed to live as he pleases, and then he is not allowed to die as he pleases: one has to have a priest, even at one's deathbed.

Hume: I heard you had a priest at your table.

Voltaire: The excellent Father Adam. He is my domestic chaplain. And he does not only sit and eat, like most of his kind. He plays chess with me, and although he is the better player, he always allows me to win.

Hume: A man of discretion. He must be a Jesuit.

Voltaire: He is. He was persecuted by the Jansenists, so it seemed very right that he should come to me. All victims of persecution have my sympathy, no matter how much I may detest their views.

Hume: I have a certain gratitude towards the Jesuits. In fact it was in the library of the old Jesuit college at La Flèche that I wrote my first book.

Voltaire: Yes, the Jesuits have undoubted charm. They have a genuine love of scholarship and culture. It is a pity they do not love truth.

Hume: It is their combination of scholarship and superstition which makes them so dangerous. They are worse than the Jansenists.

Voltaire: No one could be worse. The Jansenists do not even believe in reason.

Hume: They are enthusiasts like the extreme Protestants of England. But it is just because they believe in religious emotion rather than reason, that they are so much less harmful than the Jesuits. Because they are so interested in personal salvation, they diminish the power of priestcraft and authority. Besides, religious enthusiasm tends naturally to grow cooler and more innocuous with time, while superstition stays rigid and unyielding.

Voltaire: And superstition is the badge of the Jesuits? No one could deny it.

Hume: Yes, it is superstition which prompts them to elevate the authority of priests and to emphasize external forms and ceremonies. What is even worse is the political effect. Superstition makes Jesuits at the same time slaves of the Court and tyrants of the people.

Voltaire: That is true enough, I agree. Fortunately Father Adam is here in his slavish rather than his tyrannical role.

Hume: What are his duties, dare I ask?

Voltaire: To administer the sacraments to me.

Hume: Not an arduous task, I fancy, compared to playing chess and losing.

Voltaire: Do not let us belittle it. I often tell Father Adam about another priest I knew, who spent all his time playing backgammon, and was once called from the table to administer the sacrament: he placed by mistake a gaming counter on a woman's tongue instead of the wafer: 'Mon père,' she protested, 'thou hast given me God the Father, it is so old and tough.'

Hume: You remind me of a story I was told in Paris of a young polytheistic Indian who was converted to the Catholic faith; after his first communion his instructors asked him how many gods there were. He answered 'None'; and when they looked amazed, he explained: 'But you told me that there was only one god, and I have just eaten him.'

Voltaire: I must tell that to Father Adam.

Hume: You must not scandalize him.

Voltaire: I could not. He is the worldliest man I know.

Hume: So he would not question your fitness to receive the sacrament.

Voltaire: It is only my willingness that matters.

Hume: I can but assume that you accept the argument of Pascal's bet: that if there is no God we lose nothing by taking the sacrament, and that if there is a God we gain everything.

Voltaire: No, that is not my reason. It is not with an eye to another world that I take the sacrament, but simply for the sake of protection in this world. I have always taken care to be respectful to the Church. Do you know that I dedicated one of my finest tragedies to the Pope?

Hume: Which tragedy was that?

Voltaire: *Mahomet.* I no longer think it my best.

Hume: I know the play. Since it is a barely disguised attack on revealed religion, I cannot imagine the dedication was welcome.

Voltaire: You deceive yourself, my friend. His Holiness accepted it with 'greetings and apostolic blessings to his dear son'.

Hume: Then I can only assume he did not read it.

Voltaire: He did not read between the lines. He was too wise a man for that.

Hume: You will not expect the lesser clergy to show the same wisdom.

Voltaire: I cannot and I do not. But they can hardly accuse a man of atheism if he builds a chapel at his own expense, employs a Jesuit as his private chaplain, and receives the sacrament in public.

Hume: So long as you are not caught venerating Saint David Hume.

Voltaire: St David is my little secret. Or shall I say my big secret, for I see that you have waxed large in the land of liberty, my dear Hume, while I have shrunk after a lifetime of persecution to the bundle of flesh and bone that you now contemplate.

Hume: You bear the unmistakable lineaments of a philosopher, my dear Voltaire, while I have been immortalized in verse as the 'Fattest Hog of Epicurus' Sty'. It is for me to be envious.

Voltaire: I fear you do not approve of my chapel.

Hume: I judge such buildings purely by their architectural merits.

Voltaire: But I can feel that you reproach me for insincerity.

Hume: I would never condemn insincerity, especially in matters of religion. It is putting too great a respect on the vulgar, and on their superstitions, to pique oneself on sincerity in regard to them. Besides, a certain measure of dissimulation, or rather of simulation, is a necessary part of civilized life. A man is not a liar if he orders his servant to say he is not at home when he does not desire to see company.

Voltaire: You speak as a born diplomatist.

Hume: Of course, it might also be said that if the authorities can bring Voltaire to communion by the use of threats, then they may be all the more inclined to consider intimidation an effective means of defending religion.

Voltaire: If I think of you as a saint, my dear Hume, I do not fancy myself as a martyr.

Hume: Well, things are not so bad as they were. You can afford to be a good deal bolder than you could.

Voltaire: Not as bad? What about the case of the Chevalier de la Barre?

Hume: I am not well informed about it.

Voltaire: It is very simple. La Barre, a spirited youth, was accused of singing blasphemous songs and insulting a wooden cross on a bridge at Abbeville on the road from Paris to Calais. The judges of that place condemned him to tortures whose horror would dismay a cannibal. They cut out his tongue, cut off his ears, and hanged him. The sentence was confirmed by the Bishop of Amiens and executed on 1 July 1766.

Hume: Was that the young man who was said to have studied the works of Voltaire?

Voltaire: He was, and a copy of the *Dictionnaire Philosophique* was thrown into the flames when they cut down the corpse and burned it. That, my dear friend, is how the Christians of France deal with blasphemy. So do you wonder that I take precautions? And La Barre was a young nobleman of less than twenty. Do you think they would be more sparing towards an elderly scribe of bourgeois origins and dubious renown?

Hume: There is nothing dubious about your renown, my dear Voltaire. I can think of no author of the age more universally honoured— or more prosperous. Here you are in this magnificent estate, with your country house and your private theatre and your parklands, not to mention your private chapel, a prince among poets.

Voltaire: Perhaps, but I have also spent much of my life as a poet among princes, a very different and more humiliating situation. However, you are right to suggest that money is a great consolation for suffering, greater, I suspect, than even the most credulous believer ever derived from prayer. I was not born rich. When I was young, I never thought of material things, but then I saw so many men of letters poor and despised that I determined not to augment their number. I resolved to make a fortune.

Hume: Well, I was born in an impoverished branch of a noble Scotch family. They brought me up to believe that only inherited wealth was worth having, and then bequeathed me nothing. So I, too, had to make my own way in the world.

Voltaire: In France every man must either be a hammer or an anvil. I turned myself into a hammer in order to avoid being an anvil. The first efforts to make money are painful, but it soon becomes very satisfying to watch one's wealth accumulate; and in old age, when money is most necessary, it is almost a duty to be rich.

Hume: Especially for such as you and me. Christians can wait for their reward in heaven, but we who know there is no after-life, must find our joy in this world.

Voltaire: Indeed. And the pleasure of having a fortune is all the greater if you know that you have made it yourself.

Hume: Well, I was expected to make my pile at the Bar, but literature has always been my ruling passion, and when I quit the law to devote myself to writing, I abandoned all hope of wealth. I had to make a very rigid frugality supply my deficiency of fortune and live as the poorest of scholars.

Voltaire: Happily it did not hinder your rising to the splendours of the Embassy in Paris.

Hume: I have had several kinds of employment. My first book, my *Treatise of Human Nature*, which I composed at La Flèche, was published in London when I was aged twenty-seven. It fell dead-born from the Press, so I realized then that I should never earn even the scantiest livelihood from authorship.

Voltaire: I have no doubt you were robbed. One has to drive a hard bargain with publishers and booksellers if one is to make any money as an author.

Hume: Oh, I made a little more when I turned from philosophy to history. But that was many years later. I was once a tutor to a mad nobleman. Then I became a soldier for a time, and, as you know, I have been a diplomatist. I have also been a librarian and an under-secretary in the government service. But it was a long time before I commanded an income of a thousand pounds, and then I considered myself opulent, though some of my friends smiled at the thought. But I have never allowed my various employments to interfere for long with my attention to literature. Independence is what has always mattered to me. Or liberty, if you want another word for it.

Voltaire: And you have never burdened yourself with wife and family?

Hume: No.

Voltaire: Or the sweeter, but no less burdensome attachments, such as I have enjoyed with Madame de Châtelet and Madame Denis?

Hume: As you may know, I lost my heart in Paris to Madame de Bouf-flers, but then the Princesse de Conti died, and my love conceived the ambition of marrying the royal widower; so I was discarded. But that, like my early experiences of hardship, I regard as a good school of stoicism.

Voltaire: Stoicism? Well, doubtless there is something to be said for it. At least it is morally superior to Christianity. It breeds a better character. A Stoic must earn salvation by living well, whereas a Christian only needs a brisk repentance after thirty years of crime, and he is assured of eternal bliss. But I must confess, my dear Hume, that I am not a Stoic. I am an Epicurean. I do not believe that life is to be endured. I believe it is to be enjoyed. I approve of luxury.

Hume: I have never disapproved of luxury, as I fear that most of my fellow Scotchmen do.

Voltaire: Ah, the Calvinist imbeciles.

Hume: Yes, their minds are so disordered by the frenzies of their religion that they consider it vicious to take the smallest pleasure in meat, drink and apparel.

Voltaire: The Genevans are the same. As you know I live here near their frontier only in order to escape if the French try to arrest me again. But Geneva is unbearably provincial and puritanical. When we suggested that they might improve their amenities by building an opera house, they were filled with righteous indignation. But they are very glad to be asked out here to my own little theatre.

Hume: If not to your little chapel?

Voltaire: No, their Protestant eyes are spared the ludicrous spectacle of Voltaire on his knees.

Hume: Why ludicrous? You do, after all, do you not, believe in God?

Voltaire: There is one sun. There is one God. If only there were one religion, then men might be held together in the bond of peace. That is my creed.

Hume: You take a more sanguine view than I. Oh, I will admit I have known some religious men of excellent character. But in the main, it is abundantly clear that religion undermines morality.

Voltaire: What a staunch unbeliever you are, my dear Hume. I am sure it is due to the robust constitution which your radiant face proclaims.

Hume: I suffered torments of religious doubt when I was young. But that was due to my unfortunate upbringing in a Scotch Presbyterian home. You could never imagine the severity of that kind of fanaticism. But now I have left it all behind me.

Voltaire: I am sometimes sick and afraid. It is then that I conjure up the image of God.

Hume: No doubt such feelings explain the origin of all religions. Belief in God has nothing to do with reason.

Voltaire: I wish I had your fortitude. Next time I kneel at the altar I shall pray to you: 'Help thou my unbelief, Saint David. Let my head rest more sweetly on the pillow of doubt.'

Hume: You had better not let your Jesuit chaplain hear that prayer.

Voltaire: My prayers are silent. Besides, I always address God in English, which no one here understands. I am disposed to share the Anglican belief that God is an Englishman, for England is certainly the only country where the worship of God is properly conducted.

Hume: Well, there is more than one religion in England.

Voltaire: Of course, there must be at least thirty. But the important thing is that they have learned to live side by side. In England, everyone is allowed to go to heaven in his own way—a most enviable privilege. If we cannot have a single religion, then it is best to have a multiplicity of religions, each one of which will tolerate the others.

Hume: Or no religion at all?

Voltaire: No, no, my dear Hume. Scepticism is very becoming in a philosopher; but the ordinary man needs some belief in the supernatural.

Hume: Why, if it prompts them to torture and hang the Chevalier de la Barre for blasphemy?

Voltaire: A very good religion is needed to take the place of bad ones, including Christianity.

Hume: How is its goodness to be ascertained?

Voltaire: By its capacity to generate virtue and a love of truth.

Hume: No religion does that.

Voltaire: Exactly, and that is why we need a new and rational religion.

Hume: No religion can be rational. And why look for a new one? The only advantage of existing religions is that they are old. Men are creatures of habit and tradition, and it is fortunate that they should be, for custom is, in the main, the chief basis of morality. A new creed might promise to be better than the old ones, but the chances are a thousand to one that it would soon become every bit as absurd and intolerant as the creeds it replaced. Indeed, I am of the opinion that the best religions in human history were the earliest, which must, of course, have been polytheistic.

Voltaire: And what do you consider their advantages?

Hume: First, toleration. Where there are many gods, men do not seek to impose their own beliefs on their neighbours. Intolerance and persecution begin with monotheism. Then there is the question of morals. Polytheistic religions often encourage manliness, courage and civic spirit, whereas monotheism encourages the mortification of the flesh and the cult of monkish virtues.

Voltaire: Monotheism has, however, the advantage of being more rational, much as we may disapprove of the forms it tends to take.

Hume: There I must disagree with you. Religions are all irrational.

Voltaire: But all the logical arguments for the existence of God are arguments for the existence of one supreme being.

Hume: Have you ever reflected on the value of those arguments? The order and design we discern in the universe are said to be proofs of the existence of a creator and designer, namely God. Now, even if this were a proof of the existence of a designer, it would not be evidence of that omniscient, omnipotent, benevolent father in heaven that people call 'God'. It would be evidence only of a being with enough capacity to design and create the universe, not necessarily omnipotent, not necessarily omniscient, and certainly not necessarily benevolent.

Voltaire: But my God is not, as you know, the Christian God. I certainly do not believe in a universally benevolent providence. I see the universe as a gigantic clock, and a clock bespeaks a clock-maker.

Hume: It may, as you say, bespeak it, but it does not prove it. Even a real clock is no evidence that its maker was one man, and not several, and its continued existence is no evidence of its maker or makers being still alive. Besides, the natural universe, so far as our sense impressions entitle us to claim any knowledge of it whatever, is not in the least like a clock. It is manifestly not man-made. That is what we mean when we call it a natural, as opposed to an artificial entity. And it is surely most absurd to jump from the premise that the universe is not man-made to the conclusion that it must be God-made.

Voltaire: Not if we understand God in the proper sense, as the author of nature, the supreme being. Besides, we must not forget that God is needed to provide a divine sanction for morality. It is absolutely necessary, not only for ordinary people, but also for princes and rulers, to have the idea of a supreme being, creator, governor, rewarder and avenger, profoundly graven on their minds. As I have often said, if God did not exist, we should have to invent him.

Hume: Why?

Voltaire: For purely selfish reasons. I want my lawyer, my tailor, my servants, even my wife to believe in God, because then I think I shall be robbed and cuckolded less often.

Hume: I am not sure that I have followed your argument, Voltaire. You say the clock bespeaks a clockmaker. Very well, and now you say the important thing about this being is not that he makes the clock, but that he is a rewarder and avenger, and you want people to believe in him because you think that such belief improves their conduct.

Voltaire: The hopes and fears instilled by their religion will lead them to act well.

Hume: But my dear Voltaire, you have first to explain the logical connexion. Why is evidence for the existence of a creator of the universe evidence for the existence of a being concerned with punishment and reward? I think you will agree with me that the two beings are entirely distinct.

Voltaire: The important thing is not that such a God should be proved to exist, but that people should believe he exists. And they do.

Hume: I would agree that the propensity to believe in an invisible, intelligent power is, if not an original instinct, at least an almost universal characteristic of mankind.

Voltaire: And placed there no doubt by the supreme being.

Hume: But you will not seek to argue that universal assent is any proof of the truth of a belief? All men once thought that the earth was flat.

Voltaire: In matters of religion we must give heed to natural assent.

Hume: But the most widespread belief, in matters of religion, has never been belief in the kind of supreme being adumbrated by rationalistic philosophers.

Voltaire: That is because the natural propensity to believe in God has been distorted by priests and official cults. If we can cut out superstition, if we can destroy the Christian Church, if we can crush the infamous thing, then man's natural assent will fasten on its proper object. Not God as he is depicted in the Bible, a cruel vindictive despot, but God as he appears to the eye of reason, a God of justice and compassion, commanding men to love one another, and to admit both their ignorance and their feebleness.

Hume: Such excellent precepts are expounded in the Gospels.

Voltaire: But the Church does not teach them.

Hume: Of course not, because it is not in the nature of popular religion to uphold morality. Every religion, however sublime the verbal definition which it gives of its divinity, leads its adherents to seek the divine favour, not by decent conduct, but by frivolous observances or intemperate zeal, or rapturous ecstasies or the believing of absurd opinions. And if we consider the natural history of religion, we can, I think, see why this is so. Most men feel a natural inclination to do their duty. It is not often painful for them to do what they ought to do. Even the most austere virtues are prompted by reflection on what we owe society and what we owe ourselves. Hence, a man who does his duty and in general lives well, cannot feel he has done anything for the sake of God alone. So in order to obtain divine favour, he reaches beyond the natural field of duty to find something which will please God. The more strange the practice, the more useless it is for human service, the stronger the violence it offers to a man's natural inclinations, the more will he seize upon it as a means of demonstrating his zeal and devotion. If a man does an act of justice or kindness, he does no more than he ought to do; but if he fasts a day, or puts on a hair shirt, or gives himself a sound whipping, that has a direct reference, he believes, to the service of God.

Voltaire: All this is because men have been nurtured on false religions.

Hume: But what is the origin of all religions? Fear, anxiety and terror of the unknown. You said of yourself, my dear Voltaire, that you return to God when you are sick and afraid. That has always been so. Early men in a world they did not understand, formed grovelling and familiar notions of superior powers, who had in turn to be dreaded, appeased, and induced to intervene in human affairs. Such crude polytheistic notions became in time refined into the monotheistic one; and that in turn became refined from the Jealous God of the Hebrews into the Supreme Being of Monsieur de Voltaire.

Voltaire: But my supreme being is so perfect and metaphysical that even you, my dear Hume, could hardly deny its existence.

Hume: I would never dream of denying it. I only say that such a perfect being must be unknowable to man. Its perfection is hidden from human curiosity. Indeed it would be profaneness to attempt to penetrate its sacred obscurities. No, my dear Voltaire, I neither affirm nor deny the existence of a deity. Doubt, uncertainty, suspense of judgement is the only proper attitude in matters of religion.

Voltaire: But having weighed religion in the scales of truth, my friend, we must also weigh it in the scales of politics. Such is the miserable condition of man that the true is not always the advantageous. It would be dangerous and unreasonable to seek too swift a reform in matters of religion. I would like, as you know, to see a new religion. But the people are not yet worthy of it. For the present, it is enough to circumscribe the Church within its limits, and make it submit to civil legislation. The more the laity is enlightened, the less harm priests will be able to do. Indeed I do not even despair of enlightening the priests themselves. One day we might make them blush for their errors, and turn them into citizens. I have high hopes of my own chaplain.

Hume: He may have the same hopes of you, like the Jesuit priest who reconciled the Baron de Montesquieu to the Church on his deathbed.

Voltaire: I am not sure if the story is true. I should not be surprised. Montesquieu was never a man to miss an advantage, especially if it were free. I had never the misfortune to dine at his table, but he was one of the meanest men in France. He would do anything to save a sou, or collect a debt, or avoid paying one he owed. He even economized on his daughter's wedding.

Hume: I must confess that I have always thought him a great man. I hope that is not because he was so generous in his praise of my books. In fact, Montesquieu was the first writer of any eminence to appreciate my work. We corresponded together over the years.

I helped with the English translations of his *Esprit des Loix*, and he tried to have my *Political Discourses* translated into French—not, I am afraid, with much success.

Voltaire: I had the same feelings about Lord Bolingbroke, the first great man to praise my works. Of course Montesquieu was older than you; he was even a little older than I, but only by five years, so I could never regard him with that unqualified veneration which I might have felt if I had been younger and known him less well.

Hume: Perhaps we in the British Isles admire Montesquieu so much because he urged the world to imitate us. He called our constitution the mirror of liberty, and made it his model. That is very flattering.

Voltaire: It would have been more flattering still if the constitution Montesquieu described had really been that of England.

Hume: But in the main he says what you say, that the English understand freedom better than any other nation in Europe.

Voltaire: What Montesquieu means by freedom, and what he imagines to prevail in England, is the dominion of people like himself—the provincial aristocracy. Montesquieu has always a shrewd sense of the interests of his rank as well of his own person. In England the King is largely subordinate to Parliament, and Montesquieu imagined that Parliament was controlled by little lords like himself. That is the system he wished to prevail in France. The argument is called *la thèse noble*: and it is a very pernicious one.

Hume: And the alternative is *la thèse royale*. Do you subscribe to that, Voltaire? I suspect you do. The poet who wrote the *Henriade* must surely be a royalist.

Voltaire: I have no wish to go back to the Middle Ages. For that is what *la thèse noble* means: restoring the privileges of feudalism. I am more interested in the rights of man, and I believe they are better secured under an absolute king than under any kind of aristocratic government. A great king made France what it is, and we need another like him.

Hume: You mean Louis Quatorze?

Voltaire: Yes, has any king rendered more services to humanity than he? Or shown better taste? Or distinguished himself by finer establishments? Louis Quatorze did not do all that he might have done—no doubt because he was a man—but he did more than any other, because he was a great man.

Hume: He also persecuted the Protestants, and drove a million people from France.

Voltaire: They found refuge in England, and enriched that nation with the wealth of French industry. Do you count so many silk and crystal factories for nothing? No, even the faults of Louis Quatorze have been to the advantage of Europe. And give me the name of any sovereign who attracted to his country more able foreigners, and did more to encourage merit among his own subjects. Under Louis Quatorze, all the arts were perfected and all were rewarded. Paris surpassed Rome and Athens. Reflect, my dear Hume, that when this great prince was at war with more than half Europe, he sent geometers and physicists to the depths of Africa and America to seek for new knowledge. Not only were great things done during his reign, but it was he who did them.

Hume: I fail to see why an enlightened prince need also be a despot.

Voltaire: It is typical of your race, my dear Hume, to suppose that an absolute monarch must be a despotic one. A despot is an arbitrary ruler who puts himself above the law; an absolute king is one who keeps all political power in his hands, but rules according to the law.

Hume: The distinction is of no importance; for such kings always regard the law as whatever they choose to enact. That is one lesson of English history. You say yourself, my dear Voltaire, that liberty is better secured in England than anywhere else in Europe. The reason surely lies in the fact that England has a mixed form of constitution, neither wholly monarchical nor wholly republican. On the one hand, there is the monarch with all the traditional prerogatives of a prince. On the other hand, there is a parliament to maintain a watchful jealousy over the government, to remove all discretionary powers, to secure every man's life and fortune by general and inflexible laws which are superior even to the King. The Roman government under the emperors was a mixture of authority and liberty, where the authority prevailed; the English government is a mixture of the same kind, where the liberty predominates.

Voltaire: Then you will not disagree with me that authority and liberty can exist side by side. The aim is to have a general freedom coupled with a firm enlightened government, and the only way to achieve this in France, at any rate, is to have an enlightened absolute king. You speak of the lesson of English history. Have you ever studied the thoughts of the great Lord Chancellor Bacon?

Hume: I have read his essays.

Voltaire: Well, Bacon was an infinitely wiser man than Montesquieu. His scheme was to concentrate power in the hands of a single prince, and then direct that power to the general advantage of society. He shows that you can never do good in the modern world if you allow political control to remain in the hands of a gaggle of privileged people, each fighting for his petty rights. Such methods belong to the feudal past. The modern world calls for a strong ruler.

Hume: I doubt if we can ever do good in politics. The thing is to avoid doing harm. To right some wrongs, perhaps; but not to entertain dreams of a perfect commonwealth or utopia.

Voltaire: The philosopher-king is perhaps a dream. But it is not fanciful to speak of a king acting on the advice of a philosopher; indeed I think that is the best hope for mankind.

Hume: The experience of Francis Bacon is not encouraging. He sacrificed much to enlarge the power of his king—James VI of Scotland who became James I of England. Bacon twisted the law, he betrayed his friends, he accepted bribes, and even authorized the use of torture . . .

Voltaire: Even I must reluctantly admit that torture is sometimes permissible.

Hume: Well, my dear Voltaire, it did Bacon no good. For although he and the king could agree about enlarging the royal powers, Bacon could never persuade the king to use those powers to further any of his enlightened projects. And in the end Bacon was banished from office in disgrace.

Voltaire: Yes, it is a melancholy story. And indeed I myself had a somewhat similar experience with Frederick of Prussia. Not that I was ever in his employment, or even seriously regarded by him as a philosopher. I lodged with him at Potsdam—in extreme discomfort I may say—as a poet. He hardly ever consulted me about political questions; and any advice I gave him was received either with levity or with scorn. Frederick only listened when I tried to correct his verses; and then he resented my corrections.

Hume: Plainly he did not want your criticisms but only your approval.

Voltaire: He is a strange man. He can be very witty at times, and of course he is the most fiercely anticlerical king in Europe. When he heard about the case of the Chevalier de la Barre, he said he would have punished the youth by making him read the works of St Thomas Aquinas—a fate, as he put it, worse than death.

Hume: And was it his anticlericalism, or his love of poetry, which drew him to you?

Voltaire: It was partly his upbringing. Frederick's father was a brutal boorish man who hated anything to do with culture, and loved only his army, or rather the troopers of his guard, who were all nearly seven feet tall. His son, by way of contrast, became a man of exquisite culture, and thus able to discern the merits of my writings. But like his father, unfortunately, Frederick loves soldiers, not such huge ones, it is true, but he loves them more tenderly. His court at Berlin when I was there was packed with handsome young lieutenants, ensigns, pages and cadets. When he held a levee he would throw a handkerchief at the one who pleased him, and the favourite would stay ten minutes in *tête-à-tête* with his Majesty. In the evenings, Frederick would compose verses or listen to music or play the flute himself, and then dine in a little hall decorated with the most indecent pictures, but where the conversation was always rarefied and decorous.

Hume: How unlike Paris, where the furnishing of the dining rooms are always decorous, and only the conversation is indecent.

Voltaire: Yes, and you can imagine how much I yearned for Paris. Besides, for a man of my sensibilities, to live without the company of women was most uncongenial.

Hume: You can hardly deny an absolute monarch the right to be a paederast.

Voltaire: I doubt if Frederick should be called one. Indeed I think he was so severely punished during his father's lifetime, that he has been effectively cured of love in his *amours de passade*.

Hume: It is only a pity that his attachment to the military should have found expression in wars of conquest.

Voltaire: Yes, that is the thing for which I shall never forgive him. He has treated me disgracefully, betrayed my years of friendship for him, had me seized and kept in custody on preposterous trumped-up charges, threatened my person and my property—but all that, I could overlook, but not his having plunged Europe into war for the aggrandizement of his bleak and barbarous kingdom.

Hume: I once read Frederick's essay against Machiavelli. It struck me as paradoxical that a king who adopted all the more iniquitous advice that Machiavelli offers to princes should attack Machiavelli as immoral.

Voltaire: Remember that Machiavelli himself might have urged him to do so. If you want to gain a reputation as a virtuous prince, attack the author who upholds vice.

Hume: Or who is thought to uphold vice.

Voltaire: Which Machiavelli undoubtedly does.

Hume: Not altogether. He says there are two moralities—one for the private person and the other for the prince or ruler. A double standard, if you like, but clearly a justifiable one.

Voltaire: Frederick of Prussia could never be accused of having a double standard. He is unscrupulous as a prince, in matters of state, and equally unscrupulous as a man, in private dealings. A model of consistency.

Hume: But of course it is his private morality which shocks the world. As a prince his crimes are condoned; indeed we already hear him being spoken of as Frederick the Great. And of course this is readily explained. In the condition of anarchy which exists between nations, where indeed a state of war is almost endemic, there is little room for that moral code which prevails among individuals, who live under systems of law.

Voltaire: So much the worse for the condition of anarchy among nations. If there were respect for moral principles among states, peace would be more secure.

Hume: I doubt it. The state which kept its word would be swallowed up by the one which broke it; the lamb would be consumed by the lion. We may deplore the lack of a system of law superior to nations, but in the absence of such a system, it would be folly for the rulers to act as if one already existed.

Voltaire: It is a painful reflection on mankind.

Hume: Assuredly it is; and that is why Machiavelli is so much disliked, for drawing attention to a painful truth. Men prefer to deceive themselves into thinking that they uphold the same moral standard in national and private life, whereas in reality they do not and could not afford to do so. It strikes me that there is a certain analogy between the two standards of political and private morality, and the standard of chastity as we apply it respectively to the female and the male. A woman we expect to be absolutely chaste and modest; the smallest departure from the strict rule of purity, and society punishes the sinner severely. And for a good reason: the integrity of the family depends on it. But we expect a man to be chaste only to a moderate degree. We condemn debauchery in him, but, at the same time, we do not admire virginity or total abstinence from the pleasures of the flesh. We are indulgent towards the peccadilloes of the male. In a similar way, it seems to be appropriate to be strict and exacting in the moral principles we impose on the private person, and indulgent towards the prince who, for reasons of state, resorts to deceit, at times, or falsehood, or breaks his promises.

Voltaire: I disagree profoundly. The 'reason of state' I consider one of the most sinister phrases in the language.

Hume: But you yourself have said, in defence of Francis Bacon that torture can sometimes be justified. I am sure you do not hold that torture is ever permissible in private dealings; so if it is ever to be justified at all, which I doubt, it can only be in the political realm, by an appeal to the reason of state.

Voltaire: I appeal only to public utility or social advantage. Those who invoke the reason of state think always of the advantage of the ruler. However, I might agree with you that there is a certain difference between the province of morality and that of administration. It is a great mistake to regard courts of criminal law as courts of punishment. Prisons and other penalties should not be used as forms of retribution, but only as means of deterrence and perhaps of reform. Society must protect itself, but no man is entitled to perform the office of God and judge or inflict punishment on sinners. Penalties can be justified only in terms of utility to society. The death penalty, for example, I conceive to be very rarely, if ever, justified. And do not exaggerate my suggestion that torture might, exceptionally, be admitted. That would be only in the very rare case of an overwhelming social benefit. That is very different from Machiavelli's doctrine of the reason of state, which allows a man like Frederick to set the world in flames with impunity.

Hume: I disapprove of Frederick as much as you do. But I merely remark, as a natural feature of moral codes, that they must lie heavily on the individual, and bind him in conscience, but must rest more lightly on a civil ruler, who, in his duty to his nation, cannot allow his private scruples to have a larger voice than the public interest. This is not difficult to understand if we consider what is the foundation of all moral law.

Voltaire: Reason, my dear Hume. The essential principles of morality are revealed to men by the light of reason which the supreme being has implanted in them.

Hume: And there I think you are mistaken. The basis of morality is not reason, but interest. How do you think that the notion of justice arose among men?

Voltaire: Many philosophers could give you an answer to that question—all equally speculative.

Hume: Of course the idea that men once lived in a state of nature is a fiction, but we can fairly say that the natural world in which men found themselves was characterized from the first by scarcity or shortage. There was not an abundance, for nature is not generous to man. There was not enough to go round. So men had the choice of fighting over the little there was, and probably dying in the process, or of working together to improve the scarce resources of nature, and each respecting what others accumulated. The idea of justice must have arisen with the institution of property.

Voltaire: Then you appear to assert, my dear Hume, what your writings deny: that society is based on a contract, or promise, entered into by all its members.

Hume: No, it is not a case of a contract or promise. It is simply a sense of a common interest, which all the members of society express to one another, and which induces them to regulate their conduct by certain rules. I observe that it will be to my interest to leave my neighbour in the possession of his goods, provided that he will act in the same manner towards me. He, for his part, is sensible of the same interest in the regulation of his conduct. We are like two men who pull the oars of a boat; they do it by agreement or convention, although they have given no promises to each other.

Voltaire: They might alternatively be said to act from a sentiment of mutual benevolence.

Hume: Benevolence is assuredly a social sentiment. But it is far too weak in itself to compete with the passion of self-love or avidity. Indeed the only passion strong enough to restrain self-interest is self-interest itself, enlightened and altered in its direction. It is when men understand that they can gratify their appetites better in a system of ordered society than they can gratify them amid the violence of universal anarchy, that their self-interest itself becomes the foundation of morality. As it is man's strongest passion, it makes civil society secure.

Voltaire: You speak of understanding, and I am sure you are right to do so. But understanding is a rational thing; and only rational beings can be moral beings. Man is virtuous only when reason is sovereign.

Hume: I have said before, and I say again, that reason is, and ought to be the slave of the passions.

Voltaire: A truly blasphemous remark, if I ever heard one.

Hume: But surely you must agree, Voltaire, that reason is only a faculty. It can show us how to realize what we desire, or avoid what we fear; but desire and fear are not part of reason, they are feelings or passions. One's moral experience, of course, has its reflective side. But reason itself is not the seat of man's generosity or probity or courage any more than it is the seat of his cowardice or meanness or untruthfulness. Passion prompts a man to act charitably towards a friend in need, and reason tells him how to execute such an act. Reason is thus the tool of the sentiments, or, as I expressed it before, the slave of the passions.

Voltaire: But you yourself speak of enlightening and directing the passions, and what assumes this role if it is not reason? If reason is in a position to instruct and direct, it is in a superior position.

Hume: The office is not superior, but subordinate, like that of a lawyer to his client, or that of a minister to an absolute king. Reason does not compete in any way with men's self-love; it simply teaches them how best to achieve the satisfaction they desire.

Voltaire: But that in itself is a triumph of reason over passion.

Hume: It is a mistake to talk of a conflict between reason and passion. The conflicts which take place within a man are conflicts between one passion and another. Some passions are calm and tranquil; and it is perhaps natural that every action of the mind which operates with the same calmness as reason, should be confused with reason. What we call strength of mind is not strength of 'mind' understood as the strength of reason, but simply the prevalence of the calm passions above the violent passions.

Voltaire: Well, perhaps we may find ourselves in some measure of agreement. I should not call your calm passion a 'passion'. I should call it a reflective disposition.

Hume: Then you have no occasion to speak of rational moral knowledge.

Voltaire: As you know, I agree with the greatest of English metaphysicians, Locke, that there are no innate ideas. It follows that there is no moral proposition innate in our souls. But because men are born without beards, does it follow that they are not born to be bearded at a certain age?

Hume: If moral ideas come later, as of course they do, then this is because they derive from experience, and not from rational knowledge.

Voltaire: It is clear that God—or, as you might prefer to say, Nature—intended men to live in society. And since society cannot exist without ideas of justice and injustice, God or Nature, gave men the means of acquiring those ideas. Our different customs, it is true, will never allow us to attach the same idea of justice to the same notions. What is a crime in Asia will not necessarily be a crime in Europe. All societies will not have the same laws, but no society will be without laws.

Hume: Yes, there I think I agree with you. I think that Montesquieu exaggerates the differences between societies when he says that social norms are as variable as the climates they depend on.

Voltaire: Anything Montesquieu says should be regarded with some mistrust. It is true that societies have different moral codes. We are told, for example, that theft was permitted in Sparta. But why? Because property was held in common and because to steal from a miser who kept to himself what belonged to society was to do a service to the state. We are told that there are savages who eat men and think it no crime. I reply that these savages have the same idea of justice and injustice as we have. They make war, as we do, from madness. War is universal, and eating one's enemies is merely an additional ceremony. The crime is not putting them on the spit, but killing them in the first place. And savages justify the killing by the same excuses with which we justify our foolish European wars: that the enemies of the state must be put to the sword.

Hume: It appears to me, my dear Voltaire, that you are of my own opinion, that what is called morality is nothing other than those rules which are necessary for the life of man in society.

Voltaire: In a sense, yes. Place two men on earth; they will call good, virtuous, and just, only that which is advantageous for both. Place four men on earth, and there will be nothing virtuous except that which is suitable for all four—and if one of the four eats another's supper, or cheats him or kills him, he will undoubtedly arouse the other two. What is true of these four men, could be said of the whole universe. And that, my friend, is roughly the plan of my moral philosophy.

Hume: If that is so, my dear Voltaire, I do not see why you should dispute my suggestion that morality is based on utility or interest.

Voltaire: You spoke of a selfish interest; I speak of a social interest.

Hume: Every man tenders the social interest only because it coincides with his selfish interest.

Voltaire: Reason teaches him that what is to the common advantage is also to his own advantage. But passions blind men.

Hume: Violent passions blind them. The calm passion of cool self-love prompts a man to obey rules which are in his own interest as well as that of everyone else.

Voltaire: It appears to me, Hume, that you escape the familiar conflict between reason and passion only to be confronted by a conflict between the calm passions, as you like to call them, and the violent passions; and whereas I look for the sovereignty of reason you look for the supremacy of cool self-love. Both of us seem at least to be agreed that some kinds of passion must be subdued if morality is to be upheld.

Hume: Yes, of course, the violent passions are dangerous to a man and still more dangerous to society. And since most men are prone to be governed as often by their violent as by their calm passions, there has to be force behind the law, and penalties for those who break it.

Voltaire: I think it more important to prevent crimes than to take it upon ourselves to punish them. That is another reason why I think a powerful and enlightened government is so necessary. The state could then be ordered in such a way as to give people incentives to obey the law and diminish the attractiveness of crime.

Hume: So we return to your absolute monarch. Of course, I would never deny that some peoples are not fit for anything better. Machiavelli said so, and most of the Roman authors say the same. If there is to be liberty in the state, there must be a certain moral character in the citizens. If there is no civic virtue, then the people will have to accept despotism.

Voltaire: The modern world needs a king to teach men what civic virtue is. French patriotism did not exist before Henri IV instilled it in men's hearts.

Hume: I am glad you talk of hearts and not men's minds.

Voltaire: That is because I do not exaggerate the value of patriotism. There are other, even more important virtues.

Hume: Such as . . .?

Voltaire: Humanity, tolerance, compassion, intelligence, the love of truth and the hatred of cruelty.

Hume: I fear they are not widespread virtues.

Voltaire: Alas, they are not; and that is another reason why strong government is necessary. The mob is stupid and barbarous.

Hume: That is perhaps because the mob is poor. The ownership of property is the best school of civic virtue. Naturally so, since the law originated from the need to protect possessions, those who have property understand justice best, and are less likely to be swayed by intemperate passions. I do not believe in Utopias, but if I were to design a perfect commonwealth, I would prefer to see the legislation confined to an aristocracy of substantial property-owners.

D

Voltaire: You would perpetuate what already exists in England.

Hume: Yes, I am in favour of perpetuating a system that works well. I certainly would not wish to see any more revolutions. Great upheavals always bring the violent passions of the multitude to the surface. There is something alarming about the very thought of democracy.

Voltaire: Oh I could adapt myself easily to democratic government. As you know, there is a fair amount of it among the Swiss. And it has its advantages. I like to see free men make the laws they live under, just as they make the houses they live in. It pleases me that my mason, my carpenter, my blacksmith, my neighbour the farmer and my friend the manufacturer, all raise themselves above their trade, and they know the public interest better than the most insolent Turkish official. In a democracy, no labourer, no artisan need fear either molestation or contempt. To be free, to have only equals, is the true natural life of man.

Hume: But it is a life which very few men have ever lived. How many democratic governments has the world witnessed?

Voltaire: A bare handful as yet.

Hume: Then history does not suggest that it is a very practicable form of government. And if it is not workable, why stir up the passions of the populace by suggesting that they might accede to so ideal a form of constitution?

Voltaire: I have never done so. I realize that the French are not ready for democracy. They are not even ready for a mixed constitution of the kind you have in England. You favour an aristocracy of property, my dear Hume, and I suppose that is more or less what exists in England since James I started selling peerages and the upheavals of the seventeenth century made the occupation of estates the only effective test of nobility. But here in France there is still only an aristocracy of blood and ancient lineage; and the man of mere property is just a *bourgeois* like myself.

Hume: You speak of yourself as a bourgeois, but were you not elevated to the dignity of Sieur de Voltaire as Gentleman in Ordinary to Louis Quinze?

Voltaire: That means that I became a courtier, not a nobleman. Besides it did not last long. I lived at Versailles as historiographer to the King —lived, I should say, in a stinking privy on the kitchen court— until the politeness I showed the King's mistress antagonized the Queen, and I was banished. Yet without politeness to the King's mistresses, advancement would never have been possible for me.

Hume: For a royalist, my dear Voltaire, your experience of royalty has been less than fortunate.

Voltaire: And what of your experience with the English aristocracy?

Hume: Scarcely happier. When I wrote my *History of England*, I sought only to record the truth. I was without interest, and, I hope, without partiality; in consequence I was accused of bias by everyone. I was, I own, sanguine in my expectations of that work. I thought I was the only historian in the kingdom who had at once neglected present power and the cry of popular prejudices, and I expected proportional applause. But miserable was my disappointment. I was assailed by one united cry of reproach, disapprobation and even detestation. English, Scotch and Irish; Whig and Tory, churchman and sectary; freethinker and religionist united in their rage against me.

Voltaire: Fortunately your book is better appreciated in France.

Hume: Perhaps that is because it does not deal with French history.

Voltaire: Undoubtedly it is. Otherwise you might have been persecuted as I have been. However, I hope you found enough admiration among the more discriminating members of the British aristocracy to sustain you in your political beliefs.

Hume: As much as you have found for yours among the crowned heads of Europe.

Voltaire: We have talked too much about Frederick of Prussia. You must not forget that there is also the Empress Catherine of Russia and King Stanislaus of Poland—not to mention your sovereign or mine. Somehow I feel the present trend of modern kings is towards enlightenment. And if it is not, they are doomed.

Hume: Which is more likely?

Voltaire: I believe in progress.

Hume: I have mixed feelings about progress. In England today you cannot fail to observe the great decline, if we ought not rather to say, the total extinction of literature. And I am afraid that this prognosticates a very short duration of all our other improvements.

Voltaire: I agree with you that there is no progress in the arts. Literature in France is in even greater decline than it is in England. My own writings, alas, mark the end and not the beginning of a great creative movement. But we must be careful to draw a distinction between the arts, which are in decay, and the practical sciences, which are everywhere improving.

Hume: I am certainly not one of those who regard the old days as superior in every way. Indeed I would say of England that when Queen

Elizabeth was on the throne, there was very little good roast beef in the land and no liberty at all. And imagine what daily life must have been like. Even castles were no better than dungeons. No chimney to let out smoke and no glass windows to keep out air; a glimmering candle to see by, and no diet but salt beef and mutton for nine months of the year, and no vegetables of any kind.

Voltaire: England is uncomfortable enough today. Considering how prosperous the kingdom is, the standard of living is wretched. London is the rival of Paris in size, but by no means its rival in splendour, or taste, or amusement, or the arts, or society. I believe that there is five hundred times more silver plate in the private houses of Paris than in those of London. In Paris a mere notary or attorney or woollen draper is better housed, has much better furniture and is much better served than a great magistrate in London. The English are rich, but they do not enjoy their riches.

Hume: I could never bring myself to live in London. But then I am a Scotchman.

Voltaire: I could, and I have done. The English have many great merits. They know how to think, where the French can only talk. English science and industry are unrivalled. So is their commerce; their liberty is a priceless possession, and their literature is magnificent.

Hume: Did you not once say that English books were better than English men?

Voltaire: I would say the same of French books and French men. And you know, my dear Hume, it was I who introduced English literature to France. Before I translated passages from Milton, Dryden and Pope, forty years ago, no one in France knew anything of English poetry. As for English philosophy, I was the first to explain Newton and Locke to my fellow-countrymen, and Swift, the English Rabelais, would never have been read here but for me.

Hume: I realize that apart from Shakespeare, English literature has no more fervent champion . . .

Voltaire: Not apart from Shakespeare. I have always said that his virtues were his own, and that his faults were those of his age. His work has such a beautiful, but wild nature; no regularity, no propriety, no art; baseness mixed with grandeur, buffoonery with the sublime—barbarous, low, extravagant, absurd—but still great literature.

Hume: I confess I have no liking for Shakespeare. The truth, I suspect, is that the English have so little delicacy of taste, so little sensibility to the charms of the muses, that their comic poets must have recourse to obscenity to move them, and their tragic poets must wallow in blood and slaughter.

Voltaire: I think you are unfair to the English. If their taste in dramatic poetry is bad, that is because Shakespeare has corrupted it. In the field of politics the English are the most civilized people in Europe; the most disposed to moderation and forbearance and the least inclined to excess.

Hume: That is because they exhausted themselves and their fanaticism in the civil wars and revolutions of the seventeenth century. What you see as moderation is perhaps better understood as fatigue.

Voltaire: But none the less admirable for that reason.

Hume: Indeed. And perhaps all the more useful. For a people which has exhausted its energies is likely to be proof against new enthusiasms as well as old ones.

Voltaire: I would, however, prefer a lively to a weary scepticism.

Hume: We should be grateful for what we have. If polite society is no longer religious, it is not because its members have become persuaded by the arguments of philosophy, or excited by Encyclopaedias, but rather because they have grown bored with sermons. It is not the influence of your books, which they do not understand, my dear Voltaire, or mine, which they do not read, which is undermining orthodox faith today, but the failure of the clergy to make it attractive. But we should not complain. Toleration flourishes, where it does flourish, in the soil of religious indifference.

Voltaire: You do less than justice to philosophy, Hume.

Hume: We should not pay too much regard to philosophy, my dear Voltaire. From the perspective of philosophy, your so-called natural religion is no more rational than orthodox Christianity, your ethical principles are no more demonstrable than any others. Philosophy ends where it begins, in doubt and uncertainty. And the only escape from it is to abandon philosophy altogether, and turn one's mind to other thoughts; and get on with the business of life, sharing the common sense opinions of the ordinary man.

Voltaire: I agree with you. Let us each cultivate our garden: that is the golden rule. But for you or I to pretend to be ordinary would be putting too great a strain on people's credence.

Hume: We are men, too, like others.

Voltaire: We are men, but very unlike others. You, my dear Hume, are a genius, and so am I.

Edmund Burke, Tom Paine and Mary Wollstonecraft

A dialogue on Revolution

In the spring of the year 1790, Edmund Burke was writing his
Reflections on the Revolution in France. He was then aged sixty-one,
and had been a Member of Parliament for the better part of
twenty-five years. He had a considerable reputation as a reforming, liberal and independent Whig; but his attitude to the French
Revolution was from the beginning uncompromisingly hostile.
Some people fancied that he was becoming reactionary as he was
growing old. In truth Burke's views on the question of revolution
in politics had never changed. He had always been as much the
conservative as he was the reformer. In the dialogue which follows, Burke is presented defending his views against the ideas of
two left-wing friends, Thomas Paine and Mary Wollstonecraft.
Thomas Paine, who was the same age as Burke, was an East-
Anglian boy of humble origins who had made his name in
America as the author of the revolutionary tract, *Common Sense*.
He had served in the rebel army, and as an American diplomatist
in France. In 1790 he was in England as a visitor from Paris.

The third voice in the conversation is that of Mary Wollstonecraft, who subsequently married William Godwin. In the year
1790 she was barely thirty; she had only just begun to work as a
publisher's reader in London and to move in radical society, but
she was already a woman with forceful opinions of her own.

Paine: Well, Mr Burke, I understand you are no longer with us.

Burke: I do not follow you, Mr Paine.

Wollstonecraft: He means you have turned recreant to the idea of social justice;
that you are no friend of the French Revolution.

Burke: I am certainly no friend of that Revolution, Miss Wollstonecraft.
I do not see how any person of discrimination and the smallest
moral insight could be.

Wollstonecraft: And I do not see how anyone could fail to be.

Paine: You have been a friend of other revolutions, Mr Burke.

Burke: Which revolutions?

Wollstonecraft: You supported the revolution which took place in America sixteen years ago, when the colonists rebelled against the British
crown.

Paine: And you have often spoken with the warmest approval of the English revolution of 1688.

Burke: You believe that because a man supports some revolutions he should support all?

Paine: No one has suggested such a thing, Mr Burke. We spoke only of 1688 and 1775; that is, of revolutions conducted on the same principles as the new revolution in France.

Wollstonecraft: Yes, and it is extremely inconsistent to support the earlier ones and resist the new.

Burke: The *same* principles did you say, Mr Paine?

Wollstonecraft: Yes, he did. And what is more, each revolution inspired, to some extent, the ones which followed. We English gave the lead, we established, so to speak, the precedent.

Burke: Well, madam, you have been a governess and a schoolmistress, so you ought to know more history than I, who have only been a student of Law and a member of Parliament and a Grub Street hack. But you, Mr Paine, who have actually witnessed the events of 1775 in America, and have been so much in Paris—that you should say that these movements are animated by the same principles, that does surprise me.

Wollstonecraft: Then a manifest truth surprises you, Mr Burke.

Paine: The principles are identical.

Burke: But what are these principles, Mr Paine?

Paine: The rights of man, Mr Burke.

Burke: I will admit I have often heard that expression, though I have never been told precisely what it means. But one thing is luminously clear; the Revolution of 1688 was not designed to realize the rights of man. It was done to restore the rights of Englishmen.

Wollstonecraft: What is good for the English is good for the French. They saw what we did a hundred years ago, and they read the theory of it all in Locke and others. It inspired them. French writers like Montesquieu are full of English inspiration. How can we criticize them now for trying to be like us?

Burke: But there is no real resemblance between the two revolutions, madam. The French Revolution is designed to introduce a new social system, a new ethos and a new mode of life. Our revolution of 1688 was designed to restore an old system and an ancient mode of life which James II was trying to destroy. The King was the innovator. He attacked the constitution. And the people of England, from dire necessity, took up arms to uphold the law against a lawless monarch.

Paine: The French have done the same.

Burke: Nonsense; the French have taken up arms against the law itself.

Paine: I would agree with you that the English revolution stopped short where the French revolution has gone forward. The landed and property-owning interest in English society put on a brake in 1688. The glory of the French Revolution is that it is overcoming this kind of sectional interest. It is finding a new national morality. And what we see in France is, I agree, something more than has ever been seen in England: it is nothing less than the regeneration of man.

Burke: You speak of morality, Mr Paine. You will find no support for the French Revolution in that.

Wollstonecraft: The French may affront backward and undeveloped systems of morality; but as man goes forward he discovers new principles.

Burke: The principles of morality do not develop, madam. They are unchanging. The philosophers of the French Revolution may think they have made discoveries in morality, but they deceive themselves, because there are no discoveries to be made.

Wollstonecraft: What authority have you to say that?

Burke: The laws of morality have been laid down for us for all time by God himself. They were understood long before we were born as well as they will be after the grave has heaped its mould on our presumption, and the tomb has silenced our pert loquacity.

Wollstonecraft: So you think there is no progress?

Burke: I know there is no perfectibility.

Paine: Or no improvement?

Burke: Some wrongs may be corrected, and it is our duty to correct them. But we shall never enter the millenium in this world.

Wollstonecraft: You may sneer at the millenium, Mr Burke; but the prospect of greater purity in morals may not be a mere poetic fiction.

Burke: That is an odd way of expressing the ambitions of the French Revolution. But there is one thing we must remember. Evil will never be banished from the universe; and perhaps the sum total of it may never be diminished. It is the result of the Fall.

Wollstonecraft: To teach men to be resigned to evil is short-sighted benevolence, Mr Burke. How much better to labour to increase human happiness by extirpating evil.

Burke: By seeking to introduce the millenium you do not extirpate evil. On the contrary you destroy or undermine the very institutions which mankind has built up over the centuries to ward off evil and prevent it from increasing.

Paine: The evil in the universe is one thing, Mr Burke, and perhaps, as you say, it will never be banished. But the particular injustice and iniquity and oppression of the *ancien régime* in France was remediable, and the people of France have sought a remedy.

Burke: A remedy indeed. They sought a remedy and they have inherited a whirlwind. Two years ago the people of France gave their representatives to the States General a mandate to reform the government. There was not the remotest suggestion of a design to destroy it. Had such a design been then even insinuated, I believe there would have been but one voice in France, and that voice would have been for rejecting it with scorn and horror.

Paine: The old system had to be destroyed because it was too corrupt to be reformed.

Burke: To hear some people speak of the late monarchy in France you would imagine that they were talking about the barbarous, anarchic despotism of Turkey or Persia, where arts are unknown, and manufactures languish, and the human race melts away under the eye of the observer. Was this the case in France? Facts do not support the resemblance. Along with some evil, there was much good; and the French monarchy had some corrective to its evil from religion, laws, manners and opinions. It was by no means a free constitution, and therefore not a good constitution, but it was a despotism in appearance rather than reality.

Paine: It is not for us foreigners to distinguish between appearance and reality. I am not a bookish man, Mr Burke, and I have not read the ancient Greek writers as you have; but I think it is Aristotle who says that it is the wearer who knows where the shoe pinches. It is the people who live under a despotism who can tell whether it is a reality or not.

Wollstonecraft: And the people of France decided that the despotism of Louis XVI was a reality, just as the people of England decided that the despotism of James II was a reality.

Burke: You are still wedded to the notion that there is a real resemblance between the French Revolution and our own?

Wollstonecraft: It is more proper than the comparisons you make between France and Turkey or Persia. Both the English and the French Revolution have the same supreme objective, and that is liberty. If you deny that, Mr Burke, you are closing your eyes to history.

Burke: And if you assert it, madam, you are closing your mind to reason. If we are to make an objective of liberty we must ask what *kind* of liberty is in question. For I cannot believe that liberty of all kinds is to be counted a blessing. Am I seriously to felicitate a madman, who has escaped from his cell, on his restoration to light and liberty? Am I to congratulate the murderer, who has escaped from prison, upon the recovery of his natural rights?

Wollstonecraft: You are not speaking to the House of Commons now, Mr Burke. You will not enlarge our understanding of the problem of human freedom by asking rhetorical questions about the restraint of exceptional persons who are not fully rational.

Burke: But it is you, madam, who make an abstraction of liberty, and invite us to love it without any concrete knowledge of the specific freedom we are confronted with. I mean, not you alone, but all theorists and apologists of the French Revolution. I flatter myself that I love a manly, moral, regulated liberty as well as any gentleman in France—and perhaps I have given good proof of my attachment to it in the whole of my public life. But I cannot stand forward and give praise or blame to an object which is stripped of all concrete relations and stands in all the solitude of a metaphysical idea.

Paine: So you will not agree that freedom in general is good?

Burke: Generally speaking, for what that mode of speaking is worth, I would agree that freedom is good. I would also agree that government is, generally speaking, good. But I hardly fancy, Mr Paine, that you will wish to persuade me that all and every actual form of government is good. Nor would you succeed in persuading me that all and every actual form of liberty is good. Before I venture to congratulate a person on a blessing, I must be tolerably sure that he has really received one. So I should suspend my congratulations on the new liberty in France until I had been informed how it had been combined with government, with public force, with the discipline and obedience of armies, with effective revenue, with morality and religion, with solidity and property, with peace and order, and with civil and social manners. All these things in their way are good things, too; and liberty without them is not much of a benefit while it lasts, and, in any case, it is not likely to last long.

Wollstonecraft: When the French speak of liberty they do not mean a cold and speculative abstraction. What they ask for is such a degree of freedom, social and religious, as is compatible with the freedom of every other individual with whom he is united in a social compact.

Burke: Ah, Miss Wollstonecraft; you are already putting limitations on

your freedom, and very large ones. A freedom which is circumscribed by the needs of others in society is far from being absolute
and indefeasible.

Paine: Miss Wollstonecraft has never said, and I do not think any friend
of the French Revolution has ever said that men have the right to
an absolute and indefeasible liberty. They have said, what Locke
said, that men have an absolute and indefeasible right to liberty;
but that liberty in each case is qualified by the rights of others.
When the Declaration of the Rights of Man was before the
National Assembly some of its members remarked that if a Declaration of Rights was published it ought to be accompanied by
a Declaration of Duties. But one who reflects enough will see that
a Declaration of Rights is in itself a Declaration of Duties also.
Whatever is my right is the right of another man also, and it
becomes my duty, not only to enjoy, but also to guarantee and
protect the rights of all.

Wollstonecraft: That is true. It is in this kind of reason that one can observe the
moral nobility of the French Revolution.

Burke: The *moral nobility*, madam! You can contemplate all the frauds,
impostures, violences, rapines, burnings, murders, confiscations,
compulsory paper currencies, and every description of tyranny
and cruelty employed to bring about and uphold the Revolution,
and you can talk of 'moral nobility'!

Wollstonecraft: If there has been violence in France, it is because the privileged
orders refused to give up their privileges.

Paine: I can see now why you hate the French Revolution, Mr Burke. If
it had confined itself merely to the destruction of a flagrant
despotism, perhaps you would have been silent. What upsets you
is that it has gone too far. That is, it has gone too far for you. It
stares corruption in the face, and answers vice with virtue. It
offers a new image of social justice, of friendship and freedom and
equality in place of the old social order of hierarchy and privilege.

Burke: Assuredly, Mr Paine, among the revolutions in France must be
reckoned a revolution in manners. History will record that on
the morning of 6 October 1789, the King and Queen of France,
lay down to rest, after a day of confusion, alarm, dismay and
slaughter—lay down, under the pledged security of public faith.
From this sleep the Queen was first startled by the voice of a
sentinel, who was instantly cut down. A band of cruel ruffians and
assassins, reeking with blood, rushed into the chamber of the
Queen. She, her husband and their infant children were then

forced to abandon the most splendid palace in the world (now polluted by massacre) to be conducted as captives on a journey of twelve miles, amidst the horrid yells and frantic dances of the vilest of women, to be lodged in one of the oldest palaces in Paris, now converted into a Bastille for Kings.

Wollstonecraft: By the 'vilest of women', Mr Burke, I presume you refer to the poor. It is true that poverty and oppression does brutalize its victims; but it is not for you, who speak as a champion of the *ancien régime* to complain of its consequences. When the social changes now beginning in France have achieved their full effects, the unseemly expression of poverty will be wiped from the face of the lower orders, and the true beauty of their humanity will once more shine in their eyes.

Paine: It is certainly a disagreeable experience to be arrested, Mr Burke. I have been arrested myself, so I can speak from experience. But I cannot see it is any worse for a queen than for any other mortal. What is so remarkable about Marie-Antoinette?

Burke: Remarkable? It is now sixteen or seventeen years since I saw her, but I shall never forget that vision. There she was like a morning star, full of life and splendour and joy. Little did I dream that I should live to see such disasters fall upon her in a nation of gallant men, of men of honour and cavaliers. I thought ten thousand swords must have leaped from their scabbards to avenge even a look that threatened her with insult. But the age of chivalry is gone, it seems; and the age of economists, and sophisters and calculators has come in its place.

Wollstonecraft: I notice that the brief discomfort of a queen can move you to great emotion, Mr Burke. Do the long and patient sufferings of the poor have no power to touch your heart? In France millions lived in darkness of oppression and injustice until the Revolution recognized their rights and brought them into lightness and the hope of happiness.

Burke: Lightness? What we see in France is a people possessed by a dark spirit of fanaticism, which denies both reason and morality. The activities of agitators, with their writings and speeches, have filled the populace with a black and savage atrocity of mind, which is fast driving out the common feelings of nature as well as all sentiment of religion.

Wollstonecraft: You said yourself, Mr Burke, that some evil is inevitable in human life, so why do you become so indignant about the wrong there may have been among all the good done in France?

Paine: Force, in greater or lesser degree, must be exercised in any revolution. It is part of normal politics.

Burke: How can I make you understand that revolutions are not a part of normal politics. Revolution is the most extreme medicine for the most grievous sickness in the constitution. You talk as if it were its daily bread.

Wollstonecraft: France under Louis XVI was suffering from a most grievous sickness.

Burke: It is suffering from an infinitely worse one now, madam, under a popular tyranny.

Paine: It is clear why you detest the democratic system in France, Mr Burke. You despise the common people.

Burke: You must forgive me if I cannot always follow you in argument, Mr Paine. You tell me I despise the common people because I deplore the fanaticism and irreligion of a mob. And you tell me I detest the democratic system in France, where there is in fact no democratic system to detest. What we see in France is not a democracy, or even anarchy; but rather a succession of short-lived tyrannies, each enjoying a fluctuating and unstable popular support.

Wollstonecraft: Be frank with us, Mr Burke; even if you were satisfied that the system were democratic you would still oppose it.

Burke: I should still criticize it, I imagine. Democracy as a method of government does not strike me as ideal. Hairdressers and tallow-chandlers ought not to be oppressed by the state, but the state itself is oppressed if such as they, individually or collectively, are permitted to rule.

Wollstonecraft: You have confessed your prejudice at last, Mr Burke. What I believe, and what the French of today believe, is that a hairdresser or a tallow-chandler is as good as a marquis or a duke and very probably better.

Burke: As good, perhaps, but not as wise. And wisdom is what is needed in a voter or a legislator.

Paine: What makes you think the rich have wisdom?

Wollstonecraft: They have wealth, which is a very different thing.

Burke: Wealth buys leisure, and leisure enables a man to reflect. You will find it well said in the Scriptures: 'The Wisdom of learned men cometh by opportunity of leisure. How can he get wisdom that holdeth the plough . . . that driveth the oxen, and is occupied in their labours?'

Paine: Well, I have never been a hairdresser or a tallow-chandler, but I left school at the age of thirteen to be apprenticed to a corset-maker, so no doubt you will consider me one of that same kidney . . .

Burke: You are no longer a corset-maker, Mr Paine. You are a journalist like myself. You are not someone ill-qualified by your station to do good for the state, but someone exceptionally enabled, by your talents, to do both good and harm; you have done both; more recently, if I may say so, the latter.

Wollstonecraft: You claim that the rich have wisdom, Mr Burke. I should agree that they often show skill in legislating in their own interest. But the higher orders in France can scarcely be said to have done even that. They brought about their own ruin by their own short-sightedness and folly. I think we should find more wisdom, and certainly more commonsense, in your hairdressers and tallow-chandlers.

Burke: It is true that the poor know what oppression feels like. But they are too ignorant to know how to cure it. Besides, in lacking property they also lack a sense of responsibility.

Paine: So you mistrust the people, Mr Burke, even if you do not actually despise them?

Burke: Mr Paine, I assure you that I reverentially look up to the people and with an awe that is almost superstitious. But I should show them little respect if I said what I do not mean. Of one thing I am certain; and that is that in a democracy the majority of citizens is capable of exercising the most cruel oppression on the minority. And such oppression is worse than can almost ever be apprehended from a single ruler. In such a popular persecution, individual sufferers are in a much more deplorable condition than in any other. Under a cruel prince they have the balmy compassion of mankind to assuage the smart of their wounds; but those who are subjected to wrong under multitudes are deprived of all external consolation. They seem deserted by mankind, over-powered by a conspiracy of their own species.

Wollstonecraft: Mr Burke, you speak with eloquence, but you may remember that Locke once said that eloquence was not worth much since it was generally employed to make the worse look the better part. You attack the imaginary defects of democracy in order to cloak the real evils of . . . I know not by what word to name the monstrous engine of corruption and privilege by which we are ruled in England.

Burke: But I understood you to say that the revolution of 1688 had established the reign of liberty and the rights of man in this kingdom.

Wollstonecraft: It was intended to, but we have suffered from a century of such corruption that the good which was then achieved is rapidly slipping from us . . .

Paine: Yes, how can we in England criticize the French? Do not all our inhabitants agree that English politics is a market where everyone has his price?

Burke: That may be the popular, or democratic, delusion, Mr Paine. But you should look at the English constitution as it is in reality.

Wollstonecraft: What is that constitution?

Burke: To begin with, government by the King in parliament.

Wollstonecraft: Well, let us look at the system, then, Mr Burke. The King is an unfortunate man who appears to be going out of his mind. So let us look at Parliament. Look at it: two houses—one an assembly of hereditary noblemen, so called, the descendants of the robber barons who helped William of Normandy to ravish and subdue the English people. They fill the upper and superior house. The other house is supposed to contain representatives of the commons, of the great mass of the English people. Since you are a member of the House, Mr Burke, I shall not deny its merits. It may well contain everything that is illustrious in rank, descent and in opulence, both hereditary and acquired. Whether it contains everything that is illustrious in talent and distinction is more problematical. But one thing is abundantly clear: the House of Commons is not representative of the ordinary people.

Burke: You say that because you do not know it well.

Paine: Miss Wollstonecraft is right. The House cannot be representative, Mr Burke. You have only to consider the means by which it is elected. In France the new constitution provides that the number of representatives for any place shall be in ratio to the number of taxable inhabitants. What article of the English constitution can you set against that? The county of Yorkshire which has nearly a million souls sends two members to Parliament, so does the county of Rutland which has not a hundredth part of that number. The town of Old Sarum which has not three houses sends two members, and the town of Manchester which contains upwards of 60,000 souls, is not permitted to send any. Is there any principle in these things? Is there anything by which you can discern wisdom or 'measured liberty' in this?

Burke: It seems to me that you are excessively concerned with the irregularities in parliamentary boundaries. The important matter here is not formal parity, but moral equality. If all the representatives are equally devoted to the well-being of the whole country, it is of no matter whether they receive their suffrage in Old Sarum or in Manchester. When I was the Member for Bristol, I had occasion to remind my constituents that I was their representative, but not their delegate. I was not bound then to their particular will as an advocate is bound to his client. I had their mandate only to obey my most pondered and impartial judgement as to which policy would best serve the interests of the kingdom.

Paine: But, it is not just a question of one place being better represented than another place. In the House of Commons, so-called, it is the landed and commercial interests which are represented. The poorer people, who are vastly more numerous, are not represented at all.

Burke: What do you mean, they are not represented?

Paine: They have no vote.

Burke: If they have no vote that is because they are not taxpayers.

Paine: That is a fallacy, Mr Burke. The poor are the greatest taxpayers. The beer tax, for example, produces more revenue than the land tax. And it is the working men who pay the beer tax, not the aristocracy. If the rich want beer, they brew their own, and escape the tax. It is hardly credible that you, after all your years in Parliament, could say that the poor are not taxpayers.

Burke: They are not direct taxpayers. The taxes they pay are indirect.

Paine: Yes, concealed taxes, so that they do not realize the unjust burden which is placed on them.

Burke: There is no other way of collecting the pennies of the poor. It may well be, since the poor are so numerous, that their pennies do sometimes add up to as much as the sums collected from the rich. But in the case of the rich, the contribution of each is substantial.

Paine: The poor pay substantial sums as well; it has been reckoned that the average English working man pays eight pounds a year, or a quarter of his income in hidden taxes.

Burke: If you think they would rather pay direct taxes, Mr Paine, you do not know them as I do. In any case, a man does not need a vote to be represented. The women and children of the country have no vote, but they are represented, so long as members of Parliament understand that it is the nation as a whole, and not any partial interest, that commands their service. Besides, the interest of the rich should not be seen as a separate interest. In society, as in the family, the stronger and wiser and more opulent speak for the weaker; they guide, enlighten and protect the rest. The rich look after the poor.

Wollstonecraft: What rubbish, Mr Burke. The rich do not look after the poor; they exploit them. Look at what happens when a man gets rich. He builds himself a fine house with a good stable and a splendid garden; he lavishes his care and solicitude on his trees and lawns and horses and dogs. But what care does he take of his tenants? He merely subjects them to the grasping hand of an avaricious steward.

Burke: You paint a vivid picture of the newly rich, Miss Wollstonecraft. You make us all the more sensible of the value of an old family and a natural aristocracy.

Wollstonecraft: The rich are the same, whether they are old or new. They have one concern in life, and that is the protection and extension of their own fortunes. That is the curse of England; the demon of property which has ever been at hand to encroach on the sacred rights of man.

Burke: But I always understood that the rights of man included the right to property. Locke says it plainly enough: life, liberty and property—these are our natural rights.

Paine: When Locke said that men had a natural right to property he explained what he meant—that men have a natural right to the fruits of their own labour. He did not say they have a natural right to the produce of rent, usury, interest and the exploitation of the labour of others.

Burke: You are quite right in the sense that Locke distinguishes between property in a state of nature and property in more advanced societies which followed the invention of money. He shows how the right to these more elaborate forms of property derives from the natural right to the simpler forms of property.

Wollstonecraft: I do not see how one man's right to the product of another's labour can possibly be derived from the right of every man to the product of his own labour.

Burke: I admit it is a complicated argument. And you might be well advised to let metaphysics alone, madam; sometimes nature is a better guide than speculative reason.

Wollstonecraft: I have noticed before that you have a marked antipathy to reason, Mr Burke. I grant that the cultivation of reason is an arduous task, but it is not, on those grounds, to be shirked.

Burke: Nature, madam, is wisdom without reflection, and often above it.

Wollstonecraft: I am well aware that people find passion an easier impulse to follow than reason; and so they persuade themselves that it is the more natural.

Burke: I suggest that we must have both nature and reason. Reason becomes impertinent when it is invoked against nature, just as it does when it is invoked against religion.

Paine: They are all abstractions, Mr Burke, and you have said that you do not like abstractions. I am as ready as you to respect nature and religion; but not if nature means a 'natural aristocracy', as you call it; or religion, if religion means bishops.

Burke: What is wrong with bishops? Are the sheep to have no shepherds?

Paine: Privilege, Mr Burke.

Burke: Privilege?

Wollstonecraft: Yes, he said privilege. Do you see nothing wrong with a system where the bishops live like oriental potentates in palaces, while the souls of the people are tended by impoverished curates, who run from one parish to another, bilked of their stipends by rapacious diocesans. The poor clergy do all the work; the rich take all the Church's income.

Burke: A fitting arrangement, one might fancy. The poor clergy look after the poor; the rich look after the rich.

Wollstonecraft: Indeed they look after the rich. Otherwise they would never become bishops. Few priests would gain the mitre if they did not show a due servility to those who possess the greatest fortunes and dominate the kingdom.

Burke: You speak as if the rich had no need of religion, Miss Wollstonecraft. You must remember that the great and the opulent are also among the unhappy. They feel personal pain and domestic sorrow. They need the consolation of religion as well as its instructions. It is just those who have nothing to do, who feel the killing languor of lassitude, just those whose material wants are satisfied, whose every desire is anticipated, just those who call for the charitable balm of salvation.

Wollstonecraft: I do not see how the spiritual needs of the idle rich can justify the impoverishment of the lower clergy and the accumulation of fortunes by the bishops.

Burke: How could a priest influence a great man if he could not appear before him as an equal? We all know in what contempt a poor curate is held in the houses of noblemen. He sits at the table well below the salt; he is little above the rank of a domestic servant.

Could such a person instruct the soul and conscience of a marquis or a duke, let alone a person newly rich? No, Mr Paine. The people of England understand that well. They make sure that their higher clergy shall be on a footing with the greatest of the hereditary nobility. They are content to see a Bishop of Durham or of Winchester in possession of ten thousand pounds a year because they will not have the landed interest look with scorn on the Church. It is not our English habit to confine religion to obscure municipalities and rustic villages. The Church must also have its mitred front in courts and parliament. The Church must have its dignity if it is not to suffer the insolence of wealth and titles.

Wollstonecraft: So the duty of the bishops is to outshine the haughty brilliance of secular patricians, and also to console them in the spiritual anguish which lies behind their arrogant pretensions. I shall not dispute that such is what they do, Mr Burke. Only I shall say that that is not what Christ meant when he told his apostles to 'Feed my lambs'.

Paine: Perhaps, Mr Burke, you think that Christ was enjoining us to feed the dogs and horses in the bishops' palaces while the children of the poor go hungry.

Burke: It may well be that many dogs and horses are nourished by victuals that might serve to feed the children of the poor. It is certainly true that the whole Church revenue is not employed in charity, nor perhaps ought to be. But it is better to cherish virtue and humanity by leaving much to free will, rather than to attempt to make men mere machines of political benevolence.

Wollstonecraft: I am not sure what you mean by 'political benevolence' though I am sure that if our system of government were democratic, it could serve the interests of the poor as it now serves the interests of the rich. It could become an instrument of the people for their own ends.

Burke: But the people of England do not want a democratic government, madam. It is alien to their traditions.

Paine: Not at all, Mr Burke. In 1688, the English people took the decisive step in the direction of democracy. It was then that they asserted their right to choose their own kings and cashier them for misconduct.

Burke: They did nothing of the kind. In 1688 the people of England reaffirmed the principle of hereditary monarchy. James II forfeited the right to rule by the unlawful nature of his conduct; and he was succeeded by those persons closest to him in blood in the Pro-

testant succession: namely his daughter Mary and her husband
William, who was also his nephew.

Wollstonecraft: William and Mary were put on the throne by popular force in the
lifetime of James II and of his son, the heir.

Burke: Assuredly there was some temporary departure from the strict
order of regular hereditary succession, by reason of the exclusion
of Papists. But it is against all principles of jurisprudence to regard
some exceptional deviation as a rule of law.

Wollstonecraft: But even the great jurist Blackstone seems to agree that the succession to the throne depends on the choice of the people. He says
that the doctrine of hereditary right by no means implies an indefeasible right to the throne.

Burke: No right is indefeasible, and no law is indefeasible except the law
of God. But it is arrant folly to suppose on those grounds that the
people of England in 1688 acquired the right to elect their kings
and to cashier them for misconduct. On the contrary, in the Acts
of Parliament of the Revolution Settlement you will see that both
Houses affirmed—and here I quote, for I have memorized the text
of the enactments—'The lords spiritual and temporal, and commons, do in the name of the people aforesaid, humbly submit
themselves, their heirs, and posterities for ever to defend their
majesties and the limitation of the crown.' So you see, that if the
English people ever had the right to elect their kings, they did
then most solemnly renounce and abdicate it.

Paine: Mr Burke, there never did, and never will, exist a Parliament with
the right to bind and commit posterity 'for ever'. Every age and
generation must be free to act for itself in all cases, just as the
generations which preceded it were free in their turn. Man has no
property in man, neither has any generation a property in the
generations which follow. Those who have quitted the world and
those who have not yet arrived in it are as remote from each other
as the utmost stretch of imagination can conceive. What possible
obligation then can exist between them? It is often said that the
government cannot take money out of a man's pocket without
his consent, so how can you claim that the Parliament of 1688 had
the right to take away the freedom of posterity?

Burke: But the people of England do not feel *bound* and *constrained* by past
enactments. They look upon the frame of their commonwealth
as it stands, to be of inestimable value. They look upon an un-
disturbed hereditary succession to the throne as a pledge of the
stability and perpetuity of that constitution. You talk much of

rights, both of you. But the English people look upon the hereditary monarchy as one of their rights, as a benefit, not as a grievance, as a security for their freedom, not as a badge of servitude.

Paine: The English people do not need a king as a pledge of their liberties. In fact, the hereditary nature of the crown is the one thing which has chiefly jeopardized their liberties, as the instances of Charles I and James II—to go back no farther—amply prove. You talk of the hereditary crown as if it were some production of nature; as if it had power to operate, like time, independently of human will. The propriety of such a monarchy is already being doubted; and I am sure that its legality will, before long, be generally denied.

Wollstonecraft: Yes, Mr Burke, the case for hereditary monarchy is not based on reason; it is based on superstition; a superstition which has nothing but antiquity to recommend it.

Burke: What has stood the test of time is most likely to endure. You are versed in the history of these islands, madam, so you will know that from Magna Carta to the Declaration of Rights, it has been the uniform policy of our constitution to claim and assert our liberties as an *entailed inheritance* derived from our forefathers and to be transmitted to our posterity. We have an inheritable crown, and inheritable peerage, and a House of Commons and a people inheriting privileges, franchise and liberties from a long line of ancestors. This idea of inheritance furnishes a sure principle of conservation, without excluding the possibility of improvement. It leaves acquisition free, but it secures what it acquires. You should not be insensible of the merits of such a contrivance of human wisdom.

Wollstonecraft: Hereditary government cannot be a contrivance of human wisdom, for the simple reason that wisdom is not hereditary.

Paine: In any case, Mr Burke, all hereditary government is by its nature tyrannical. To inherit a government is to inherit a people as if they were flocks and herds. Under the system which prevails in this country, a man finds himself a king or a peer not because he has any aptitude for government or legislation but simply because he is his father's son. He may well be, and often is, a fool; he may well be, and sometimes is, a rogue. But so long as he is not a Papist, the constitution calls on him to legislate or rule. He has royal blood, or noble blood, and that is all that counts.

Burke: And what innovation, Mr Paine, would you wish to introduce in place of our well-tried methods?

Paine: Representative government, Mr Burke. Republican government. That is government established and conducted for the interest of the people, both individually and collectively.

Burke: Where shall we seek our model? In ancient Rome?

Wollstonecraft: There are republics in the modern world as well.

Burke: Poland?

Paine: Now that is what is called an elective monarchy, but has an hereditary aristocracy.

Burke: Holland?

Paine: That calls itself a republic but has an hereditary Stateholdership. No, Mr Burke, America is the example we must look to, a country where you yourself are reverenced and remembered as a champion of the colonists' revolt. America is the only real republic in the modern world. Its government has no other business than the business of the nation. And the Americans have taken care to ensure that this, and no other, shall always be the object of its government by excluding everything hereditary.

Burke: 'Shall always be', did you say, Mr Paine? So the Americans have bound their posterity as we have? I am glad to hear it. To forget the future is a result of a selfish temper and confined views. An enlightened mind looks forward; but it also looks backward, and your weakness, Mr Paine, and equally yours, Miss Wollstonecraft, is that you will not look backward.

Wollstonecraft: You have not answered Mr Paine's criticism of the principle of heredity.

Burke: What am I to say? Heredity is a feature of nature and society as well as of the constitution. The awful Author of our being is the Author also of our place in the order of existence. All men are born with the social state of their parents, endowed with all the benefits and loaded with all the duties of their situation.

Wollstonecraft: That does not justify the institution of an hereditary monarchy or hereditary nobility.

Burke: Our manners, madam, our civilization in this European world of ours, have depended on two principles—the spirit of a gentleman and the spirit of religion.

Paine: In America we recognize a gentleman by his conduct, not by his birth.

Wollstonecraft: If the idea of a gentleman means anything at all, that is the only way one could be recognized.

Burke: But it is from an aristocracy that a system of manners originates, and spreads its civilizing influence on society at large.

Wollstonecraft: The conduct of our own aristocracy is no model to society at large, Mr Burke. Those who are not boorish dullards in the country are foppish libertines in the city. Drinking, hunting, gambling and fornication is the measure of their lives.

Burke: Let us not judge the institution of nobility by the intemperance of some individual nobleman. Surely you can see in the tradition of chivalry one of the glories of Europe? A generous loyalty to rank and sex, a proud submission, a disciplined obedience, a subordination of heart which kept alive, even in servitude itself, the spirit of exalted freedom?

Wollstonecraft: You talk of the past, Mr Burke.

Burke: Yes, I fear that that manly sentiment has vanished from the modern world. That sensibility which felt a stain on its honour like a wound, which inspired courage and mitigated ferocity, which ennobled all it touched, and under which vice itself lost half its evil, by losing all its grossness: that, I fear, has gone for ever.

Wollstonecraft: Mr Burke, I despair of you. What a sentiment to come from the lips of a moral being! So vice loses half its evil and all its grossness when it is committed by the aristocracy? Vice is vice, Mr Burke, no matter who commits it. And if anyone can plead extenuating circumstances, it is the lower orders, whose circumstances are so wretched that the beauty of the virtuous life has never been revealed to them.

Burke: You think that beauty will be revealed to them in France? In France, where churches are being robbed and the skill of builders employed in the erection of opera-houses, brothels, gaming-houses, club-houses and obelisks in the Champ de Mars?

Paine: There is some difference between a brothel and a club-house.

Burke: Yes, the one debauches the body, the other debauches the mind.

Paine: A club-house is a meeting-place for public-spirited gentlemen, where new political ideas are canvassed and programmes for reform contrived.

Burke: A place where political plots are hatched, you had rather say; a place where the envious and avaricious conspire against the property and rights of others.

Wollstonecraft: You call men envious and avaricious because they wish to do away with privilege?

Burke: I call them such because they wish to possess themselves of the privileges of others. That is what lies behind all their talk of equality.

Paine: You are unjust, Mr Burke. Those who speak of equality are inspired by a great ideal. Witness the case of Monsieur de la Fayette, formerly the Marquis de la Fayette, a title he has renounced, with all his other hereditary privileges. He has done that from one motive only; and it is the motive of all who are changing the social order in France today—love of the principle of the equality of man.

Burke: There can be no such principle, Mr Paine, because there is no such fact. Men are not equal, and can never become equal.

Wollstonecraft: Inequality can be removed, and the French are already doing so.

Burke: No one can remove inequality, madam, because we cannot eradicate natural difference. By pretending that real differences are unreal, by proclaiming the stupid fiction of the equality of man, you do great social harm. You inspire false hopes and vain expectations in those destined to travel in the obscure walk of laborious life. You aggravate and embitter that real inequality which you can never remove.

Wollstonecraft: There is a difference between natural and artificial inequality, Mr Burke. The former cannot be changed, but the latter can and should be. You will find the point well made by Jean-Jacques Rousseau.

Burke: Rousseau, madam? I can think of no worse authority to look to. But I can see that the French Revolution owes much of its theory, not to our own excellent John Locke, but to that Swiss professor and founder of the philosophy of vanity. A man who abandoned his children to an orphanage, and then preached fraternity and mutual devotion to the whole of the human race. A hater of his kindred, and a lover of his kind.

Wollstonecraft: I am not concerned with Rousseau's character, or his unhappy circumstances. I am concerned with the truth of what he wrote. He said that some forms of inequality are the result of natural differences, and cannot be removed; others are the consequences of social institutions, which it is within the power of men to change.

Burke: The people of France may be taken in by such sophistry, but the people of England are not. They discern the true motives of the spokesman of equality. They can recognize the patois of fraud and the cant and gibberish of hypocrisy.

Paine: Will nothing persuade you of the sincerity of the revolutionists, Mr Burke?

Burke: Yes, I shall believe in their good faith when they throw their own goods in common, and submit their own persons to that austere discipline which they recommend to others.

Wollstonecraft: It is not clear to me, Mr Burke, whether you are saying that the idea of equality is a delusion, or merely that the French exponents of equality are hypocritical.

Burke: I am saying both.

Wollstonecraft: You provide no proof of either.

Burke: If you want proof of the natural inequality of man, look around you; look to human nature for it. If you want to know more of the petulant, assuming, short-sighted coxcombs of Jacobin philosophy, you had better go to Paris and make their acquaintance.

Wollstonecraft: I can assure you that I have every intention of doing so. I have studied their writings, and I can only say that they seem to me to appeal to the highest principles which operate in man.

Burke: In *words*, assuredly. Morality, religion, law, liberty, justice, fraternity, the rights of man; these are the pretexts of the revolutionists. These are the colours they nail to the mast. But look a little deeper, madam, and you will see that the *causes* of the revolution are somewhat different; they are men's vices—pride, ambition, avarice, revenge, lust, sedition.

Paine: Mr Burke, you do not see avarice in the hearts of those who have acquired private fortunes in the past, and cling to them. You see envy in those who seek to limit the privileges of the opulent. But I suggest to you that nothing could be more in harmony with the ideal of justice than to mitigate the gross inequalities of property.

Burke: It is the characteristic essence of property to be unequal. How could it be otherwise? You will find it well explained in Locke's writings on the origin of property. Property is created by industry, and some men are more industrious than others; hence, property from its earliest beginnings is unavoidably unequal.

Wollstonecraft: That does not make it right.

Burke: But we cannot alter what is unalterable. What we can strive to do is ensure that those who have accumulated the larger fortunes conduct themselves with a sense of responsibility towards society as a whole. It is not by fanciful dreams of equality that the good of the commonwealth can be promoted. It is by seeking to effect, within a pattern that is by its nature unequal, that the most powerful element is also the most virtuous. You levellers do nothing to further that objective.

Paine: You call us levellers. But what could be more levelling than the hereditary system you uphold? It indiscriminately admits every species of character to the same authority. Vice or virtue, ignorance or wisdom—every quality, good and bad, is put on the same level. Nothing else counts. Kings and lords succeed each other, not as rational beings, but as animals.

Wollstonecraft: We should all like to see power and virtue go together, Mr Burke. And surely the only way to achieve this is to give power to those who have proved themselves virtuous, rather than to suppose that those who are already powerful can somehow be made virtuous. You remember the words of the Gospel: 'It is easier for a camel to go through the eye of a needle than for a rich man to enter into the kingdom of God.'

Burke: I notice, madam, that you are sensible only of the virtues to be found in the lowly and the poor. I do not belittle those virtues; I share your admiration for them. But remember it is a consequence of a humble station; once the people concerned are elevated from obscurity to prominence and authority, the virtues we so much admire fall from them.

Paine: Well, if your aim is to breed virtue in those already rich and powerful, you had better tell us how it is to be done.

Burke: How else than by religion? By that very institution which your friends in France are determined to subdue, if not finally to suppress. They are already taking education out of the hands of the clergy and putting it into those of secular and atheistical professors.

Wollstonecraft: The clergy may teach religion; but they cannot well be expected to teach morals, especially to the rich. You yourself remarked just now that the chaplain in the household of the great is held in the smallest respect. And you were right; the family chaplain today is the modern counterpart of the court jester of Gothic memory.

Paine: The intellectual part of religion is a private affair between every man and his Maker, and in which no third party has any right to interfere. The practical part consists in doing good to each other. But since religion has been turned into a trade, the practical part has been made to consist of shows performed by priests, and ceremonies and processions and bells. By devices of this kind true religion has been banished; and all manner of means have been found to extract money from the poor to maintain the commerce of priestcraft.

Wollstonecraft: Yes, Mr Burke, it is not by means such as these that we can hope to uphold morality. The superstitious instruments of the old religion are a hindrance to virtue. Let us look rather to the inner light of reason, the stern imperatives of conscience, the natural love of man for his fellows, the ardour and compassion of the uncorrupted heart. These are the factors which are making possible the moral regeneration of man that Mr Paine has spoken of.

Burke: The Church in Europe has a long tradition of learning, madam. We should be slow to pit our minds against it. We must not be too much in love with our own conjectures. We too, must strive to be humble.

Paine: We learn to be humble in seeking fraternity, in preparing ourselves for the brotherhood of man, in treating as equals people we had once thought of as inferiors.

Burke: What is the use of seeking the brotherhood of man if you forget the fatherhood of God? The one has meaning only in relation to the other.

Paine: I have never denied the fatherhood of God. I have criticized only those who claim to be his ministers on earth.

Wollstonecraft: The basis of fraternity is, in any case, friendship; and friendship can only be enjoyed between equals. That is another reason why the hierarchies of the past must be abolished.

Burke: Abolish. Abolish. That is your continuing cry, Miss Wollstonecraft. Oh, how the language of destruction grates upon my ears.

Paine: Then you would leave all things as they are, good and bad?

Burke: No, Mr Paine, I would not exclude alteration; but even when I changed, it should be to preserve. I should be led to my remedy by a grievance. In what I did I should follow the example of our forebears. I would make the reparation as nearly as possible in the style of the building. A politic caution, a guarded circumspection, a moral rather than a complexional timidity were among the ruling principles of our ancestors in their most decided conduct. Let us imitate their caution if we wish to deserve their fortune and to retain their bequests.

Wollstonecraft: But what if we do not want to retain their bequests? The French people inherited a system of government that was riddled with injustice, and they have very reasonably made up their minds to set up a different and a better one.

Burke: 'Riddled with injustice' is an extravagant phrase. There is not, and never was, a principle of government under heaven that does not, in the very pursuit of the good it proposes, naturally and inevitably lead into some inconvenience. There is a radical infirmity in all human contrivances. The French system was no worse than most and a good deal better than many.

Wollstonecraft: I notice you talk much of our ancestors, Mr Burke; and your argument seems to be that we should reverence the rust of antiquity as if it were the sage fruit of experience.

Burke: It is natural to do so; as it is natural for the young to respect the old.

Wollstonecraft: The analogy is absurd: the elderly are venerable because they are alive; that which belongs to antiquity has been dead for centuries. No, you speak from a Gothic fancy, Mr Burke. The ivy is old and beautiful, but when it insidiously destroys the trunk we do not hesitate to grub it up.

Burke: When we are talking of government, it is an argument in favour of any settled scheme that a nation has long existed and flourished under it. It is a better argument even than the choice of a nation, for it is not the choice of one day, or of one set of people. It is the deliberate election of ages and of generations.

Paine: It strikes me, Mr Burke, that the error of those of you who reason from antiquity is that you do not go far enough into antiquity. You stop in some of the intermediate stages of a hundred or a thousand years, and produce what was then done as a rule for the present day. This is not authority at all. But if we travel yet further into antiquity, we shall do better. For we shall come to the time when man first came from his Maker. Who was he then? Man: that was his high and only title. God created no kings or bishops or marquises or dukes. He created man simply, and created him in his own image.

Burke: But man at that time was in a state of innocence; political societies had not come into being.

Paine: Man already had his rights, God given.

Burke: But we are told that when man entered into political society he gave up his natural right of self defence for the sake of the advantages of a system of justice. He gave up his right to unlimited liberty for the sake of a secure and measured liberty, or social liberty, where the freedom of each is assured by an equality of restraint. In other words, man acquired the rights which are peculiar to life in a commonwealth, rights which are ascertained by wise laws and secured by well-constructed institutions.

Paine: But what if the institutions are not well-constructed?

Burke: Then they should be corrected. But they should be corrected slowly, Mr Paine. Political arrangement, being a work for social ends, is to be wrought only by social means. Mind must conspire with mind. Time is needed to produce that union of one man with another which alone can yield the good we seek. Patience will achieve more than energy. We are most successful when we compensate, and reconcile, and balance. That is why you will find you cannot do positive good by revolutionary methods. They are too swift. They are too violent.

Wollstonecraft: Well, Mr Burke, the English government you admire so much did not originate in patience, reconciliation, moderation and balance. It stems from conquest and robbery.

Paine: Yes, Mr Burke, look to its origins. It dates, as Miss Wollstonecraft reminds us, from 1066; from the Norman conquest. William of Normandy, the son of a prostitute and the plunderer of England, is the founder of our royal house and the fountain of our noble honours. Admittedly, once having plundered the nation, and divided the spoils among his banditti of ruffians, he lost the name of robber in that of king. And his henchmen, having first plunged the country into several centuries of strife by quarrelling over the spoils, did ultimately settle down to live in peace together, and even to acquire that polish of good manners they display in courts. Or rather, their successors tried to cut off the entail of their disgrace, by cultivating these more civilized appearances. But history does not forget.

Burke: History teaches us to be cautious in judgement.

Wollstonecraft: What is wrong is wrong whenever it was committed. I can think of no opinion more subversive of morality than the idea that time sanctifies crime.

Burke: But the criminals, if they were criminals, are dead. I do not see why their descendants should be held culpable.

Paine: They cling to the spoils; that is why, Mr Burke.

Burke: Now it is my turn to protest that *you* do not go back far enough in time, Mr Paine—or look wide enough. If we contemplate the whole history of mankind, we shall see that the victory of William of Normandy in these islands was a wholly typical feature of that recurrent pattern of war and conquest between prince and prince, between lord and lord which is endemic in the life of nations. Between one political society and another, war is recurrent precisely because there has been no system of law between nations, no commonwealth of states. This example should make us all the more mindful of the value of that peace between individuals which is made possible by the existence of law and government. Between nations there is war because there is anarchy among them; in society there is tranquillity, because there is a system of law. And there, Mr Paine, is a ready answer to your case for revolution. Law is the most priceless possession of mankind; and revolutions, which overthrow the law, rob men of that possession.

Wollstonecraft: Political societies are based on the system of law; we are all agreed about that. But the contract binds the ruler as well as the ruled; if the ruler betrays his trust, and takes away the rights of the people, he dissolves the commonwealth.

Burke: Society is indeed a contract, but it is not a contract which can be so easily dissolved. Subordinate contracts for objects of mere occasional interest may be dissolved at pleasure, but the state ought not to be considered as if it were like a partnership in a trade of coffee or pepper, or tobacco or calico. The state is to be looked on with other reverence, because it is a partnership in all things. Political leaders are not morally at liberty to undo the bonds of society at will. To tear asunder the community, to resort to anarchy, is to plunge from a world of reason and order and peace and virtue and fruitful penitence into the antagonist world of madness, discord, vice, confusion and unavailing sorrow.

Paine: The people of France are not tearing asunder the community. They are working together to build a new community. And it will not be a levelled-out society. It will be a free society in which talents will rise, and social merit will be rewarded; and reason, not superstition, will be men's guide in all their most important conduct. There will be a chance for the peasant and the artisan to enjoy the product of his industry instead of having to surrender the greater part of it in rent to the landlord and in taxes to the King. The labouring multitude can look forward, to a better livelihood, and a new dignity; and common soldiers will bear arms more gladly because the state they fight for will be their own.

Wollstonecraft: Yes, Mr Burke, a new nobility is being created in France, and it is a nobility of the entire population; a whole people which has recovered its rights to freedom, equality and brotherhood. And what is happening in France will happen soon in the rest of Europe. The days of the old order are numbered everywhere.

Paine: Yes, revolution on the broad basis of national sovereignty and government by representatives is making its way in Europe; France has followed America; and soon it may be England's turn. But it would be an act of wisdom to anticipate the approach of the new order and produce revolutions by reason and accommodation rather than to submit them to the issue of convulsions. But in whichever way they happen, come they will.

Burke: So that is your prediction, Mr Paine? It is not my own. So I do not fear what you hope to see. It seems to me certain that some military leader will emerge in France, some popular general who understands the art of conciliating the soldiery and who possesses the true spirit of command. And he will draw the eyes of all men on himself. Armies will obey him on his personal account. But the moment in which that event shall happen, this person who commands the army, will be the master of France, the master of your whole republic. And that, Mr Paine, will be the end of your 'democratic' revolution: a despotism worse than anything that went before.

Karl Marx and Michael Bakunin

A dialogue on Anarchism

On 3 November 1864, Karl Marx and Michael Bakunin met for the last time. Their conversation took place in Bakunin's lodgings in London, where the Russian anarchist leader was paying a short visit, and where Marx was living in exile. They had known each other for twenty years, but their friendship was precarious. Each was wary of the other, and both were competing for leadership of the workers' international. Marx had the stronger following in northern Europe; Bakunin in the south. Their theories of socialism were sharply opposed, but each still regarded the other as a possible ally in the struggle against the bourgeoisie. In time they were to become bitter enemies; but their meeting in London was, in the eyes of both, a success.

Bakunin: My dear Marx, I can offer you tobacco and tea; but otherwise I fear the hospitality of these lodgings is frugal. I am at the moment impoverished.

Marx: I am always poor, Bakunin. There is nothing I do not know about poverty. It is the worst of evils.

Bakunin: Slavery is the worst of evils, Marx, not poverty. A cup of tea then? I always have it ready: these London housemaids are very kind. When I lived in Paddington Green there was one called Grace— a *bonne à tout faire*—who used to run up and downstairs all day and most of the night with my hot water and sugar.

Marx: Yes, the working classes have a hard life in England; they should be the first to revolt.

Bakunin: They should be. But will they be?

Marx: They, or the Germans.

Bakunin: The Germans will never rise. They would sooner die than rebel.

Marx: It is not a question of national temperament, Bakunin; it is a matter of industrial progress. Where the workers are class conscious . . .

Bakunin: They are not class conscious here. That housemaid I spoke of was entirely docile, resigned, subdued. It pained me to see her so exploited.

Marx: You appear to have exploited her yourself.

Bakunin: London is full of exploitation. This vast city, full of misery and squalor and dark, mean streets—yet no one seems to want to throw a barricade across them. It is no place for a socialist.

Marx: But it is almost the only place that will have us. I have been here for fifteen years.

Bakunin: A pity you never came to see me in Paddington Green, my dear Marx. I was there for more than twelve months. When I found your card yesterday, I realized our paths had not crossed since the old days in Paris. When was it we last met . . . in 1848?

Marx: I had to leave Paris in 1845.

Bakunin: Ah, yes. I remember. I stayed on until 1847. It must have been a year after that we met in Berlin—a little before the rising in Dresden, when I fell, so to speak, into the enemy's hands. They kept me in prison for ten years. Then they sent me to Siberia; but as you know, I escaped, and made my way to London. Now I have a place to live in Italy. I am going back to Florence next week.

Marx: Well, at least you keep moving.

Bakunin: I have to. I am not so discreet a revolutionary as you are. The crowned heads of Europe have kept me moving.

Marx: The crowned heads of Europe have expelled me from several countries, too. And poverty has forced me out of several homes.

Bakunin: Ah yes, poverty, too, in my case. I am always penniless, always having to borrow money from friends. Indeed I suppose I must have lived on borrowed money for a large part of my life—except when I was in prison—and now I am fifty. But I never think about money. It is very bourgeois to think about money.

Marx: You are fortunate. You have no family to keep.

Bakunin: You must know that I acquired a wife in Poland. Though it is true that we have no children. Have some tea? I shall. A Russian cannot live without tea.

Marx: And you are very much the Russian, Bakunin; very much the Russian nobleman, to be more precise. It must be difficult for someone of your temperament to enter into the mind of the proletariat.

Bakunin: And what of yourself, Marx? Are you not the son of a prosperous bourgeois lawyer? And is your wife not Freiin von Westphalen, daughter of Baron von Westphalen and sister of the Prussian Minister of the Interior? That is hardly a plebeian background.

Marx: Socialism needs intellectuals as well as working men. Besides, I have learned a lot from persecution and hunger, in the cold and sleepless night of exile.

E

Bakunin: The night of imprisonment is longer and colder. But I am so accustomed to hunger that I scarcely even notice it now.

Marx: I think the worst thing is to see one's children die because one has not enough money to feed them properly.

Bakunin: Yes, I can believe that. To be condemned to death oneself is not as bad as you would think. In a way I found it exhilarating.

Marx: Since I have been in London, I have lived in cheap and sordid furnished rooms. I have had to borrow and buy food on credit, and then pawn our clothes to pay the bills. My children are used to answering the door and telling creditors I am not at home. All of us, my wife and I, and the children and an old servant are still crowded into two rooms—and there is not a clean or decent piece of furniture in either of them. I try to work at the same broken table where my wife sews and the children play, and often we sit for hours without light or food because there is no money to pay for either. My wife is often ill, and so are the children, but I cannot call a doctor, because I could not pay his fees or buy the medicines he would order.

Bakunin: My dear Marx! But surely some kind friend—does not your collaborator Engels?—I always understood . . .

Marx: Engels is extremely generous, but he has not always been able to help me. Believe me, I have suffered every kind of misfortune. My greatest unhappiness came eight years ago, when my son Edgar died at the age of six. Francis Bacon says that really important people have so many contacts with nature and the world, and have so much to interest them, that they easily get over a loss. I am not one of those important people, Bakunin. My son's death affected me so greatly that I feel the loss as bitterly today as I did on the day when he died.

Bakunin: If money is what you need, Alexander Herzen has plenty. I usually turn to him first. I see no reason why he should not help you too.

Marx: Herzen is a bourgeois reformer of the most superficial kind. I really have no time for the society of such people.

Bakunin: If it had not been for Herzen, I should not have been able to translate your *Communist Manifesto* into Russian as I did a year or two ago.

Marx: A belated translation; but I am grateful for it. Perhaps you might think next of translating *The Poverty of Philosophy*.

Bakunin: No, my dear Marx, I do not rank that among your greater works. It is altogether too hard on Pierre-Joseph Proudhon.

Marx: It is intended to be hard on him. How could it be otherwise since it is a refutation of his *Philosophy of Poverty?*

Bakunin: It is a work of polemics against another socialist.

Marx: Proudhon is not a socialist. He is an ignoramus—a typical lower-class autodidact, a parvenu of economics who makes a great show of the qualities he does not possess. His loudmouthed, boastful, blather about science is really intolerable.

Bakunin: I admit Proudhon is limited. But he is a hundred times more revolutionary than all the doctrinaire and bourgeois socialists. He has the courage to declare himself an atheist. Above all, he has come out for liberty against authority, for a socialism which is to be entirely free from any kind of government regulation. Proudhon is an anarchist, and admits it.

Marx: In other words, his ideas are very like yours.

Bakunin: I have felt his influence, but Proudhon never goes far enough for me. He shrank from action and violence. He does not see that destruction is itself a form of creation. I am an active revolutionary. Proudhon was a theoretical socialist, like yourself.

Marx: I do not know what you mean by a theoretical socialist, Bakunin; but I venture to claim that I have been as active a socialist as you.

Bakunin: My dear Marx, I meant nothing disrespectful. Indeed I remember that you were removed from Bonn University for duelling with pistols, so I know you will be a useful soldier of the revolution if we can ever get you out of the library at the British Museum and on to the barricades. When I spoke of you as a theoretical socialist, I meant only to say that you are a theorist of socialism as Proudhon is. I could never write a long philosophical treatise of the kind that you and he write. A pamphlet represents my limit.

Marx: You are an educated man. You could not write in the vulgar way that Proudhon writes.

Bakunin: Well, it is true that Proudhon is the son of a peasant, and a self-taught man, whereas I am the son of a landowner, though I suppose what you are thinking of, Marx, is that I studied Hegelian philosophy at Berlin University.

Marx: You could not have had a better education. And I should expect a socialist of your culture to do more than shoulder a rifle at the barricades or set fire to the Opera House at Dresden.

Bakunin: You flatter me, Marx. I did not personally set fire to the Opera House. And I was certainly not acting in Dresden on behalf of anarchism. The fact of the matter, as you ought to remember, is that the Saxon Diet voted for a federal constitution for Germany.

The King of Saxony would have nothing to do with any kind of unification, and dismissed the Diet. The people were indignant, and in May of that year they began to put up barricades in the streets of Dresden. The Parliamentary leaders—who were, of course, bourgeois liberals—entered the Town Hall and proclaimed a provisional government.

Marx: Not, I should have thought, an inspiring cause for one so opposed as you are to all forms of government.

Bakunin: Well, at any rate, the people had taken arms against a king. They had rebelled. That was something. So, as I happened to be in Dresden, I put myself at the disposal of the revolution. After all, I was trained for the army. The Saxon bourgeois liberals had no knowledge of arms whatever. I and a couple of Polish officers formed the general staff of the insurgent forces.

Marx: Soldiers of fortune, eh? But, then, you were not very fortunate.

Bakunin: No, it did not last more than a few days. The King found Prussian reinforcements, and we had to evacuate Dresden. As you said, some of our men set fire to the Opera House. I was all for blowing up the Town Hall with ourselves in it. But the Poles had disappeared by that time, and Mohner, the last of the Saxon liberals, wanted to remove his government to Chemnitz. I could not desert him, and so I was led like a lamb to the slaughter. At Chemnitz the local burgermeister arrested us in our beds.

Marx: So you went to prison, Bakunin, for the cause of German unity; and for trying to establish by force a bourgeois liberal government. I find that ironical.

Bakunin: I might well have been shot for it. But I am a far wiser man now than I was then. Indeed I have learned a lot from you, Marx. I disagreed with you in 1848, but now I see that you were far more right than I was. I am afraid that the flames of the revolutionary movement in Europe went to my head, and I was more interested in the negative than the positive side of the revolution.

Marx: I am glad you put your years of enforced reflection to good use.

Bakunin: Still, there was one point where I was right, and you wrong, Marx. As a Slav, I wanted the liberation of the Slav race from the German yoke. I wanted this to be brought about by a revolution —that is, by a destruction of the existing regimes of Russia, Austria, Prussia and Turkey; and by the reorganization of the people from below upwards in complete liberty.

Marx: So you have not thought better of your old Panslavism? You are still the same old Russian patriot you were in Paris.

Bakunin: What do you mean by 'Russian patriot'? Be frank, Marx, you still believe that I am some kind of Russian government agent?

Marx: I have never believed it, and one of the reasons why I have come here today is to clear away any lingering vestiges of that unfortunate suspicion.

Bakunin: But the story was first published in the *Neue Rheinische Zeitung* when you were the editor.

Marx: I have explained that before. The story came from our Paris correspondent that George Sand had said you were a Russian spy. Afterwards we published George Sand's denial and your own in full. We could do no more. I have also expressed my own regret.

Bakunin: But you haven't succeeded in killing the rumour. Even though I was sent from an Austrian prison to a Russian one, kept for years in solitary confinement and then sent to Siberia. You have never been to prison, Marx. You will never understand what it feels like to find yourself buried alive. To have to say to yourself every hour of the day and night 'I am a slave; I am annihilated'. To be full of devotion and heroism to serve the sacred cause of liberty, and to see all your enthusiasm break against four bare walls. That is bad enough. It is worse to come out and find you are pursued by the wicked libel that you are an agent of the very tyrant who has persecuted you.

Marx: But nobody believes that story any longer.

Bakunin: Alas, my dear Marx; it is circulating afresh here in London. It has been printed in one of those papers, published by Denis Urquhart —an English friend of yours I am sorry to say.

Marx: Urquhart is a monomaniac. He loves everything Turkish and hates everything Russian—indiscriminately. He is not altogether sane.

Bakunin: But you write for his press and you appear on his platforms, my dear Marx.

Marx: He is a likeable eccentric. And since he shares my views of Palmerston—or thinks he does—he provides a medium for the publication of my work. It is propaganda. And it pays a little, just as the *New York Tribune* does. But let me assure you, Bakunin, that the reappearance of that idiotic story of your being a Russian spy has distressed me more than it has distressed you. And I hope you will allow me to apologize once more here and now, for ever having had anything to do with the circulation of it. I have never ceased to regret it.

Bakunin: Of course I accept your apology, Marx.

Marx: But one thing that I must in honesty add, is that I regard your Panslavism as being entirely inimical to the interests of socialism, and only conducive to the sinister growth of Russian power in Europe.

Bakunin: Panslavism—and I mean, of course, democratic panslavism—is one part of the great movement of European liberation.

Marx: Nonsense, nonsense.

Bakunin: Prove that it is nonsense, my dear Marx. Justify your criticism.

Marx: The proper age of panslavism was the eighth and ninth centuries, when the southern Slavs still occupied all of Hungary and Austria and threatened Byzantium. If they could not defend themselves then, and win their independence when their two enemies, the Germans and the Magyars, were hacking one another to pieces, how can they expect to do so now, after a thousand years of subjection and denationalization? Nearly every country in Europe contains minorities, odd ruins of people, left-overs of the past, pushed back by the nations which became the carriers of historical development. Hegel, you will remember, called them ethnic trash.

Bakunin: In other words, you see such peoples as wholly contemptible, as having no rights to live.

Marx: I do not understand the language of rights. The very existence of such peoples is a protest against history; and that is why they are always reactionary. Look at the Gaels in Scotland—supporters of the Stuarts from 1640 to 1745; look at the Bretons in France, supporters of the Bourbons from 1792 to 1800. Or the Basques in Spain. And look at Austria itself in 1848. Who made the revolution then? The Germans and the Magyars. And who provided the armies which enabled Austrian reactionaries to crush the revolution? The Slavs. The Slavs fought the Italians and stormed Vienna on behalf of the Hapsburg monarchy. Slav troops keep the Hapsburgs in power.

Bakunin: Naturally there are Slavs in the Emperor's armies. But you know very well that the Panslavist movement is a democratic one, determined to oppose the Hapsburgs just as much as the Romanovs and the Hohenzollerns.

Marx: Oh, I have read your manifestos, Bakunin. I know what you would *like* to achieve.

Bakunin: Then you will know what I have advocated: the abolition of all artificial frontiers in Europe and the creation of boundaries which are traced by the sovereign will of the people themselves.

Marx: That sounds very well. But you simply ignore the real obstacles that stand in the way of any such scheme—the completely different levels of civilization that different European peoples have achieved.

Bakunin: I have always seen the difficulties, Marx; and I have said that the only way of surmounting them is by a policy of federation. The Slav is no enemy of democratic Germans or democratic Magyars —we offer them a brotherly alliance on the basis of liberty, fraternity and equality.

Marx: But those are mere words. They tell us nothing about facts. And the facts are quite brutally simple. Except for your own race and the Poles, and perhaps the Slavs of Turkey, no other Slavs have any future whatever, because those other Slavs have none of the historical, geographical, economic, political and industrial prerequisites of independence. They have no civilization.

Bakunin: And the Germans have? Is that it? You think that their greater civilization gives the Germans the right to dominate Europe, and commit any crimes against the rest.

Marx: What crimes? So far as I read history, I find that the only crime that the Germans and the Magyars have committed against the Slavs is to prevent them from becoming Turkish. What would have happened to those scattered little nations if they had not been held together and led by their so-called oppressors?

Bakunin: They were not defended as allies. They were subdued and exploited.

Marx: I dare say a few delicate national flowers were trodden underfoot. But without force and ruthlessness, nothing is accomplished in history.

Bakunin: You speak, as usual, like a true German, Marx.

Marx: On the contrary, I have always been opposed to German national prejudices. I have always said that Germany is backward compared to the great historic nations, England and France. It is because I am unsentimental about my own country that it benefits me to resist the sentimental illusions of the Slavs.

Bakunin: And I suppose you supported the Prussian war against Denmark for the same reason?

Marx: I supported the Prussian war against Denmark for the same reason that I supported the French war in Algeria. The spread of industrial progress speeds the coming of socialism.

Bakunin: Well, my dear Marx, I have always said of Germany what Voltaire said of God: if it did not exist we should have to invent it.

For there is nothing so effective for keeping Panslavism alive as hatred of Germany.

Marx: There you have another proof that your wretched Panslavism is reactionary. It teaches people to hate the Germans instead of hating their real enemies, the bourgeoisie.

Bakunin: The two go together. That is where I have advanced beyond the crude nationalism of my youth. Now I say that liberty is a lie for the great majority of people if they are deprived of education, leisure and bread.

Marx: I consider you a friend, Bakunin, as you know, and I do not hesitate to call you a socialist, in spite of everything . . .

Bakunin: In spite of what?

Marx: Well, you are clearly not interested in politics.

Bakunin: I am certainly not interested in parliaments, and parties, and constituent assemblies or representative institutions. Humanity needs something altogether more inspiring. A new world without laws and without states.

Marx: Anarchy?

Bakunin: Yes, anarchy. We must overthrow the whole political and moral order of the world as it is today. We must change it from top to bottom. It is no good just trying to modify existing institutions.

Marx: I do not wish to modify them. I simply say that the workers should take them over and transform them.

Bakunin: They should be completely abolished. The state corrupts our instincts and will, as well as our intelligence. The first principle of any valid socialism is to overthrow society.

Marx: I should call that a curious definition of socialism.

Bakunin: I am not interested in definitions, Marx. That is where I differ from you. I don't believe that any ready-made system is going to save the world. I have no system. I am a seeker. I believe in instinct rather than thought.

Marx: But you cannot be a socialist without a policy.

Bakunin: Of course I have a policy. And if it impresses you to have things set out point by point, I will tell you what my programme is. First it is to do away with man-made laws.

Marx: But you cannot do away with laws. The whole universe is governed by laws.

Bakunin: Natural laws assuredly—they cannot be done away with. Indeed I agree with you that men can enlarge their liberty by extending their understanding of the natural laws which rule the universe. Man cannot escape from nature, and it would be absurd to try to do so. But that is not what I proposed. I said we should abolish man-made laws—artificial laws—in other words, political and juridical laws.

Marx: You cannot seriously believe that society should impose no laws on its members?

Bakunin: Society should have no need to impose laws. Man is by nature a social creature. Outside society he is either a wild beast or a saint. There have to be laws in capitalist society because capitalist society is competitive, acquisitive, and sets one man against another. Freedom will only be possible when all men are equal. That is why there cannot be liberty without socialism.

Marx: There I entirely agree with you.

Bakunin: You say you agree with me, Marx. But when I say that there cannot be freedom without socialism, I also say that socialism without freedom is slavery and brutality.

Marx: I have never advocated socialism without freedom.

Bakunin: You have, my dear Marx. You ask for the dictatorship of the proletariat.

Marx: The dictatorship of the proletariat is a part of freedom too because it is part of the process of liberation.

Bakunin: When I speak of liberty, I have in mind the only freedom worthy of that name—liberty consisting in the full development of all the material, intellectual and moral powers latent in man—a liberty which does not recognize any restrictions but those traced by the laws of our own nature. I think of a freedom which, far from finding itself checked by the freedom of others, is, on the contrary, confirmed and extended by the freedom of all. I think of freedom triumphing over brute force and the principle of authority.

Marx: I hear your words, Bakunin, but I do not know what meaning to ascribe to them. But one thing, I will say, and that is you will never hasten the coming of socialism, or achieve anything else in politics unless you have a principle of authority.

Bakunin: Socialism will need a principle of discipline, but not authority. And not the kind of discipline which is imposed from outside; but a voluntary and reflective discipline which a man imposes on himself, and which harmonizes perfectly with the principle of freedom.

Marx: You do not appear to have learned much from your experience of rebellions, Bakunin. Such movements could not prosper without a principle of authority. There must be officers even in the armies of anarchism.

Bakunin: Naturally at a time of military action, in the midst of a struggle, the roles are distributed in accordance with everyone's aptitudes, evaluated and judged by the whole movement. Some men direct and command, and others execute commands. But no function remains fixed and petrified. Hierarchic order does not exist, the leader of today may become the subordinate tomorrow. No one is raised above others, and if he does rise for some little time, it is only to fall back later, like the waves in the sea, to the salutary level of equality.

Marx: Well, Bakunin, if you admit that direction and command are necessary during the struggle, then perhaps we may agree after all. I myself have always said that the dictatorship of the proletariat will only be needed during the preliminary stages of socialism. As soon as the classless society is matured, there will be no need for a state; in a phrase of my collaborator, Engels, the state will wither away.

Bakunin: There is not much indication of the state withering away in the *Communist Manifesto* that you and Engels wrote together. That is a marvellous pamphlet, and I should not have translated it if I did not admire it. But the fact remains that of the ten points for a socialist programme which you outline in those pages, Marx, no fewer than nine call for the enlargement of the state—the state is to possess all the means of production, to control all commerce and credit, it is to impose forced labour and collect taxes, it is to monopolize the land, it is to control all means of transport and communication, and also it will run the schools and universities.

Marx: If you do not like that programme, you do not like socialism.

Bakunin: But that is not socialism, Marx; it is the most far-reaching form of *étatisme*—the usual German hankering for the big stick of the magnified state. Socialism means the control of industry and agriculture by the workers themselves.

Marx: A socialist state is a workers' state; they will control things indirectly.

Bakunin: But that is a typical illusion of bourgeois democratic theory that the people can control a state. In practise it is the state that controls the people, and the more powerful the state, the more crushing its dominion. Look at what is happening in Germany. As the state grows, all the corruption that goes hand-in-hand with political centralization is sweeping over a public that used to be the most honest in the world. What is more, monopoly capitalism is growing as fast as the state grows.

Marx: The growth of monopoly capitalism is paving the way for the coming of socialism. The reason why Russia is so far from socialism is that it is only beginning to emerge from feudalism.

Bakunin: The Russian people are closer to socialism than you realize, my dear Marx. The Russian peasants have their own tradition of revolution, and they have a great role to play in the liberation of mankind. The Russian revolution is rooted in the whole character of the people. In the seventeenth century the peasants rose in the south-east; and in the eighteenth century Pugachev led a peasants' revolt in the basin of the Volga which lasted for two years. The Russians will not shrink from violence. They know that the living fruit of human progress is watered with human blood. Nor do they shrink from fire. There was something truly Russian about the setting fire to Moscow which led to the defeat of Napoleon. Such are the fires in which the human race will be purged of the dross of slavery.

Marx: That sounds very dramatic, my friend; but the plain fact remains that socialism depends on the emergence of a class-conscious proletariat; and that is something which we can only expect in highly industrialized countries like England and Germany and France. The peasantry is the least organized and the least ready of all social classes for revolution. Peasants are even more backward than the Lumpenproletariat of the towns. They are natural barbarians or troglodytes.

Bakunin: That shows how much we differ, Marx. To me the flower of the proletariat does not consist, as it does for you, in the upper layer, in the skilled artisans of the factories, who are, in any case, semi-bourgeois in their outlook. I have known such men in the labour movement in Switzerland; and I can assure you that they are permeated with all the social prejudices, all the narrow aspirations and pretensions of the middle-classes. The skilled artisans are the least socialistic of the workers. To *my* eyes, Marx, the flower of the proletariat is the great mass, the rabble, the disinherited, wretched and illiterate millions that you speak of so contemptuously as the peasants and Lumpenproletariat.

Marx: You have clearly not given much thought to the concept of the proletariat. The proletariat is not the poor. There have always been poor people, but the proletariat is something new in history. It is not their poverty or wretchedness which makes men a proletariat. It is their indignation against the bourgeoisie, their defiance, their courage and their resolution to end their condition.

A proletariat is created only when this inner indignation, this class-consciousness is added to poverty. The proletariat is the class with revolutionary ends, the class which aims at the destruction of all classes; the class which cannot emancipate itself without emancipating mankind as a whole.

Bakunin: But your socialist state will not eliminate classes, Marx. It will create two classes; the rulers and the ruled. There will be a government which is to do much more than is done by any government known to exist at present. Then there will be the people who are governed. On the one hand the Left-wing intelligentsia—the most despotic, arrogant, self-opinionated kind of men who exist—they will command, in the name of knowledge; and on the other hand there will be the simple ignorant mass, who will obey.

Marx: The legislators and administrators of the socialist state will be the representatives of the people.

Bakunin: But that is another liberal illusion namely, that a government, issuing from popular elections, can represent the will of the people. Even Rousseau saw the folly of that idea. The instinctive aims of governing *élites* are always opposed to the instinctive aims of the common people. Looking at society from their exalted positions, they can hardly avoid adopting the perspective of the schoolmaster or the governess.

Marx: Liberal democracy cannot work because the political institutions are always manipulated by the financial power of the bourgeoisie.

Bakunin: Socialist democracy, so-called, would be vitiated by other pressures. A parliament made up exclusively of workers—the selfsame workers who are staunch socialists today—would become a parliament of aristocrats overnight. It has always been the way. Put radicals in positions of power in the state, and they become conservatives.

Marx: There are reasons for that.

Bakunin: The chief reason is that the democratic state is a contradiction in terms. The state entails authority, force, predominance, and therefore inequality. Democracy by definition entails equality. Therefore democracy and the state cannot exist together. Proudhon never said a truer word than when he said that universal suffrage is counter-revolutionary.

Marx: That is an exemplary half-truth, a characteristic product of Proudhon's journalistic mind. It is true that the workers are usually too oppressed by poverty, too easily influenced by the propaganda of the bourgeoisie, to make good use of the vote. But universal suffrage can be exploited for a socialist end. We can go into politics and help to make what is nominally democratic actually democratic. We cannot achieve all our ends by parliamentary means; but we can achieve a great deal.

Bakunin: No state—not even the reddest political republic—can give the people what they most need—that is freedom. Every state, including your socialist state, my dear Marx, is based on force.

Marx: What is the alternative to force?

Bakunin: Enlightenment.

Marx: But the people are not enlightened.

Bakunin: They can be educated.

Marx: Who is to educate them, if the state does not?

Bakunin: Society will educate itself. Unfortunately the governments of the world have left the people in such a state of profound ignorance that it will be necessary to establish schools not only for the people's children, but for the people themselves. But these schools must be free from any taint of the principle of authority. They will not be schools at all in the conventional sense; they will be popular academies, and the pupils, being rich in experience, will be able to teach many things to their teachers, even as they are taught. In that way there would develop a sort of intellectual fraternity between them.

Marx: Well, at least you admit the two categories of teachers and taught. I do not myself see any great problem of education, once the socialist society has been created.

Bakunin: Yes, the first question is economic emancipation; and the rest will follow of itself.

Marx: It will not follow of itself unless the socialist state provides it. You have all the evidence of history to prove it. The most educated people in Europe today—the French and the Germans—owe their education to a strong state system of public instruction. In countries where the state provides no schools, the people are hopelessly illiterate.

Bakunin: The great schools and universities here in England are not controlled by the state.

Marx: They are dominated by the Church of England, which is worse; and which is part of the state, in any case.

Bakunin: The colleges of Oxford and Cambridge are governed by independent and self-perpetuating societies of scholars.

Marx: You know little of English life, Bakunin. Both Oxford and Cambridge have had to be radically reformed by Acts of Parliament. The state has intervened to save them from complete intellectual decay. They are backward enough as it is compared to German universities.

Bakunin: But their existence shows that it is possible for scholars to control their own colleges. And there is no reason why the workers should not administer their own farms and factories in the same way.

Marx: One day, no doubt, many such things will come about, but in the meantime a workers' state must replace the bourgeois owners until a better system is prepared.

Bakunin: That is the great difference between us, Marx. You believe that you must organize the workers to take possession of the state. I want to organize them to destroy, or, if you prefer a politer word, to liquidate the state. You want to make use of political institutions. I want to see the people federate themselves spontaneously, freely.

Marx: What does it mean to federate spontaneously?

Bakunin: Labour will organize itself. Productive associations based on mutual aid will be joined together in districts, and these districts will be freely combined in larger units. All power will come from below.

Marx: Such projects are utterly unrealistic. They are no different from the *phalanstères* and other duodecimal editions of the New Jerusalem proposed by utopian Socialists. They are all foolish, but they are not, unfortunately, harmless; because they introduce a spurious notion of socialism which may take the place of the real thing. And in diverting men's attention from the immediate conflict, their effect is conservative and reactionary.

Bakunin: One thing you cannot say about me, Marx, is that I divert men's attention from the immediate conflict. What is more, I think, as you do, that there are only two parties in the world: the party of revolution and the party of reaction. The peaceful socialists, with their co-operative societies and their model villages, belong to the party of reaction. The party of revolution is unfortunately already dividing itself into two factions: the champions of state socialism, which you represent, Marx, and the libertarian socialists of which I am one. Your side has the greater following, naturally, in Germany, and also here in England. But the socialists of Italy and Spain are libertarians almost to a man. So the question before us is: which side is going to prevail in the international workers' movement?

Marx: The genuinely socialist side, I hope; and not the anarchist side.

Bakunin: You call yours the genuinely socialist side because you deceive yourself about the nature of popular dictatorship. You do not realize the danger, but it would bring enslavement just as all other states have done.

Marx: You suppose that because the state has always been an instrument of class oppression, that it always must be? Can you not imagine the possibility of a different *kind* of state?

Bakunin: I can imagine one so different that it could not be called by the same name. There is room for something on the lines proposed by Proudhon—a sort of simple business office, a central clearing house at the service of society.

Marx: Perhaps that is all that every socialist society will ultimately have. There will come a time when the government of people will give way to the administration of things. But before the state can wither away it must be magnified.

Bakunin: That is not only paradoxical; it is contradictory.

Marx: But what if it is ? You know your Hegel as well as I do. You know that the logic of history is the logic of contradiction. What we affirm, we also deny.

Bakunin: The argument may be good Hegel, but it is not good history. You will never destroy the state by enlarging it. I am your disciple, Marx. The longer I live, the more certain I am that you were right when you followed the great high road of economic revolution, and invited others to follow. But I shall never understand, or agree with, any of your authoritarian proposals.

Marx: If you are an anarchist, you cannot be my disciple. But perhaps I had better tell you in greater detail just where you go wrong. First of all, you speak of the principle of authority as if it were everywhere and in all circumstances wrong. This is a very superficial view. We live in an industrial age. Modern factories and mills where hundreds of workers supervise complicated machines have superseded the small workshops of the individual producers. Even agriculture is falling under the dominion of machines. Combined action displaces independent action by individuals. Combined action means organization and organization means authority. In the mediaeval world, the little craftsman could be his own master. But in the modern world, there must be direction and subordination. If you are going to resist any kind of authority, you will have to live in the past.

Bakunin: But I do not resist any kind of authority, Marx. In the matter of boots, I refer to the authority of bootmakers; in the matter of houses, I refer to the authority of architects; in the matter of health, I refer to the authority of physicians. But I do not allow the bootmaker or the architect or the physician to impose his authority on me. I accept their opinions freely; I respect their expert knowledge, but still reserve to myself the right of criticism and censure. Nor do I content myself with consulting a single authority. I consult several; I compare their views; for I recognize none as infallible. I know that I cannot know everything; and I also know that no one else can know everything. It is because there is no universal and omniscient man, that my reason forbids me to accept any fixed, constant and universal authority.

Marx: But if you eliminate authority from political and economic life, nothing will ever be done efficiently even if it is done at all. How could a railway, for example, run, if there were no one with power to keep people off the lines, no one to decide at what hours the trains should start; no one to lay down the order in which they should run, if only to avoid accidents; and no one to decide who should be admitted to the carriages.

Bakunin: The railway workers would elect the guards and signalmen and obey their instructions freely. As to the question who is to stoke the engines and who is to travel in the first-class compartment—well, that is a question for you to put to any socialist. Under my kind of socialism, people would take it in turns to do the work and enjoy the comfort, by mutual agreement. But under your kind of socialism, Marx, I fancy we should see the poor old-fashioned kind of locomotive fireman still stoking away at the engine, and only a new kind of privileged passenger, the administrator of the socialist state smoking a big cigar in the first-class compartment.

Marx: Listen, Bakunin, I am no more in love with the state than you are. All socialists are agreed that the political state will disappear as soon as the success of socialism makes it unnecessary. But you demand that the political state shall be abolished overnight, and the workers left without any kind of leadership or discipline or responsible control. The truth of the matter is, that you anarchists have no plans for the future whatever.

Bakunin: That is because we cannot foretell exactly what the future will hold. All recorded history is the history of class struggles, as you yourself have shown, Marx. But the future is going to be quite different. When the proletariat has eliminated its oppressors, there will be only one class left. Then, provided no new state arises on the ashes of the old, the people will be able to arrange their affairs on the principles of mutual aid. According to the economics of socialism, the true interests of men do not conflict with one another. So there will be no economic drive to aggression, and therefore no need for an external authority to keep the peace between hostile neighbours. Neighbours will no longer be hostile. But precisely how men can best arrange their affairs in a socialist society is something that can only be worked out when the socialist society has been established. I am mistrustful of all detailed schemes, Marx. When competitive instincts have given way to fraternal instincts, I believe that the technical problems of production and distribution will be solved by the common intelligence and good will of the people themselves.

Marx: Your troubles, Bakunin, are partly psychological and moral; but they are also intellectual. You seem to be under the gross mis-apprehension that it is the state which has created capital, or that the capitalist has his capital only by grace of the state. This accounts for the almost stunning simplicity of your views; as you see it, we have only to do away with the state, and capitalism will go to blazes of itself. Now the truth, I have to tell you, is the other way round. Do away with capital—do away with the concentra-tion of the means of production in the hands of the few—and the state will no longer be an evil.

Bakunin: But the evil lies in the very nature of the state. All states are the negation of liberty.

Marx: But by taking this extreme and emotional attitude towards the state, you do great harm to the cause of the workers. You are using your influence, Bakunin, to prevent them taking part even in elections.

Bakunin: I tell the workers to do more than take part in elections; I tell them to fight.

Marx: You tell them to fight even before there is any prospect of victory. And that is another form of irresponsibility. I said just now, that your defects were partly moral. One of them is that you have no patience. You like shooting rifles at the barricades, even for causes you do not really believe in, because that satisfies your emotional craving for violent action, for excitement at all costs. You will not dedicate yourself to real political activity because that requires patience, order, reflection.

Bakunin: My whole life is dedicated to political activity.

Marx: Your life is dedicated to political conspiracy, but that is not the same thing.

Bakunin: My whole life is spent among the workers. Organization, propaganda, education . . .

Marx: Education for what?

Bakunin: For the revolution. I certainly do not think the workers should waste their energies in the bogus institutions of representative government, so called.

Marx: I can understand that such ideas have a following in Italy and Spain, among lawyers and students and other intellectuals. But the workers will not allow themselves to be persuaded that the political affairs of their country are not also their own affairs. To tell the workers to abstain from politics is to drive them into the arms of the priests and the bourgeois republicans.

Bakunin: My dear Marx, if you have read my published writings you will know that I have continuously and passionately opposed both the Church and the republicans. Your own opinions are very guarded in comparison to mine.

Marx: My friend, I do not for a moment deny that you do really hate both the priests and the republicans, but what you do not realize is that your own thinking is permeated by their assumptions.

Bakunin: You are jesting, my dear Marx.

Marx: No, I mean it quite seriously. First, take all your talk about liberty. It is abundantly clear that the only freedom you believe in is individualistic liberty—in fact the same freedom which is advocated by bourgeois theorists like Hobbes and Locke and Mill. When you think of freedom you think that nobody should be ordered about by anyone else. You think of each separate man, standing with all his rights, being menaced by social and collective institutions like the state. You never think, as a real socialist must think, of humanity as a whole, or of man as a creature inseparable from society.

Bakunin: There again, Marx, you show that you have either not listened to me or not understood what you have heard.

Marx: I fancy I have understood you better than you have understood yourself. If you cannot conceive of a state as anything but oppressive, that shows you cannot think of men as being anything but isolated units, each with his own private will and desires and interests. This is how the theorists of bourgeois liberalism think; and you anarchists have just the same image of the human being and society. Your anarchism is only liberalism pushed to an extreme, pushed to a somewhat hysterical extreme, I might add. Your philosophy is essentially egoistic. You have a conception of the self, and of freedom for the self, which belongs to the metaphysics of capitalism.

Bakunin: I am not interested in metaphysics.

Marx: But anarchism has its metaphysical assumptions, whether you choose to understand them or not. It also has its own ethics, which are very like Christian ethics. 'Mutual aid', I hear you repeating; or you might put it in more conventional Christian terms and say 'Love your neighbour' or 'sacrifice yourself for others'. But real socialism needs no such precepts because it does not recognize the isolation of the individual. In a socialist society, man is no longer alienated either from his neighbour or himself.

Bakunin: Since the state is the cause of their alienation—the obvious remedy is to eliminate it.

Marx: But we cannot eliminate it until we have removed the conditions which make the state a necessary outgrowth of society.

Bakunin: As soon as the workers' movement has recruited enough power to remove it, the state will cease to be necessary.

Marx: You admit it is necessary at present?

Bakunin: It is necessary to a property-owning society. Once private property has been redistributed; once socialism has triumphed . . .

Marx: But it is a very vulgar kind of socialism which is bothered about the redistribution of property. Surely, Bakunin, you are not one of those who thinks that socialism consists in the fair sharing of goods among individuals?

Bakunin: That is certainly one of its aims.

Marx: My friend, the aim of socialism is far more radical than that. Its aim is to bring about a complete transformation of human nature, a change of the self, the creation of a new man. The individual will be fused into society. Each will be freed from his self-alienation. You tell me your own goal is freedom. Socialism will bring a freedom which is quite unknown in the past experience of mankind.

Bakunin: You make freedom too mysterious a thing.

Marx: And you make it too commonplace a thing. As you look at the world, Bakunin, you imagine that some people are free today and some oppressed.

Bakunin: I do not imagine it. It is so. The few are free—the rich.

Marx: I tell you that *nobody* is free in the world today. Not even the richest bourgeois. Morally speaking, the capitalist, as a man, is as much a slave of the system as the workers are. This is what enables us to say, with truth, that the emancipation of the proletariat means the emancipation of mankind.

Bakunin: But the hard fact remains that at present the rich man can do what he likes, while the poor man cannot even get what he needs.

Marx: But the rich man's choice is governed and restricted by the bourgeois culture, by a system which denies the humanity of everyone. Besides, it is a very narrow theory of freedom which defines it as doing what you want to do.

Bakunin: But it is better than the theory of freedom which defines freedom as doing what you ought to do. That is what the priests say—the service of the Church is perfect freedom; and what Hegel says, obedience to the state is perfect freedom. Personally I'd rather have the plain man's notion that liberty is doing what you want to do.

Marx: But you yourself have just defined liberty as the fulfilment of the potentialities in man. And that is much closer to the goal of socialism. The socialist man will be free because he will be a changed man.

Bakunin: But if men are not left alone to develop themselves they will not realize the best that is in them.

Marx: There you are, Bakunin, betraying your bourgeois liberal philosophy in bourgeois liberal words. For is that not just what Adam Smith and all his kind say? Leave men alone and each will do the best he can for himself? The economic man will have his own incentive to self-improvement? What is the phrase?—'*Laissez nous faire . . .*'

Bakunin: Of course, if you choose to ignore the fact that the liberals stand for private property and a competitive economy, while I believe in everything being held in common . . .

Marx: But if your overriding principle is that every man must have his precious private right to freedom unrestrained, then you will soon find there are those who want to abstract something from the common pool and claim it as their own. For you cannot have at the same time complete individual liberty and no individual property. For what could you say to the man who claimed the right to property? Or rather, not what would you *say* to him, but what would you *do* to him, if you had no state or any other instrument of socialist authority to restrain recalcitrant or antisocial individuals?

Bakunin: But you yourself, Marx, have said that socialist man will be a changed man. He will no longer have the egoistic, acquisitive, unnatural impulses which are generated by life in bourgeois society.

Marx: *My* kind of socialist man will be changed, Bakunin. But I do not recognize your kind as socialist man at all. You think of men as individuals, each with his little empire of rights. I think of humanity as a whole. Freedom, as I see it, is the liberation of mankind; not the liberty of the individual.

Bakunin: But that is Hegel's notion of freedom again. The idea that acting freely is acting morally, and acting morally is acting in accordance with the principle of reason which is embodied in the state.

Marx: Hegel was not altogether wrong. Only a rational being can be free because only a rational being can make a choice between alternatives. An irrational choice is not a free choice. To act freely is to act rationally. And to act rationally is to acknowledge the necessity of nature and of history. There is no real antithesis between necessity and freedom.

Bakunin: But we are not talking about the question of the freedom of the will, Marx. What we are considering is political freedom. There is nothing metaphysical or difficult about that. Political freedom depends on the removal of political oppression. One does not need any philosophical training to see that. A child of nine can see who is oppressed and who are the oppressors.

Marx: And a child of nine might well suppose that the situation could be briskly remedied by doing away with the state. He might well become an anarchist. And his tender years would excuse his folly.

Bakunin: There is the folly of the philosopher as well as the folly of the child. All your abstruse reasoning about liberty can only take you where it took Rousseau and Hegel: to the belief that men can be forced to be free.

Marx: Of course men can be forced to be free, in the sense that you can force them to act rationally—or at any rate prevent them from acting irrationally.

Bakunin: But a freedom which can be imposed on a man is not worth the name of freedom.

Marx: It is reality that matters, not names.

Bakunin: Well, look at reality then, if you talk about forcing men to be free you must be thinking about two classes of people—the one who does the forcing and the one who has his freedom forced upon him. And there you have the two types who make up the so-called classless society of authoritarian socialism: the rulers and the ruled, those on top, and those below.

Marx: Of course some people must be superior to others. As I have said to you before, a socialist society must be regulated, especially in the early stages. The alternative is the Tower of Babel, a world in which no one knows what to do, or what to expect; a world where there is no order, no security, or reliance on settled and fixed arrangements. Anarchy means chaos; and chaos appals me. If it appeals to you, Bakunin, it is because you are susceptible to the meretricious charm of Bohemian or gypsy life. After the rigidity of your early home, with your upper-class family and your military schools, it may be only natural that Bohemian disorder should attract you. But if you reflect upon it you will see that Bohemianism is really only an elaborate tribute to the bourgeois ethos, studiously defying and outraging it. But I tell you, the bourgeois ethos is not worth such attention. The socialist has more serious things to think about.

Bakunin: You speak of 'vulgar socialism', Marx, but you yourself have a vulgar notion of what anarchism means. To the uneducated mind the word 'anarchy' means just chaos or disorder. But an educated man must know that the word is only a transliteration from the Greek and that it means nothing more than opposition to government. It is pure superstition to assume that the absence of government means the presence of chaos or disorder. The most orderly nations in Europe today are not those where the government bears most heavily upon the public, but those where its pressure is felt the least. As for what you say about Bohemianism, I do not understand you; I certainly have no relish for disorder.

Marx: But you have spoken eagerly enough about blood and fire and destruction.

Bakunin: That is mere zeal for battle. I may be more impatient for the coming of the revolution than you are, Marx; but I can assure you that the anarchist yearns as much as you do for the tranquillity of socialist order.

Marx: It is no use you yearning for it; because without the socialist state you will not have it. Your kind of revolution will bring blood and fire and destruction, assuredly; but it will not bring much else.

Bakunin: And your kind of revolution, Marx, will bring something infinitely worse, and that is slavery.

Marx: Well, my friend, I fancy it is fortunate that we have both been persecuted by the bourgeois; otherwise, if we continued this conversation much longer, we might cease to be socialist comrades.

John Stuart Mill and James Fitzjames Stephen

A dialogue on Liberty

John Stuart Mill (1806–1873) was already a famous writer and philosopher when he published his essay *On Liberty* in 1859. He had sketched it out some years before in collaboration with his wife, Harriet Taylor. What prompted him to finish it for publication was the experience, to him unnerving, of finding the statues and other works of art on view in Naples being subject to a 'fig leaf' censorship. The main argument of the essay, however, is directed not so much against the constraints of the state as against the constraints of society, which Mill believed were taking away the freedom of the individual. Mill believed as strongly as his liberal predecessors in freedom from the state; but he went beyond them in insisting that it was equally important for men to be free from the dictates of convention. taboo and unwritten law.

Sir James Fitzjames Stephen (1829–1894) was an eminent legal theorist who published an essay *Liberty, Equality, Fraternity*, attacking Mill's concept of freedom. Having been a judge, professor, administrator, educationist and journalist, Stephen brought as much breadth of experience to the debate as did Mill himself, although his voice remained essentially that of a lawyer rather than a philosopher. He was more than twenty years younger than Mill, but in the imaginary conversation which follows, the two men meet on equal terms.

Stephen: Has the success of your *Essay on Liberty* surprised you, Mr Mill?

Mill: I am not altogether sure what you mean by 'success', my dear Stephen. It has been vigorously attacked in many quarters; in others it has been kindly received. I cannot say that the hostility exceeded my expectations; neither can I say that my hopes have been disappointed. I felt, and still feel, that the time was ripe for such a publication.

Stephen: Yet many people might have assumed that the cause of liberty, in England at any rate, had been won. All the things that the philosopher Locke, for example, understood as the essentials of freedom have been achieved; indeed most of Locke's thinking about liberty has become part of the thinking of Englishmen of every walk of life today.

Mill: In a sense, you are right. The situation of England in the 1860s is very different from what it was in the 1680s. The freedom that was needed then was, in the first place, freedom from the oppression of James II. The freedom that is needed today is not freedom from the oppression of Queen Victoria. Her Majesty does not oppress us. We are hardly aware of her existence. We are more conscious of her government, but even that is not the chief source of the constraints which bear upon us.

Stephen: I am not very clear, sir, as to what are these 'constraints which bear upon us', as you call them. But I certainly agree that the word 'freedom' or the word 'liberty'—and I take the words to be synonymous—must bear a different meaning in different situations. Indeed I suppose one must say that there are as many varieties of freedom as there are constraints to which it stands opposed. Yet the word seems to have the same exalted emotional appeal in every context in which it is used.

Mill: When I wrote the *Essay on Liberty* I was thinking of the question of freedom as it confronts, in the first instance, English people, but in effect, most Western European and North American people at the present day. In fact the resolution to publish the essay as a separate volume came to me when I was travelling in Italy in 1855. I had been working in very close collaboration with my late wife—and she, I may say, had an almost greater share in the writing of the essay than I had myself—in drafting what was intended to be a general work on problems of social philosophy, with chapters on socialism, religion, population, education and so forth, as well as liberty. Then it struck me that the question of liberty was somehow much more pressing and urgent than the others. The spirit of censorship had spread, I noticed, even to Italy. For example, I found the Venus of the Capitol had been removed from public gaze in Rome, and the Venus Callipyge withdrawn from the galleries in Naples. Both in the name of public decency.

Stephen: And both presumably in response to some sort of public demand. Both may have been official acts, but they can hardly be described as oppressive acts.

Mill: But that is the chief point I am making, my dear Stephen. Kings, governments, official bodies are no longer the chief source of constraint, no longer the primary enemies of liberty. The oppression today comes from public opinion, from society itself.

Stephen: I do not see how society itself can be regarded as a tyrant, comparable to a tyrannical monarch, such as James II. The objection to James II was that he was felt to be oppressive by the general body of Englishmen. Now what is 'society' in England if it is not precisely that same general body of Englishmen? And how can they be said to oppress themselves?

Mill: I use the word 'society' in this connexion to mean the majority. The oppression we witness today is the oppression of the individual by the mass. And this tyranny of public opinion is just as bad as, even worse than, the tyranny of the state. Society can and does execute its own mandates, and if it issues wrong mandates instead of right, or any mandates at all in things with which it ought not to meddle, it practises a tyranny far more formidable than many kinds of political oppression.

Stephen: It is not upheld by such extreme penalties.

Mill: True, but it leaves fewer means of escape; it penetrates more deeply into the details of life, and enslaves the soul itself. So you see, the cause of liberty cannot stop short at resistance to the tyranny of political rulers; there needs to be protection also against the tendency of society to impose, by other means than civil penalties, its own ideas as rules of conduct on individuals who dissent from them.

Stephen: What you say, sir, provokes a great many doubts in my mind. Perhaps that is because you are a philosopher, and I am a lawyer. You are concerned with universal ideas, and I am concerned with the particular significance of particular terms. These words 'liberty', 'society', 'enslavement', 'tyranny', 'resistance' are so highly-coloured, so poetic, so dramatic. They do not lend themselves easily to rational discourse.

Mill: The analysis of such terms is just as important to philosophy as it is to jurisprudence. In a sense you might say that my *Essay on Liberty* was an attempt to explain the meaning of the word 'liberty'.

Stephen: Then you will be agreeable to my analysing some other words you use. It seems to me very necessary not to confuse 'society' with 'the majority'. I am as apprehensive as you are of the tyranny of the majority which would come about if democracy were introduced as a system of government in this country. The majority of people are uneducated, and the introduction of democracy would be the enthronement of ignorance. There is surely a vast difference between this ignorant majority and what we mean when we speak of society in England, by which we mean

the general body of Englishmen, led by the educated classes, but
with all classes sharing the same basic religious and moral principles. Some Englishmen are Anglicans, some Catholics, some
Quakers, and so forth; but apart from very few exceptions, they
have the same simple notions of conscience and morality and God.

Mill: Those 'very few exceptions' you speak of are of the utmost importance, Stephen. If all mankind minus one were of one opinion,
and only one person were of the contrary opinion, mankind
would be no more justified in silencing that one person, than he,
if he had the power, would be justified in silencing mankind.

Stephen: I was not talking about anybody silencing anybody else; I was
talking about the right of society to uphold its deepest religions
and moral convictions against those who offend or defy them.

Mill: Well then, let us consider some examples of society exercising
this right which you say it possesses. In ancient Athens, a society
not lacking in culture exacted the penalty of death from Socrates
because he had offended its deepest religious and moral convictions. At Calvary, five centuries later, a society inflicted the
penalty of death on another person who offended its deepest
religious and moral convictions. If you identify morality with the
will of society, you must say that these were deeds well done.

Stephen: Both were perhaps necessary to the salvation of mankind. Society
learns from experience; the teachings both of Christ and of
Socrates have both become part of the thought of modern Europe.
But I cannot honestly say that I see the force of your examples,
Mr Mill, unless you wish to suggest that the people who dissent
from the generally accepted moral principles of the present age
are the Christs and the Socrateses of the nineteenth century.

Mill: If Socrates or Jesus of Nazareth were to reappear in England
today, they would not be found in the ranks of respectable and
conventional society. Neither would be members of the
Athenaeum Club. Socrates would be outlawed because of his
teaching and practise on matters of sexual morality. Jesus would
be outlawed as a blasphemer. Remember that England is only
nominally a Christian country. Every Sunday people pay lip
service to the teaching of Gospels. They say that the blessed are the
poor and humble; they say that they should not judge lest they
be judged; they say that if a man take their cloak, they should
give him their coat also; they say that they should take no thought
for the morrow; they say that if they would be perfect they should
sell all they have and give it to the poor. They say these things,

but they do not believe them, because if they believed them, they would do them. And if Christ were to appear among us and reproach his followers for not taking his precepts seriously, as rules of life to live by, would he not be imprisoned as a blasphemous and dangerous agitator, an enemy of our sacred middle class institution of property?

Stephen: But perhaps the texts you quote were not meant to be rules of life to live by, but counsels of perfection to which only the saintly few among Christ's followers could aspire. Private property is certainly a necessary institution if there is to be economic growth, and no one has demonstrated that fact more convincingly than yourself, Mr Mill, in your *Principles of Political Economy*.

Mill: I certainly see no conflict between the moral philosophy of Jesus of Nazareth, in its simple Gospel form, and the ethics of utilitarianism. Both teach the love of one's neighbour, in other words, that the highest moral good is not that which promotes one's own immediate satisfaction, but that which contributes most to the welfare of humanity at large. My objection to the self-styled Christians of the present-day is that they will not have any of the notions they choose to regard as Christian notions challenged in any way. You will remember the case of Thomas Pooley, who, a year or two ago, was sentenced to twenty-one months' imprisonment for uttering and writing on a gate some words which were critical of Christianity; yet he was said to be a man of unexceptionable conduct.

Stephen: I do not think the case was typical. Besides, within six months, the man received a free pardon from the crown. His crime was blasphemy, not reasoned criticisms of Christian theology.

Mill: But why should an attack on the tenets of the established religion be silenced as a crime? If the principles are true, they will gain all the more significance from being challenged and defended against the challenge. It is precisely because criticism is at present stifled that the Christian creed is repeated parrot-fashion in our churches every Sunday; nobody thinks about it because nobody is allowed to question it.

Stephen: In saying that the crime of Thomas Pooley was blasphemy one says that he did something different from questioning the truth of Christian teaching, or criticizing it in a reasonable manner. He attacked people's sacred institutions in an acutely offensive manner.

Mill: I recognize the point, my dear Stephen. It is often said that liberty of speech should be permitted only on condition that the manner is temperate and does not pass the bounds of reasonable discussion. Much might be said on the impossibility of fixing where those supposed bounds are to be placed, for if the test is to be offence to those whose opinions are attacked, I think experience testifies that this offence is given whenever the attack is telling and powerful, and that every opponent who pushes them hard, and whom they find it difficult to answer, appears to them an intemperate opponent.

Stephen: It ought not to be difficult for the atheist to put his case against religion with moderation; we are always being told how rational that case is; indeed it seems that atheists prefer nowadays to be known as 'rationalists'.

Mill: Most atheists do put their case with moderation. And can you pretend that religious people put their case against atheism moderately? They certainly do not do so in England at the present time. The very word 'atheism' evokes bitter invective and blind hatred, emotions which are dignified with the name of 'honest zeal' or 'righteous indignation'. You are a lawyer, Stephen. You will not need me to tell you how any person without theological belief is received if he appears as a witness in a court of law. He is refused a hearing. Because he will not take the oath he is assumed *a priori* to be a liar. Is this attitude on the part of society towards the free-thinking minority a moderate or temperate attitude?

Stephen: If we look at human history, Mr Mill, we see that every society holds certain persons and certain principles peculiarly sacred, that is, those persons each society believes to be divine, and those principles which it believes to be inviolable. Without this special belief in the supernatural, and the special attitude of reverence to the supernatural, I do not think there could be an effective moral code. At least you will agree with me that every society must have a moral code.

Mill: I do agree, but I do not see why any special attitude to the supernatural is a necessary condition of obedience to a moral code.

Stephen: Not in your own obedience to a moral code, Mr Mill. Once again, let me remind you that you are a philosopher. The general run of men are not philosophers. They have not the wit to think out moral codes of their own, nor the strength of character to obey such a code if they had one. For the great mass of mankind some external sanction is needed, some system of punishment and reward. Heaven, and still more hell, is a very necessary part of

Christianity. The prospect of a reward in the life to come induces men to behave well in this world; and fear of punishment after death deters them from acting ill.

Mill: I should say that is something which stands in need of proof.

Stephen: But it is not difficult to see, men being what they are, liking pleasure and disliking pain, that belief in punishments and rewards is bound to play a large part in governing their conduct. Remove the belief in the immortality of the soul and judgement after death, and morality ceases to be compelling for a vast number of simple, unsophisticated people. And perhaps for sophisticated people, too. Think of *The Republic*, for example; Plato promises to prove that justice is its own reward, but he also finds himself obliged to insist that justice is rewarded with happiness, both in this life and in the life to come. In this way, Platonic teaching and Christian teaching are much the same.

Mill: I am not quite clear when people speak of the necessity of belief in rewards and punishment after death, whether they mean that they themselves would not be virtuous if there were no such supranational sanctions, or whether they are simply afraid that *others* would not be virtuous if there were no supranational sanctions. I should not like to suspect, my dear Stephen, that the excellence of your own conduct in life was in any way due to fear of the torments of hell. I think your character is better than that. In fact I think the character of men in general is better than that.

Stephen: I am not exposed to grave temptations, Mr Mill. For the most part my interests coincide with my duties. When we think of moral discipline we have to think of less sheltered persons and more of those who are exposed to temptations. I do not think one can learn much about the character of men in general from observing the behaviour of members of a privileged class.

Mill: Your sentiments remind me of Calvin. And it seems to me that there is no notion more inimical to the cause of liberty than Calvin's belief that human nature is intrinsically wicked. Now, according to the Calvinistic theory, the one great offence of mankind is self-will. All the good of which humanity is capable is comprised in obedience. You have no choice; thus you must do and no otherwise. 'What is not a duty is a sin.' Man needs no capacity but that of surrendering himself to the will of God, and if he uses his faculties for any other purpose but to do the will of God, he is better off without those faculties. What is known as Christianity today is far closer to this teaching of Calvin than it is to the teaching of the Gospel; and that is one of the chief reasons why liberty is so much in peril.

Stephen: I do not profess to have any deep acquaintance with Calvin's writings, but it strikes me that his general argument is both straightforward and valid. He says that the one great offence of man lies in the fact that, having before him good and evil, his weaker and worse appetites lead him to choose evil. Redemption consists not in killing, but in curing his nature. Speak of Original Sin or not as you please, but the fact remains that all men are in some respects both weak and wicked. They do the ill they would not do, and shun the good they would pursue. Calvin's theory was that in order to escape from the bondage of sinfulness, men must be true to the better part of their nature, keep its baser elements in proper subjection, and look up to God as the source of the only valuable kind of freedom—freedom to be good and wise.

Mill: There are two things I might say in reply to that. The first is that I see no reason to accept Calvin's conception of what is good and what evil in human nature; the second, that there can be no freedom to be good and wise unless men have the opportunity of choosing to be good and wise, which entails the opportunity of rejecting wickedness and folly. In Calvin's own city of Geneva, any temptation for men to do what Calvin considered wicked was, where possible, removed. Nobody was allowed to enter a tavern. Dancing, games, theatres, skating; even the wearing of jewellery and the dressing of hair were all forbidden. Pictures and statues could not be exhibited. This ought to sound outrageous, but it does not, because we are rapidly moving towards the same state of affairs in England today. My argument is that the Calvinist aim is wrong, and the Calvinist method is wrong; and the two, of course, go together.

Stephen: I admit that Calvin was perhaps an extremist. I only insist that he was right in thinking that human beings need discipline, if they are not to fall prey to their own evil natures.

Mill: Why all this talk about men's evil natures, when we are told in the Scriptures that men were made in God's own image? I do not question the need, at times, for the Christian ideal of self-denial. But there is also the pagan ideal of self-development which is no less worthy. Human beings can develop what is good in themselves. And the way to achieve this is not by wearing down into uniformity all that is original and individual in people, but by

cultivating and calling it forth. It is in becoming themselves—
within the limits imposed by the rights of others—that human
beings become a noble and beautiful object of contemplation.

Stephen: I cannot see that individuality as such has any intrinsic value.
Goodness is varied, I agree, but that does not mean that variety in
itself is good. A nation in which everybody was sober would be a
happier nation than one in which half the population was sober
and the other half habitual drunkards. But the latter would be
more diversified; it would contain more variety. Are you to have
us believe that it would for that reason be the better nation?

Mill: To ask for diversity is not to ask for any kind of diversity, however bad. There are some things which I should have thought
could have been assumed, without having to be made explicit.
What is wrong with England today is that there is too much
uniformity. People are getting to be more and more alike—just
as the Chinese have become. The Chinese have resisted progress
because they have stamped out variety; they have remained
stationary for thousands of years. The modern regime of public
opinion in England is, in an unorganized form, what the Chinese
educational and political system is in an organized form. In
England it is becoming increasingly difficult for anyone who
wants to think independently or act independently to do so; the
penalties of society are too heavy; the room for free action is being
progressively narrowed.

Stephen: And what do you think should be done about it?

Mill: The great need is for individuality to assert itself; and for the
general public to learn to be tolerant. As things are, the tyranny of
opinion is so intense that it is good for people to be as eccentric as
they fancy, if only as a form of protest.

Stephen: I am afraid that if your advice were followed, sir, we should have
more oddities than men of distinction among us. Eccentricity is
far more often a mark of weakness than a mark of strength.
Originality consists in thinking for yourself, not in thinking
differently from other people.

Mill: Eccentricity has always abounded where strength of character has
abounded. The great ages in our own history were the ages which
produced the most singular English characters. The amount of
eccentricity in a society has generally been proportional to the
amount of mental vigour and moral courage it contained. That
so few now dare to be eccentric marks the chief danger of this
time.

Stephen: I am sorry, Mr Mill, but I cannot agree with you that the removal
of restraints tends to invigorate character. I would say the very
opposite of this. Habitual exertion is the greatest of all invigo-
rators of character, and restraint and coercion in one form or
another is the great stimulus to exertion. Now it seems to me that
you take so optimistic a view of human nature as to assume that,
left alone, the best that is in a man will spontaneously flow out.
Experience teaches another lesson. Many a rich man's son has been
given the means to do as he pleases, and what is the usual outcome? The young man is demoralized; his character deteriorates
with self-indulgence. On the other hand we have the example of
the young men who serve in the army or navy in battle. The harsh
discipline of active service strengthens their character, and brings
out what is best and noblest in them. Surely the most admirable
of our fellow citizens are those who have been kept under close
and continuous discipline up to the ages of twenty-two or
twenty-three.

Mill: I cannot say much about that. I myself have had to earn my living
since I was sixteen. But I would agree in principle that discipline in
childhood and youth is a necessary part of the training for freedom
in manhood. But I would certainly not favour discipline on
military lines. I do not think it at all desirable that the young
should learn to obey commands unquestioningly; on the contrary I think they should learn why certain things are enjoined
upon them and others forbidden. In that way they can learn the
principles of ethics; and so learn to govern themselves. I believe
in the discipline of enlightenment; not the servitude of blind
obedience.

Stephen: But most men are not capable of enlightenment in the full sense
you are thinking of. In fact most men, the lower classes certainly,
are very much like children.

Mill: There I disagree with you profoundly. I think there are few
greater errors than this idea that what is good for children is good
for people generally. I believe that adults must be treated as adults;
and allowed to make their own mistakes only in order that they
may learn from them.

Stephen: Can all human beings be treated in this way? You have yourself
maintained in your published writings, Mr Mill, that the backward peoples of the world need guidance, authority, supervision.
That such people are not, in a word, ready for liberty.

Mill: The argument applies to the colonies. So far as this country is

concerned—or North America or Western Europe generally—
it has no relevance.

Stephen: But is this distinction between a backward and a civilized society
such a clear distinction? Surely what we call a civilized society is
one which has a substantial educated ruling class. But there may
be many backward people in the most advanced society. The
majority of Englishmen today are still illiterate. Is not an illiterate
European more like an Indian, and hence more like a child, than
he is like an educated European adult?

Mill: I don't deny that there is something arbitrary in the way we have
of talking about backward and civilized societies. I also agree with
you that England is not yet ready for democracy, precisely because
the labouring classes are still for the most part illiterate. But the
answer to this seems to me, not to increase social tyranny, but to
spread enlightenment, to provide a system of national education
which will enable the children of the labouring classes to become
literate. Whether we like it or not, democracy is coming to
England just as it has come to America. It is the political system of
the future.

Stephen: I do not look forward to its coming.

Mill: But you are not trying to persuade me that because the English
labouring classes are not yet fit for democracy the English people
is not fit for liberty?

Stephen: I would not say that because I would not understand what it
meant. I said just now that the word 'liberty' means the absence of
restraints. More precisely, it means the absence of *injurious* restraints. The difference between you and me is not a difference as
to people's 'fitness for liberty', whatever that may signify, but as to
what restraints are desirable, and what injurious. You, sir, seem to
maintain that all social restraints are injurious; I maintain that
many social restraints are desirable, indeed imperative, in so far as
they are needed to uphold morality, and to keep society together.

Mill: I do not say that all social restraints are injurious. In fact I may
claim that my *Essay on Liberty* was written to show which social
restraints were injurious and which were not. The question as I
put it was: In which circumstances is society entitled to interfere
with the liberty of the individuals? Manifestly, freedom cannot be
absolute. Society cannot tolerate such things as murder and theft.

Stephen: But the laws against murder and theft are not felt as restraints by
the ordinary honest person, because he has no desire to murder
and to rob. And such laws cannot therefore be reasonably called

F

an abridgement of freedom. In fact, if I remember aright, the point was made by Locke himself. He said that the laws which provide for men's security enlarge their liberty, they do not diminish it.

Mill: I think the same thing. There is no necessary antithesis between law, correctly understood and confined to its proper function, and liberty. The important point is to determine what that proper function is. In general I would sum up the principle by saying that no man should be allowed to act in any way which is injurious to others. The mere fact that men live in society renders it necessary that each should be bound to observe a certain line of conduct towards the rest. Each must respect the rights of his neighbours, and those who violate that rule must be punished.

Stephen: Since I am myself a lawyer, you will forgive me, sir, if I say that 'rights' sound a very legalistic concept to make the foundation of social conduct. The Christian religion enjoins us to do something more than respect our neighbour's 'rights'; it teaches us to love our neighbour as ourselves; and you have remarked that utilitarian ethics embodies much the same idea.

Mill: I was going on to make that very point myself. The purpose of legal restraints is to protect men's legal rights and to punish those who invade them. But there is also the question of those other restraints we have been discussing, social restraints. There are certain acts of the individual which may be hurtful to others, or wanting in due consideration for their welfare, without going to the length of violating their legal or constitutional rights. Here the offender may justly be punished by opinion, though not by law. As soon as any part of a man's conduct affects prejudicially the interests of others, society has a right to intervene. In other words, in the sphere of self-regarded actions, that is, actions which concern and affect the agent alone, there should be liberty; in the sphere of other-regarding actions, that is, actions which concern others besides the agent, there is a just case for social restraint.

Stephen: I was waiting for you to formulate some such principle, Mr Mill. Your whole argument seems to turn on it, so perhaps we had better look at it rather carefully. Could you, to begin with, give me an example of a self-regarding action, that is, an action which affects no one but the agent?

Mill: If a man gets drunk it is his own business. That is, provided he is not a policeman or a soldier, and drunk on duty, which is quite another matter. Drunkenness is deplorable. If men were to learn

self-discipline it would not happen. But to stop the sale and consumption of alcoholic drink entirely, as some of our Puritan
zealots wish to do, would not teach anyone self-discipline. It
would simply narrow the field of moral choice, and take away an
important part of our freedom.

Stephen: But is getting drunk a self-regarding action? In the case of a
bachelor of means, living alone, I suppose it might be. But what of
the married man, and especially of the poor married man? Does
not his wife suffer when her husband is brutalized by drink; and
his children suffer because he has wasted his money on himself and
has nothing left to buy them food?

Mill: Drunkenness of that kind and on that scale is certainly not what I
was thinking of when I spoke of a self-regarding action. And by
locating its evil in the fact that it has prejudicial consequences for
others, you are invoking my own principle with which to condemn it.

Stephen: I was merely trying to discover what are these purely 'self-regarding actions' you spoke of, Mr Mill. And I have, I think,
shown you that, whatever other examples you may have to offer
me, the one example you have produced, that of a man getting
drunk, is certainly *not* an example—of a self-regarding action.
True, you have also spoken about the freedom of expression. But
the publication of opinions can hardly be classified as a self-
regarding action, since the whole purpose of publication is to
affect others.

Mill: But not to affect them prejudicially. In fact the first argument in
favour of the freedom of expression is that it is always in the public
interest. For if what is censored is true, then humanity is being
denied knowledge of the truth, and that is an obvious evil. If what
is suppressed is half-true and half-false, humanity is denied the
opportunity of distinguishing what is false from what is true. If
what is suppressed is altogether false, humanity is denied the advantage of re-affirming the truth of its established beliefs. Therefore censorship is always harmful to society in general.

Stephen: So you do not stress the right of an individual to express himself
but the right of society to hear what he has to say?

Mill: Yes, it seems to me that to silence a man is not only, or even
primarily, to deprive him of a right. The peculiar evil of silencing
the expression of opinion is that it is robbing the human race,
posterity as well as the present, and those who dissent from the
opinion, still more than those who hold it.

Stephen: I agree that one must distinguish between freedom of expression and freedom of action in general. But even the freedom of expression cannot be as unlimited as you seem to imply. We have spoken of blasphemy: there are also the questions of obscenity and of libel.

Mill: Libel is the abuse of the freedom of expression to injure an innocent person. That is why there has to be a legal remedy against libel.

Stephen: Obscenity, I suppose, is closer to blasphemy. It is an abuse of freedom which injures society as a whole by affronting the values it holds sacred.

Mill: But what kind of utterance is to count as blasphemy and what as obscenity? What are the tests? In the narrow-minded atmosphere we live in, any outspoken attack on the established religion is considered blasphemous, and any criticism of established sexual customs is considered 'obscene'. You may not know that I myself was once imprisoned for a day on a charge of distributing obscene literature, namely pamphlets advocating the use of contraceptive devices as a solution to the population problem.

Stephen: Society evidently feels that the general employment of contraceptive devices would both interfere with nature and remove the chief deterrent against fornication, its common punishment.

Mill: You speak of the common punishment of fornication; but if an unwanted pregnancy is a punishment you must surely agree that it is a remarkably unjust one, since it falls on the female alone. Or do you perhaps fancy that the male does not bear an equal share of guilt?

Stephen: The moral codes of all societies, sir, recognize that it is the female who suffers the evil consequences of fornication, and that is why society exacts a higher standard of chastity from the female than the male. Fornication is not one of those things which the law can properly or effectively be evoked to restrain. It is one of the functions of public opinion to enforce this particular restraint. And public opinion can afford to be more indulgent to the male, because the male does not need the same protection.

Mill: Society appears to have two standards of what is right and wrong in the matter.

Stephen: It is not a case of there being two standards of what is right and wrong, but a recognition by society of 'two standards' in biology: the biological consequences of fornication for the male are negligible, for the female they are enormous.

Mill: You seem to be saying that because the female is punished by nature, she must be further punished by society.

Stephen: I am saying that the purpose of the moral injunctions of public opinion is to uphold the basic institutions of society: and one of these is the family. In doing so public opinion seeks to engender a love of chastity and a hatred of unchastity. In our English middle classes today this sentiment has spread so far that unchastity in the male is almost as much detested as unchastity in the female, so the double standard you speak of is fast disappearing there, though a more traditional attitude may still prevail in the upper reaches of society. But let me put a question to you, Mr Mill, since we are talking of fornication: Is this, in your view, an example of a self-regarding or an other-regarding action?

Mill: That depends in the first place on whether the participants have reached the age of consent, and do consent.

Stephen: But what if there is issue? What, if as is only too likely, the action leads to the birth of a child, which for the rest of its life must bear the stigma of bastardy?

Mill: It is the crime of society that it makes the innocent suffer by attaching a stigma to one who is born in such circumstances.

Stephen: If society does not distinguish between legitimate and illegitimate issue, the family, as an institution, cannot exist; society would disintegrate. I feel, as you do, that it is a grave injustice that the innocent child should suffer. But the only way to diminish that injustice is to diminish the number of victims; and the way to diminish the number of victims is to prevent fornication, which is precisely what existing social restraints are designed to achieve. But you, Mr Mill, object to those restraints in the name of what you call liberty.

Mill: I say those restraints are too onerous; and that in any case they do not achieve their objective. Enlightenment is better than coercion.

Stephen: I am afraid I have not your faith in enlightenment, sir. One thing, Calvin, at any rate, realized was that fornication has a universal appeal. That is why he was so emphatic about the need to minimize erotic stimulation, and to train people to feel a deep distaste for what might otherwise prove too disastrously attractive.

Mill: But think of the lengths to which our Calvinists are going to 'minimize erotic stimulation' as you put it. Even the theatre has fallen in disrepute among us. Theatres are being closed in country towns and cities, and in the metropolis itself, they are shunned by a large part of the right-thinking middle class. All this, mark you, in the country of Shakespeare and Ben Jonson and Marlowe. Has any nation in Europe a more glorious body of dramatic literature than our own? Yet it is obvious, if things go on as they are going now, the theatre as such may disappear.

Stephen: Of course the dividing line between what is acceptable to public opinion and what is not acceptable is a fluctuating one. In the time of Shakespeare things gave offence which would not give offence today, and things give offence today which would not have given offence in Shakespeare's time. The pity about the theatre is that it has deteriorated morally precisely to the extent to which the serious-minded middle class has deserted it. When the theatres, which the Puritans had closed after their victory in the Civil War, were re-opened in 1660 their audiences were drawn from the libertines, the Cavaliers; and the authors who wrote for the stage wrote for that audience. You have mentioned Shakespeare and Jonson and Marlow; but there are also the names of Wycherley and Etheridge and Dryden, whose works made the English theatres temples of pornography, and abundantly justified all the strictures of the Puritans against the stage.

Mill: But by your own admission the deterioration of the stage after 1660 was the direct result of repression by the Puritans. Puritan repression did not and does not achieve its end. Drive out healthy enjoyment, and people will not become pious, they will resort to unwholesome enjoyment. Nature is not so easily thwarted. In Shakespeare's time, the English were in many ways a much freer and happier people than they are today; on a Sunday they had parish ales and wakes and games; now every Sunday they are plunged by the joint efforts of written law and unwritten law into a gloomy and demoralizing idleness. You have asked me for examples of actions which are not injurious to society, but which society tries to suppress. Well, you can see examples of this in almost all the so-called breaches of the Sabbath. If a man cuts his own lawn on a Sunday, or plays games with his children in a public place, or goes to walk in a cloth cap instead of going to church in a top hat, what happens to him? He is ostracized by his neighbours. If he is in business, he loses customers. He and his family invoke glances if not words of disapproval. He is punished in all sorts of subtle and unsubtle ways. And yet you can tell me, my dear Stephen, that the cause of liberty has been won in England.

Stephen: We live in an age of great social change, Mr Mill, and the progress which we have achieved in England, which is more than other nations have achieved, has been industrial progress; and that progress has been due to the willingness of the middle classes to turn aside from transitory pleasures and cultivate the Puritan virtues of work and thrift and abstinence and honesty. The Elizabethans could afford to enjoy their maypoles and their parish ales because the world was being won for them by a handful of bold sailors, adventurers and pirates. The Englishman of today has to win his own world, to make his own fortune. Those who have succeeded have done so by following the path of self-denial rather than that of self-indulgence. Victorian England has not the same greatness as Elizabethan England, but it has a greatness, all the same. The restraints of society may have become, as you say, more severe; but that is the price we pay for the lightness of the restraints which are imposed on us by the state. Queen Elizabeth was an arbitrary sovereign; Queen Victoria is a constitutional monarch. In that difference lies an enormous gain in real liberty. One of the factors which has made that possible is that society itself has learned to impose restraints, without resort to law, on those who defy the national morality.

Mill: When you speak of national morality you fill me with dread. The nation is not the proper seat of morality; nor can you, as a professing Christian, consistently maintain that it is. Ethics may be seated in the individual conscience, or in some principles of universal validity. But it cannot be bounded by national frontiers. If a thing is wicked in England, it is wicked in Spain, and wicked in Russia. National customs and taboos may differ. Sabbath games are taboo in England, and the eating of beef is taboo in Bombay; but precisely because these are local taboos they cannot be true moral principles. When I say that it is wrong for a man to injure his neighbour, I mean not only that it is wrong for an Englishman to injure his neighbour but for any man to do so. What is not universal in this way is not genuine morality, but only local custom, even superstition or prejudice which is mistakenly confused with morality, and mistakenly treated as if it were equally compelling. If young people are taught that Sabbath breaking and dancing and going to theatres are wicked actions like theft and cruelty and lying, their moral sense is bound to be distorted. I do not know what the English conscience is going to be like in future; but I think it only too probable that we are moving towards a state of affairs in which people will literally not know right from wrong, because the liberty of choosing and thinking for themselves is being taken from them.

Stephen: I do not wish to ride to death the analogy between disease and vice. They differ in some essential respects, but they do resemble each other in several important ones. Vice is as infectious as disease, and happily virtue is infectious, though health is not. Both vice and virtue are transmissible, and to a considerable extent, hereditary. Virtue and vice resemble health and disease in being dependent upon broad general causes which do not always force themselves on our attention. Good air, clean water, and good food are now coming to be recognized as the great conditions of health. The maintenance of a high moral standard, the admiration and honour of virtue and the condemnation of vice, is the great condition of virtue. It is what is called in a school or a regiment a good moral tone. The same thing is needed in the nation. Though when I speak of the nation, I do not wish to deny the universality of certain basic principles of morality, or for that matter, of religion.

Mill: I am not surprised, my dear Stephen, that you should invoke the model of the regiment or the school. Both are in the nature of things authoritarian institutions. In the regiment, there are officers who command and men who obey; in the school, there are masters who govern and boys who obey. Many political societies are indeed very similar; but my whole argument is that this ought not to be the case. In a civilized community, people should not be under orders; each should command himself. That is what I understand by a free society, a society which is *not* like a regiment or a school.

Stephen: It is all very well to speak of what should or should not be. But let us not forget what *is*. It is a plain fact that most people are more like children than they are like philosophers. You have spoken a great deal about enlightenment, and I certainly do not question the importance of education. But what is education except a strenuous and systematic effort to give the whole character a certain turn and bias which appears desirable to the person who teaches? A parent or school-master has to decide what is right or wrong and teach his children or his pupils accordingly. He cannot leave them to make up their own minds as to what is right or wrong. He must tell them, and tell them definitely. Legislators and the leaders of responsible opinion must perform the same function for the world at large. I suggest to you, sir, that it is an idle dream to pretend that one man in a thousand really exercises individual choice as to his religious or moral principles. He believes what he has learned from his parents or his teachers.

Mill: If people do not choose it is because choice is denied them; if they do not think, it is because they are trained to accept uncritically conventional opinion, *idées reçues*, established beliefs; and trained at the same time to be scornful and suspicious of originality and novelty. At present, yes, people *are* mostly governed as if they were children. But until freedom has been put to the test, how can you say that they can *only* be governed as children? People generally have not been given the opportunity to develop themselves; but this is no reason for saying that if they were given the opportunity, they would not profit from it.

Stephen: We see the fruits of indiscipline in individual cases.

Mill: It is not good logic to pass from particular cases which may be exceptional to general conclusions about humanity as a whole.

Stephen: I would not venture to discuss the technicalities of logic with a professional philosopher, such as yourself, Mr Mill.

Mill: I notice, my dear Stephen, that you keep on speaking of me as a philosopher, as if I were making some claim to be different from other men. I do nothing of the kind. I believe that other men are much as I am. And really it is you who are claiming to be different from others, because when you make your distinction between leaders of responsible opinion and ordinary men, you tacitly identify yourself with the former class. Admittedly your mind is directed towards the duties of an educated *élite*, but at the same time you are assuming the privileges of one, including the privilege, which you deny others, of thinking for yourself.

Stephen: If I think for myself, it is not with any ambition to be original. I do not seek to match my wits against the accumulated wisdom of the nation and the past; I am content to accept traditional ways and institutions unless I can see some overwhelmingly compelling reason for rejecting them.

Mill: When I spoke just now of the wisdom of the past—of the ethos, if you like to call it the ethos, of Elizabethan England, you told me that people's thoughts and feelings changed; and you commended instead the ethos of our own age, of Victorian England. Now, I am a quarter of a century older than you are, my dear Stephen. I can remember England as it was under the last of the Georges, and King William. It was a different place from what it has become. It has changed in some ways for the worse, I think, and in some for the better. But where it has changed for the better it is because certain people—people of vision and humanity and independence of mind—struggled to reform it. If tradition alone had served to guide them, our parliamentary system and our trading system would have been unchanged, and things be very much worse than they are today. Of course, the past has much to teach us; but it is disastrous to let it dominate us. The spirit of improvement and the spirit of liberty go together.

Stephen: Do they go together, Mr Mill? My impression is that the leading exponents of social reform today are among the keenest champions of government interference. What are socialism and communism but systems for the enlargement of the power of the state by transferring material resources from individual to public control? Are not these socialists in the forefront of reform, the very *avant garde* of improvement?

Mill: I admit there are dangers of socialism as there are dangers of conservatism, and I had those, as much as others, in mind when I wrote my *Essay on Liberty*. No scheme of reform can be truly humane if it does not put freedom among the first of all values.

Stephen: My problem, Mr Mill, and it is a problem you have not resolved for me, is what meaning to attach to this idea of yours that liberty as such is a value. I cannot see that any moral worth can be ascribed to certain kinds of freedom. Assuredly, it is good that men should be free to do what is right. But what merit can there be in freedom to do wrong? I dare say men who do well of their own accord are better than men who do well because somebody else has induced them to do so. But the real motive behind people's behaviour is something we can never really discover. We can never find out exactly why a man has done one thing and not another. But we know how to help people to do what is right; and if we can help people to do what is right by leading them in a certain direction and preventing them from going in another direction, then it seems to me manifestly our duty to do so. Your view seems to be that the more we leave people alone, the better everything will be; my view is that we ought to do all that we can to make people do what is right, chiefly by persuasion, sometimes by compulsion, if necessary, by force.

Mill: I can see, my dear Stephen, that you are not a man to be convinced by as short a book as my *Essay on Liberty*, or by as brief a conversation as we have had this evening. Indeed, perhaps nothing would convince you if you believe that morality is something which some people have to teach and others have to learn, and that the world should be a sort of school, controlled by ushers and governesses—the men and women of the right-thinking ruling class—and dominated by rigid codes of what is done and not done; a school in which those who have their own ideas about life should be cold-shouldered, despised, penalized or whipped. Perhaps to the sort of people who like the idea of being ushers or governesses, your picture may seem attractive. I find it a most disturbing one. It only comforts me to think that at least it is not an accurate picture. We have, it is true, a ruling class in this country. But its members do not owe their position to any desire for moral leadership, but to the simple fact that they have money. Their wealth has given them power, and they keep that power because they want to keep their wealth. I do not think the possessing class which dominates England today is in any way morally superior to the labouring class, and if I were to seek a moral tutor, I should seek him among the poor, and, of course, in doing so, I should be following the precept of Christ himself.

Stephen: So your objection to the moral leadership of the existing ruling class is that the ruling class is not virtuous enough.

Mill: No ruling class is ever virtuous enough, my dear Stephen. In fact, I sometimes feel that the strongest of all arguments against outside interference in purely personal conduct, is that those who interfere almost always interfere wrongly and in the wrong place.

Sir Henry Maine, Matthew Arnold and John Morley

A dialogue on Democracy

The poet Matthew Arnold (1822–1888) was one of the very few
Victorian intellectuals who looked forward eagerly to the
establishment of democracy in England. He believed that democracy was inevitable and he welcomed it as part 'of the vital effort
of human nature to better itself'. He had never been an 'ivory
tower' poet: his professional work as an inspector of schools, his
first-hand study of the educational systems of France, Germany
and America had sharpened his awareness of political and social
problems. He believed that the aristocratic tradition had exhausted
itself, and that only democracy could revitalize the nation.

Sir Henry Maine (1822–1888), anthropologist, lawyer, historian
and administrator, took a very different point of view. He held
that democracy was neither inevitable nor desirable. Maine
believed that the modern world needed modern scientific leadership, an aristocracy of brains. Democracy, he argued, meant the
reign of vulgarity and ignorance; and he was able to draw on a
wealth of historical and other evidence to support his argument.

In the dialogue which follows these two men, exact contemporaries (they were born in the same year, and died in the same year)
are brought together with a young liberal writer, John Morley
(1850–1925), who regarded democracy with less favour than
Arnold and less fear than Maine.

Morley: I hear, Mr Arnold, that you have been lecturing on democracy;
and I know that you, Sir Henry, are writing a book on the same
subject.

Maine: If it *is* the same subject, my dear Morley; a lot of people use the
word 'democracy', but they do not all use it in the same way.

Arnold: I use it as the Greeks used it. For that is what the word is, is it not,
demokratia—the rule of the people?

Maine: We have Aristotle's formula: the rule of the many, as distinct from
the rule of the one, or the rule of the few.

Morley: But Aristotle was against democracy; he gave the word a pejorative meaning. He thought there was a better form of government
by the many, the 'polity'.

Arnold: There is quite a lot to be said for *not* using the word 'democracy'.

Maine: I entirely agree, Arnold. As Morley says, I am writing a book about democracy. But I shall not call it *Democracy*. I shall call it *Popular Government*.

Morley: Well, that is certainly a more attractive title. Too many people are put off by the word 'democracy'.

Maine: Are they, my dear Morley? It is no intention of mine to alter their attitude. Though I would rather they were put off by the thing than by the word.

Morley: But surely, Sir Henry, now that the thing is becoming more and more liked, more and more wanted, the word is bound to become less and less pejorative.

Maine: The two go together, I grant you. But you will perhaps remember a pamphlet written by that great man, John Austin, just before his death—a pamphlet in which he analysed various political terms. Austin pointed out that 'democracy' is an even more ambiguous word than 'aristocracy'. There is no word that has collected around it more vague language and loose metaphors. Yet although 'democracy' does signify something indeterminate, there is nothing vague about it. It is simply and solely, as Austin said, a 'form of government'—one 'in which the governing body is a comparatively large fraction of the entire nation'.

Arnold: The trouble with Austin, it seems to me, Maine, is that he is excessively legalistic. A democracy would differ from a monarchy or an aristocracy not only in its form of government. It would be a different *kind* of society. The people would be different— precisely because they would be a self-governing people.

Morley: Yes, Sir Henry. You quote Austin. You might also quote Tocqueville. His *Democracy in America* is not just the picture of another form of government; it is a picture of another civilization.

Maine: You put your finger on what is wrong with Tocqueville's book, my dear Morley. It is ambiguous, ruinously ambiguous, because it gives us an account of what life is like in democratic America; but fails to distinguish what is characteristic of democracy as a system from what is merely characteristic of America as a country.

Arnold: Such distinctions would be purely artificial. Tocqueville shows a democratic country as it *is*, in all the fullness of its life. I would agree that some features are peculiar to America as a country; but America is not the only model of a democratic society we could look at; there is also Switzerland.

Maine: By all means let us look at Switzerland in all the fullness of its life, if you can call it fullness. Champions of democracy are only too apt to forget it. They look at America because America is exciting. It is large and rich in natural resources and almost empty. It is the New World. But Switzerland is old and small and poor and rather backward. Nobody could find Switzerland exciting.

Morley: But surely nobody has done more to make democracy exciting than Rousseau; and Rousseau was very Swiss, and the democracy he described was very Swiss, too; except that it was also extremely metaphysical.

Maine: I suppose you are right, if you mean that Rousseau excited the French. Certainly much of the current *mystique* of democracy is an inflated phantasmagoria of Rousseau-esque romanticism, blown up by French publicists and theorists.

Arnold: You speak of romanticism as if it were an evil movement, when surely if there is one thing wrong with nineteenth-century England it is our lack of romanticism; our lack of any ideal, political or social. To me it seems that just because democracy is coming to the fore as the one ideal that can stir our countrymen—the image of a better future calling us away from the moral void of selfish individualism and *chacun pour soi* and *laissez faire*; just for this reason I must declare myself ready to welcome democracy, to go forward to it with open hands.

Maine: With open hands and closed eyes, my dear Arnold? I fancy that is the usual manner in which democracy is welcomed.

Arnold: You may imagine my eyes closed, if you please. But I can assure you that I am very conscious of the dangers of democracy, and of what must be done to make its coming a blessing to the nation, and not a disaster.

Maine: You speak of the coming of democracy, as if it were something historically inevitable.

Arnold: And so I believe it is.

Maine: You astonish me. I have noticed a widespread belief that we are being propelled by an irresistible force towards an unavoidable object, towards democracy as towards death. But I did not imagine, my dear Arnold, that you would have entertained this naïve opinion.

Arnold: There are excellent reasons for entertaining it. The old political parties which have governed this country since 1688 are disintegrating. They are out of date, out of date because they are both aristocratical parties. And the aristocracy is done for. Oh, I admit there is much to be said for the English aristocracy. It is in many ways the best in Europe; and it has owed its power to some extent to its virtues, to its character and culture. But above all it has owed its power to the consent of the people it has governed. Now, Morley, you are still a young man. But you, Maine, I fancy are much the same age as I am.

Maine: I was born in 1822.

Arnold: Then we are exact contemporaries. In 1822 the English aristocracy, and the two English aristocratic parties, could still conduct and wield the nation. Today, fifty-three years later, it is becoming less and less possible. The acquiescence of the nation in the predominance of the aristocracy—and that acquiescence was the only tenure with which it held its power—that, as I say, is fast giving way. The upper class has lost its superiority over the others; and the others are no longer willing to follow it. The multitude has lost faith in its traditional leaders, and come to desire only to rule itself. That is what has been happening in your lifetime and mine, my dear Maine. Democracy is trying to affirm its own essence.

Morley: I don't think anyone could disagree with you there, Mr Arnold.

Maine: If I could understand what Arnold is saying, I dare say I should disagree with it. But I simply do not know what it means to say that democracy is 'trying to affirm its own essence'. I admit that social attitudes may have changed in the past fifty odd years. But that is nothing new. People's attitudes are continually changing; though I believe that there were far more radical changes in the seventeenth century than there have been in the nineteenth century.

Morley: The seventeenth century saw the revolt against monarchy; what we are seeing in the nineteenth century, as Mr Arnold says, is the revolt against aristocracy. The process is simply being pushed a stage further: a stage further in the direction of democracy.

Maine: I do not follow your talk about *stages*, Morley. I see no evidence in history for thinking that the English people, having abandoned one extreme form of government, absolute monarchy, is about to embrace another extreme form of government, democracy, which is nothing other than monarchy turned upside down. What has in fact been happening in England in the last two hundred years is that a moderate form of government, a parliamentary constitutional monarchy, has been repeatedly re-affirmed in the face of continuing social changes.

Morley: But what are the underlying principles of a parliamentary constitutional monarchy, Sir Henry?

Maine: The principles of 1688: freedom and consent. In a phrase used at the time, 'the only lawful title' of any ruler is 'the consent of the people'.

Morley: But surely, Sir Henry, the notion of democratic government is nothing other than the logical extension of the principle of popular consent; the fulfilment of the promise of freedom.

Maine: My dear Morley, if you believe that democracy is the fulfilment of the promise of freedom, you should re-read the words of your old friend, the late John Stuart Mill. He maintains that nothing is more inimical to freedom than the dominion of the multitude, or the rule of the majority.

Arnold: Whatever Mill may have said, it seems to me illogical to uphold the principle of popular consent in 1688, and to resist the principle of democratic government in 1875.

Maine: But the two things are quite different. Democratic government is not a *principle*, it is a *method* or form of government. And there is a very great difference between saying that the authority of a ruler must ultimately derive from the consent of the nation to be governed by him; and saying that the people ought to govern themselves. In fact, if you believe that people ought to rule themselves, the question of consent would not arise, since there would be nobody else's rule for them to consent to.

Arnold: There is a natural transition from popular consent to popular participation in government; from the system exemplified by England since 1688, towards the system exemplified in America and Switzerland.

Maine: I can see no logical connexion, or practical connexion, or indeed any connexion whatever, between the democratic form of government and the principle of consent; between democracy and freedom.

Morley: But you would not deny, Sir Henry, that America is both a democratic country and a free country.

Maine: I have no wish to deny what is asserted on every hand. America is not the most free country in the world, but it *is* a free country; and by its existence it enables our continental friends to praise free institutions without the somewhat painful necessity of praising English institutions. But if freedom flourishes in America, it is because American institutions have been so designed as to curb democratic impulses rather than to give them the rein. Nowhere are checks and balances more elaborately applied.

Arnold: But there is more than one kind of freedom, you know, Maine.

And I am as suspicious as you are of those champions of democracy who celebrate it as the mother of all freedom. *Political*
freedom—the freedom we have had in England since 1688—we
owe more to grasping barons than to the conquests of democracy.
But there is another kind of freedom which democracy alone can
bring; and that is social freedom.

Maine: I am not sure I know what 'social freedom' means, but if it is
something to be seen in America, then all I can say is that there has
hardly ever before been a community in which the weak have
been so pitilessly pushed to the wall, in which success counts for so
much, or in which there has arisen so great an inequality of private
fortune and domestic luxury in so short a time.

Arnold: Of course America has its imperfections, its great imperfections;
and we must learn from the American failures as well as the
American successes. Indeed, I sometimes feel we might express
our problem as this: how are we to democratize England without
Americanizing England? For whether we like it or not, England is
bound to be democratized, in one way or another.

Maine: I see no reason for admitting anything of the sort. Experience
offers nothing to warrant your prediction. On the contrary, it
shows that democracy is an extremely rare and fragile growth in
the history of political societies. Popular government has been
tried in France, and failed; it has been tried in Germany, and
failed; it has been tried in Spain, and failed. I do not deny its
relative success in North America, but the inferences that might be
drawn from that success are much weakened, if not destroyed, by
the remarkable spectacle of the numerous republics set up from
the Mexican border to the Straits of Magellan.

Morley: But surely, Sir Henry, it would be unfair to judge democracy by
the experience of the bogus democracies of South America,
countries which are democratic only in their pretensions.

Maine: My dear Morley, I have noticed before, that partisans of democracy will never look at instances which show democratic government to be unstable. But a sober student of history must look at
the world as it is. He must face the facts as they are. And there is
nothing in those facts to support the notion that popular government has an indefinitely long future in front of it. On the contrary,
the facts show its expectation of life to be exceedingly precarious.

Morley: It is arguable, Sir Henry, that the failures of democracy are due to
the ruthlessness of its enemies rather than to any inherent weakness
of its own institutions. And the old aristocracies are certainly not

the only enemies of popular government. There are various novel forms of military dictatorship, which are even more opposed to democracy, although they commonly usurp the name of republics. Under the old aristocracies there could be some degree of freedom, political freedom, as Mr Arnold says; while under the upstart military dictator there is neither freedom nor democracy. And I am afraid there is a particular danger of this kind of dictatorship at the present phase of western history, when the old ruling class is becoming morally bankrupt.

Maine: If military dictatorships arise, more often than not it is because the people want a military dictatorship. It is the democratic choice; and indeed the sort of foolish choice you would expect of the simple-minded multitude. Look at the way the French people used the democratic instrument of the plebiscite only the other day to give a military despot any answer he desired. And look at the consequences of that other democratic instrument, the referendum, in Switzerland, where it enables illiterate cowherds and woodcutters to put a stop to almost all enlightened legislation. Democracy is nothing other than the enthronement of ignorance. If democratic methods had been followed in England there would have been no reform of religion, no change of dynasty, no toleration of dissent, not even an accurate calendar. The threshing machine, the power loom, the spinning jenny, and possibly the steam engine would have been prohibited. In fact I would say generally that the establishment of the masses in power would be the blackest possible omen for all legislation founded on scientific opinion, which needs tension of mind to understand it and self-denial to submit to it.

Arnold: Ah, 'tension of mind' and 'self denial'—how well you express it, my dear Maine. They are assuredly the qualities most needed for effective government; but they are also just the qualities no longer found in our upper classes. Who can read the history of the flowering time of the English aristocracy, the eighteenth century, and then look at that same aristocracy today, and not be struck, even appalled, at the change? Oh, I am not thinking of private and domestic virtues, of morality and decorum: perhaps in those respects there has been a change for the better. I am thinking rather of those public and conspicuous virtues that are needed to captivate and lead the people: lofty spirit, commanding character, exquisite culture. All that has gone. I would agree that relics of the past can still sometimes be found; surviving examples of noble manners and consummate culture, but they disappear, one by one, and no one of their kind takes their place.

Maine: You say 'no one of their kind takes their place'. But surely if the English nobleman has become a somewhat diminished creature on the political scene in recent decades, the English gentleman has come forward as never before. But it must seem strange that I should be saying this to you, of all people, Arnold, the son of that illustrious pedagogue, whose aim at Rugby was precisely this, was it not?—to train a class of gentlemen qualified to accede to the ruling class, to strengthen, and perhaps in some fields to supplant the ancient aristocracy in its task of governing the nation?

Morley: But what do we mean by a gentleman? Do we mean someone who is almost, but not quite a nobleman? Someone who sets out to follow the aristocratic model? Or do we mean the whole English middle class?—and that, after all, has its own view of life and its own way of life which is quite different from that of the aristocracy. For one thing, the middle class is still predominantly Puritan.

Arnold: Puritan, yes. Yet with all its faults, the middle class is still the best stuff of the country. Some have hated and persecuted it; many have derided it . . .

Maine: None more than yourself, Arnold. You have given the English middle classes the name of Philistines, traduced them for their lack of culture.

Arnold: All the same, I have always believed in them. They are not only the best stuff of the nation; they are also the best hope for the future. But if it is to succeed, the Puritan middle class must be transformed. And transformed in the direction of democracy. Of course, the middle class does not want to be told anything of the kind. After all its sermons, its victories, its care for conduct, its zeal for righteousness, the Puritan middle class does not like the idea of being changed. But human progress itself demands it.

Maine: Well, if it is progress you want, democratic institutions are the least likely to achieve it. A democratic government may try to sweep all before it in the first flush of its enthusiasm, but it soon settles down to doing nothing. It is simply untrue that democratic republics are given to progressive or reforming legislation. You are both scholars; you do not need to be told that the ancient republics hardly legislated at all. The Americans hedge themselves around in the same way. The Swiss are the most conservative people in Europe.

Morley: You might have said the Swiss *were* the most conservative people in Europe, Sir Henry. But they have been fighting civil wars on and off since the defeat of Napoleon; they have adopted three new constitutions, and although the latest seems reasonably stable, there is a continued tension between those who want a strong centralized government and those who want to preserve the autonomy of the cantons.

Maine: Yes, 'continual tension', you will notice between those who want to preserve the old democratic institutions and those who want to introduce progressive legislation. You make the point I was trying to bring home to Arnold. Democracy and reforming liberalism do not go together; they are in fact inimical to each other. The liberal reforming Swiss of the cities who want to have the benefits of a modern, civilized, industrialized society find themselves continually thwarted by their ancient democratic institutions; progress, in a word, is made impossible by democracy.

Morley: Ah, but you cite the particular, and to be frank, peculiar case of Switzerland.

Maine: It was Arnold who invited us to look at the case of Switzerland. Really, there is no pleasing you in the matter of examples, Morley.

Morley: All I wished to say was that Switzerland is unique in the modern world in having a tradition of primitive direct democracy. The democracy we look forward to in England would be something altogether different and more modern. The Swiss cantons are rather like the Greek city-states in their size—that is, in being so small; and in their methods, in having things like legislative assemblies of the entire male population, and a part-time civil service and a popular militia, and so forth. But *our* democracy would be a representative democracy: it would *have* to be, because our population is a thousand times greater than that of a Swiss canton or a Greek city-state. Some people think we are too large; but at least being a parliamentary democracy, we should have all the benefits of parliamentary institutions.

Maine: The fact that you have a large democracy rather than a small one would hardly be relevant to the point I was making. And that point was quite a simple one: the prejudices of the multitude are far more deep-rooted and irrational than those of an educated minority. The people do not like change. Oh, I dare say that by rabble-rousing and exhortation you could produce in the mind of the common man the impression that he wants a change. But when the agitation has settled down on the dregs, when the excitement has died away, when the subject has been thrashed out, when the new thing is before him in all its detail, the common man is sure to find that it disturbs his habits, his ideas, his fears, his interests; and so, in the long run, he votes 'no' to every proposal. It is only exceptional people who want change. All that has made England famous, and all that has made us wealthy, has been the work of minorities, often very small ones.

Arnold: Of course it has, Maine. Nobody would wish to say that it has not. But the days of these splendid minorities are over. I am full of admiration for the idea of aristocracy—for the idea of being ruled by what is finest and best. And I do not deny that a divided nation —that is, a nation divided by the most signal inequalities of rank and fortune—might be a happy nation; and to the eye of the imagination it looks perhaps more pleasing, more beautiful than a popular order, pushing, excited and presumptuous, jealous of fixed superiorities, and petulantly claiming to be as good as its betters. But, my dear Maine, a popular order of that old-fashioned stamp exists today only in imagination. It is not the real force with which society today has to reckon. The spirit of democracy is something very much nobler. You tell us, Maine, that the people are prejudiced. I suggest that it is the old ruling class which is prejudiced —with all its traditional antagonism towards ideas. The old ruling class sees the people as you do, Maine, as a multitude, a crowd, a mob. That is not how I see them; and it is not what they are. They the people; and the inmost impulse of their being is leading them to assert themselves as a people, to claim an equal share in the determination of their future.

Maine: Well, my dear Arnold, of course you are a poet; and despite all your experience of administration and public education, I suppose you are bound to go on seeing the world through a poet's eyes. So that when people complain with bitterness and envy about the privileges of others, all you can see in them are the stirrings of a noble passion for equality.

Arnold: That always seems such an unfair criticism, my dear Maine. Not about being a poet, I mean; but about the desire for equality being the product of a base and malignant envy.

Maine: It was certainly Edmund Burke's view, that those who demanded equality at the time of the French Revolution were animated rather by the desire to seize privileges for themselves than to abolish privilege as such. And events in France proved Burke right.

Arnold: Oh, no doubt there is a gross and vulgar spirit of envy in the hearts of many who cry for equality. But is that a growth from the parent stock of democracy, or merely an excrescence upon it? I believe it is the latter. But in any case, even if base and blameworthy passions do sometimes accompany the claim for equality, the vital impulse of democracy cannot itself be considered reprehensible, because it is part of the vital effort of nature itself; the effort of humanity to improve itself, to expand, to reach forward to a new and better life.

Maine: You will forgive me if I do not follow you in the manufacturing of generalities. All generalization is the product of abstraction; all abstraction consists of dropping out of sight of a certain number of particular facts, and constructing a formula which will embrace the remainder. Oh, I can see this art of generalization would be an invaluable technique for the democrat. The populace—and you will notice, my dear Arnold, that I use a word favoured by you in your own writings, since you are so averse to the word 'multitude' —the populace can easily be got to assent to general statements, clothed in striking language, but unverified and perhaps incapable of verification. In this way there can be formed a sort of sham or pretence of concurrent opinion. There has been a loose acquiescence in a vague proposition; and the people, whose voice is the voice of God, is assumed to have spoken. It appears to me that this levity of assent is one of the most ennervating of national habits of mind. It has already seriously enfeebled the French intellect. It is evidently eating into the mental fibre of the English race as well.

Morley: It seems to me, Sir Henry, that your objection to democracy is very much the same as that of Plato and Aristotle; that because most people are fools, government by the people is bound to be foolish government, if not a positively evil government.

Maine: We have the advantage over Plato and Aristotle of living at a much later time, and being able to draw on the experience of a much longer period of recorded history. As you suggest, I may not be saying anything they did not say; only I can offer more evidence to support it.

Morley: But you will also remember, Sir Henry, that there are certain arguments Aristotle finds—though Plato finds none—in favour of democracy. The people, he says, are not wise; but they do have a certain common sense which is very valuable in politics. They have not the skill to devise legislation, but they can judge the success of legislation which others devise. They have enough wits to make a sensible choice between alternatives. Then, the people have a certain common decency. They cannot be corrupted easily; and in any case there are too many of them to bribe!

Maine: Perhaps we are not at liberty to forget, my dear Morley, that there is more than one kind of corruption. It can be carried on by promising, or giving to expectant partisans, places paid for out of the public revenue; or it may consist in the more direct process of legislating away the property of one class, and transferring it to another. It is this last which is likely to be the corruption of democracy.

Arnold: I hardly imagine Plato would have objected to the legislating away of property. On the contrary, he clearly thought that property itself was a corrupting institution.

Maine: It has never been any intention of mine to defend Plato. Though I have a great admiration for Aristotle, and one of the most effective points that Aristotle makes against Plato is in showing the unnaturalness and absurdity of Plato's communistic attitude to property. However, they were both agreed, as Morley said, in their criticism of democracy. In fact, *all* the best Greek philosophers and historians were agreed in thinking that democracy was a bad system of government. They had the experience of Athens to draw on.

Morley: The difficulty with Athens, it seems to me, is that the only historians we have are just the ones who are hostile to democracy. There are no impartial witnesses for us to look to. But obviously most of the finest intellects of the fifth century must have been sympathetic to the system. And if nothing else, the cultural achievement of Athens under the democratic state was something unsurpassed in history. Besides, it is not enough to say that the best philosophers of the time thought democracy a bad system unless we consider what they thought was bad about it. One of the things that stuck in their throats was that democracy entailed equality. And they did not like equality. They complained that it 'distributed a kind of equality to the equal and the unequal alike'. But why should equality as such be objectionable? I'm not sure that I object to it. In fact, I must say that I'm extremely attracted to the idea of equality.

Arnold: And there, my dear Maine, we must recognize the voice of the future; the voice of hope and courage and aspiration. And why should we cast on it the scorn of the ageing? I think we should open our minds to the thought that the pressure for equality is a natural, instinctive demand of that same impulse which drives society as a whole? Here we have an ideal which no longer touches individuals and limited classes only; but which urges the whole mass of the community to develop itself with the utmost possible fullness and freedom.

Maine: Oh, my dear Arnold, nature, impulse, instinct, fullness, expansion! So many generalities make my head spin.

Arnold: But surely, even you, Maine, must agree that to live in a society of equals tends in general to make a man's spirits expand and his faculties work easily and actively. Living in a society of superiors may be occasionally a very good discipline, but in general it tends to tame a man's spirits, and the play of his faculties becomes less forceful and active. Can you deny that to be heavily over-shadowed, to be profoundly insignificant, has a depressing and benumbing effect on the character?

Maine: Yes, I do deny it. Being born in a humble place, among superiors, has repeatedly spurred men to make efforts to improve themselves, to work and strive to win a higher place in the world. If there were no higher places to reach, there would be no incentive to endeavour.

Arnold: Oh, I know that *some* individuals do react like that against the strongest impediments and owe their success to the efforts they are forced to make. But the question is not about exceptional individuals. It is about the common bulk of mankind, persons without extraordinary gifts or extraordinary energy, people who will always need encouragement and favourable circumstances to make the best of themselves. You will surely admit that for most people the spectacle of a condition of splendour, grandeur and culture which they cannot possibly reach has the effect of making them flag in spirit; and disposes them to sink back into their own condition.

Morley: Well, Tocqueville certainly thought so, Mr Arnold, even though he had so little love for democracy. He noticed that where there is inequality 'the lowly and poor feel themselves, as it were, overwhelmed by their own inferiority'.

Arnold: Tocqueville also thought there was such a thing as 'a manly and legitimate passion for equality' as he called it, 'something which makes men desire to be, *all of them*, in the enjoyment of power and consideration.'

Maine: As I said before, I am more interested in the facts that Tocqueville accumulated, as an observer of political societies, than in his speculations about the inner workings of men's souls.

Arnold: Let us look at the facts, then. Let us look at France. Can you deny that the very equality which you decry has had a remarkable effect on the common people there? It has hardly improved the upper classes of French society, but it has given to the lower classes, to the body of the common people a self-respect, an enlargement of spirit, a consciousness of counting for something in their country's actions. And this consciousness has raised them in the scale of humanity. The common people of France have come to be the soundest part of the French nation. They are more free from brutality and servility and they have more of what elsewhere distinguishes the cultured classes from the vulgar than the common people of any other country I know. In France, the landowner and the farm-worker can talk to each other; in England, a factory owner and a factory worker could not meet without constraint on either side.

Maine: My dear Arnold, I have as great a respect for the virtues of the common people of France as you have; and I rather fancy I have more respect than you have for the virtues of the common people of England. But these virtues are hardly what is relevant to the duties and responsibilities of government. Rousseau himself could see this. He praised the moral excellence of the common people. He even seems to have thought the common man might be entirely good. But he did not think the common man was entirely wise. The people, he said, always means well. But it does not judge well. He evidently had the gravest misgivings about the practical possibility of wise legislation in a democratic republic, hence his belief in the need for a law-giver. Rousseau has inspired a great deal of nonsense, and done a great deal of harm; but he was a penetrating thinker, and we do not always give him his due.

Morley: I am not surprised that Rousseau should command such respect from you, Sir Henry. I can see he is bound to have a special charm for people who dislike democracy, if only because he refines the concept of democracy to such a degree that it becomes absolutely unrealistic, an ideal which is manifestly unattainable. That is why I think it is so important to distinguish our modern English—or American—notion of parliamentary democracy from this metaphysical notion of Rousseau's. After all, Rousseau was not a political man. He was a philosopher, with a problem which has exercised the minds of philosophers for centuries:

namely, how can men be both free and at the same time subject to a political commonwealth. It is the theoretical question which interests him; and it is a theoretical answer that he gives. People call Rousseau romantic; but his method is almost excessively rationalistic. He says people can be free and at the same time members of a political commonwealth, only if they rule themselves, since to be free is to be subject to no one but oneself. This, Rousseau adds, excludes any kind of representative government, because nobody can really represent anyone else; and it also excludes majority government, because then the minority would not be ruling itself. In other words, what is excluded are all the institutions of modern democracy.

Maine: But that did not stop Robespierre and St-Just from trying to adapt Rousseau's teaching to the modern nation state. However, I will admit that they may not have read Rousseau as closely as you.

Arnold: I am not sure you are quite fair to Rousseau, my dear Morley. You seem to think that democracy is only a matter of revising our existing parliamentary institutions, of enlarging the voting register to bring everybody in. I rather feel that Rousseau goes nearer the heart of the matter when he says that people must be united by a common moral general will if they are to retain sovereignty over themselves.

Maine: At all events, Rousseau is not so unrealistic as you say, Morley. He had, in truth, a very clear idea of how to ensure that everyone was moved in the same direction by the same moral will. It was all to be done by—and why should we hesitate to pronounce the word?—by the *state*: the omnipotent, people's state—the state which enforces morality and equality, which makes laws for its subjects, ordaining what they shall drink and eat, and in what way they shall spend their earnings; the state, which can confiscate all the land of the community, and which may force us to work when other incentives to labour have disappeared. The omnipotent democracy is the King-Proprietor, the lord of all men's fortunes and persons. It is a formidable conception; and I can understand why you shrink from it. The one thing I do not understand is why you should say you would welcome democracy, when you resist what democracy entails.

Morley: But I deny that democracy does entail the alarming things you speak of. In England a workable democracy could be achieved without any great enlargement of the powers of the state. All that is needed is that the state should be radically reformed so as to become the instrument of the nation as a whole, and not the instrument of the property-owning classes. The Englishman is proverbially hostile to the state, and that instinct is a healthy one. The democratic spirit is just as opposed to the intrusions of the government as the liberal spirit is; in fact, one of the reasons why we ask for the extension of the suffrage is to put the executive in awe of the population as a whole.

Arnold: My dear Morley, you disappoint me; I had hoped for something less—how shall I say?—less conservatively liberal, less Whiggish and materialistic—from a champion of the new democracy. My own imagination kindles more to the vision of Rousseau. It strikes me that both you and Maine are too readily, too conventionally horrified by the very name of the state. Oh, I can understand why you feel as you do. The genius of the English race has shown itself in its individualism and self-reliance; and these merits are not at all conducive to democracy, which requires people to work collectively, and feel collectively rather than individually. But I believe the attitude of our countrymen is changing in spite of their individualism; they are becoming more and more sensible of the seductiveness of democratic ideas; and more attuned to the changes that the future will demand of them.

Maine: Well, at any rate Arnold, you and I are agreed that individualism and democracy do not go together.

Morley: And I disagree with both of you. I believe it is the very individualism of our countrymen which is leading them towards democracy. The average English working man is becoming aware of himself as a responsible person, with a mind of his own, and he is claiming the right to express it just as the property-owning classes claim the right to express theirs.

Maine: I dare say your average working man may *think* he is a responsible person, just as he thinks himself a knowledgeable person. But the important question is: is he?

Arnold: Of course the average man at present is not. The mass of people are still ignorant. But this is something that can be remedied. The people can be led; they can be educated. That is precisely where the state comes in. The state is one thing that can fill the moral void caused by the disappearance of the aristocracy. As I said just now, I can understand why so many people dislike the idea of the state. The aristocratic class has always been suspicious of a political executive, which has often been the tool of the King. The middle classes have always been suspicious of the state because the government has too often lent its machinery to the interests of the prelatical and Tory party. In the minds of the English middle-class, state-action—in social and domestic concerns at any rate—has become inextricably associated with the idea of Acts against Puritan Dissenters and Acts against Free Trade. Hating this kind of state action, the middle and lower classes have come to hate state action in general. Having no experience of a beneficent state-power, they have come to think that state-power as such is not to be trusted. But they must be made to realize that they have no need to fear the state, once they have made it their own.

Maine: My dear Arnold, you have already asked us to forsake the condition of Englishmen to embrace the condition of the French and the Swiss and the Americans; now it seems you would have us learn to venerate and worship the state, like the Prussians.

Arnold: Perhaps I ought not to expect that an enlarged and beneficent state would have much charm for you, my dear Maine. It could do nothing to better the condition of the upper classes. Its advantage is that it could do much, by institution and regulation, to better the fate of the middle and lower classes. The state can bestow broad collective benefits, and these things which are meant for the many could never be so requisite as those which are meant for the few. Perhaps I am appealing to a different range of values. To sympathize with what I am thinking of, one has to care about the common, ordinary mass of mankind. A beneficent state could redeem such people's lives from ignorance and poverty and inferiority; and give them a new dignity, though no more than that dignity to which their humanity entitles them.

Maine: Oh, I think I follow the thread of your argument, Arnold. If a democratic state is the people's state, the more power it has, the more power *they* have; the more dignity it has, the more dignity *they* have. You have only to add the grand paradoxical conclusion to the argument: that the more absolute the action of such a state, the more complete the liberty of the people.

Arnold: Paradoxical as you make it sound, Maine, what you are saying, in a sense, is true. A state need not be an instrument of oppression. It can become an ideal of right reason and right feeling; it can represent the best self of the nation; it can form a rallying point for the intelligence and the worthiest instincts of the community, a true bond of union.

Morley: I must confess, Mr Arnold, that I am positively alarmed by your exaltation of the state. But perhaps if you were to tell us the kind of things you think the state should actually do, the notion might not seem so appalling.

Arnold: The omission was deliberate. I was concerned with the idea; I wanted to keep that apart from the question of the way in which the world of facts is to adapt itself to the world of ideas. But I will mention one institution which I can hardly avoid mentioning, in view of my own profession; and that is the intervention of the state in public education. Nothing seems to me more urgent than that, both to prepare the way for democracy, and to make democracy work when it comes.

Maine: Have you any definite proposals?

Arnold: Yes, I think the state should set up national secondary schools on the model of the French *lycées*. You, Maine, have raised many objections to democracy, but only one of them seems to me at all compelling; and that is the point that the great body of Englishmen are not educated for democracy. The French *lycées* may not be as splendid as Eton and Harrow, or even perhaps Rugby, but they are very much better than any of the schools the middle and lower sections of the English public is at present able to enjoy. It is the *lycées* and the *lycées* alone, which have made the common people of France, as they are, so much more cultured than the common people of England. And what is so interesting about French culture is that it is a national culture; whereas the only culture we can boast of England—and God knows it is little enough—is class culture. A class culture and a democracy simply do not go together.

Morley: What you say, Mr Arnold, reminds me of what John Stuart Mill used to say; that he considered himself a democrat, only he insisted that the universally voting public should first be made a universally educated public.

Maine: Well, my dear Morley, you knew Mill better than I did; but I do not think you will find any warrant in his writings for thinking he would approve of Arnold's doctrine of a magnified state or share Arnold's views on equality. Indeed, Mill was very emphatic that the vote should be confined to taxpayers, because it was immoral, he said, that those who pay no taxes should dispose of other people's money. He was extremely critical, I remember, of American democracy precisely because it allowed such things to happen. There is a phrase of his where he says 'the people ought to be the masters, but they are masters who must employ servants more skilful than themselves'. And you will know the elaborate plans which set out to ensure that the ordinary people were to be prevented from meddling in legislation, which he wanted to confine to highly specialized bureaucrats. I remember another phrase of Mill's: the common people 'do not need political rights in order that they may govern, but in order that they may not be misgoverned'. If anybody thinking that, called himself a democrat, I can only say he did not know what the word 'democrat' means.

Morley: I don't think you are entirely fair to Mill, Sir Henry. It is true that he thought the vote should be confined to taxpayers, but he wanted the method of taxation reformed so that virtually all the adult population should become taxpayers, and thus potentially responsible citizens. And, like Mr Arnold, he proposed that the government should prepare the way for universal suffrage by universal education. He was critical of the working classes as he found them; but he believed that an educated proletariat would be a very different proletariat from the one he knew. In any case, Sir Henry, he believed, as you do not, that democracy was coming; and that we had to prepare for it.

Maine: All I can say, Morley, is that I wish Mill were still alive and here this evening. I should like to hear what he would have to say to all this talk about equality. He was rather contemptuous, I remember, of people who ranked equality higher than liberty. Indeed I have a suspicion, my dear Arnold, that he might have persuaded you that you do not really believe in equality at all, any more than he did. Oh, I am ready to believe you cannot endure existing inequalities. But what you are groping towards all the time is not, I suspect, equality, but another set of inequalities: a hierarchy based on intelligence and drive rather than one based on family and rank. The 'beneficent state' you talk of, if it is anything other than a pure Hegelian abstraction, must be a bureaucratic state of the kind Mill envisaged: a state controlled by an *élite*, which would know what was best for the people, and give them what was good for them. But at least in Mill's proposals, the state is elaborately circumscribed in its functions and its powers; checked, so to speak, by Mill's passion for individual liberty. But you, my dear Arnold, with your zeal for collectivism, you place no limitations on the state whatever.

Arnold: My dear Maine, it seems to me that you know too much about what states have been, and not enough about what states could be. The state could become the best self of the nation; all that is needed is the will to make it so. Much depends on the middle classes. If they will not seek the alliance of the state for their own elevation, if they persist in their jealousy of all governmental action, if they go on exaggerating their spirit of individualism, then there is a real danger of anarchy.

Morley: You spoke of the middle class needing to transform itself, Mr Arnold. In what way do you think its members must change?

Arnold: They must rise above their present narrow, harsh, unintelligent, unattractive, spirit and culture. Otherwise they will never assimilate the masses; for the sympathies of the working classes at the present moment are actually wider and more liberal than those of the classes immediately above them. And these masses are eager to enter into possession of the world, to gain a more vivid sense of their own life and activity. But this very eagerness might well turn into something destructive if the middle classes prevent the state from becoming a powerful instrument of self-governing democracy.

Morley: So your idea is, Mr Arnold, that the middle class ought to reform itself, both for its own good, and to bring about a peaceful transition to democracy?

Arnold: Yes. A democracy needs leadership, as much as any other kind of society. Only it needs the leadership of intelligence; and that is to be found, for the most part, in the middle classes. But our English middle classes are not ready for leadership; they must broaden and deepen their culture if they are to fulfil their historic role.

Maine: So you have an image of an enlightened middle class, which the working classes will promptly recognize, admire, and seek to emulate and follow?

Arnold: If not promptly, then gradually. It depends on how quickly a new form of national education can be set up.

Maine: Well, Arnold, I have not had your long experience in the field of public education, but I have had some, in India; and I would never underestimate the things that education can do. But if we speak of national education, there is one question that must be answered before any other . . .

Morley: You mean the question of who is to pay for it?

Maine: No, I mean the question of what is to be taught.

Arnold: I would say that the young should be taught to know, and to love, the best that has been said and done.

Maine: Exactly. We must pass on to the young something of the wisdom of the past, and teach them the lessons of experience. And one of the lessons of experience, Arnold, is that England has achieved something rare and precious in the matter of government. Discriminating visitors, such as Montesquieu and Chateaubriand, even Voltaire himself, all remarked on what they found in England: a country where all men were free under the rule of law, where the powers of king and parliament were decently balanced, and where arbitrary arrest was a thing unheard of. And all this is something to marvel at; our ancestors achieved it with great difficulty; and our manifest duty is to preserve it. The whole art of politics lies, I should say, in a judicious combination of conservatism and reformism. It is just as much a matter of understanding what is good and worth keeping, as it is a matter of detecting what is wrong, and in need of correction. The idea of throwing away our whole English heritage for the sake of democracy, of abandoning a well-tried system of constitutional balances for an extreme form of popular sovereignty, is to my mind, a most foolish and mischievous proposal.

Morley: But I do not think the introduction of democracy, providing it were done by stages, and not too precipitately, need upset our system of constitutional balances. It is only a question of reforming things; it is not a revolutionary idea.

Arnold: Ah, my dear Morley, it will need more changes than you imagine. Democracy cannot live on the narrow liberalism of your Liberal Party, with its mean conception of *laissez faire*, and leave-us-to-ourselves. It must discover its own new social values.

Maine: Then you look for a great moral change in mankind?

Arnold: Democracy itself demands it.

Maine: But I hope at least you will be content to wait for democracy until that great moral change has taken place.

Arnold: There is a wise saying, my dear Maine, 'treat men as if they were better than they are, and they will become better than they are'.

Morley: You seem very hard on Liberal Party liberalism, as you call it, Mr Arnold. You must not forget the Liberal Party also has its radicalism, which is very much concerned with legislating in the interests of the poor and needy.

Arnold: Such niggling patronizing legislation is not enough. Democracy will call for something more like socialism.

Maine: And there I agree with you entirely, Arnold. If we have democracy, we shall certainly have socialism. The two certainly go together. But, for myself, I only pray that we have neither.

Morley: But I shall pray that we have democracy without socialism.

Arnold: And I shall pray that we have both.

Short Bibliography

SAVONAROLA

1. Works

Prediche e scritti. Ed. M. Ferrara. Florence, 1930.

Lettere. Ed. R. Ridolfi. Florence, 1933.

2. Commentaries

J. Schnitzer: *Savonarola.* London, 1924.

R. Ridolfi: *Studi Savonaroliani.* Florence, 1935.

P. Villari: *Girolamo Savonarola.* Trans. L. Villari. London, 1889.

H. Lucas, S. J.: *Girolamo Savonarola.* London, 1899.

R. R. Madden: *Life and Martyrdom of Savonarola.* London, 1853.

MACHIAVELLI

1. Works

Art of War. Trans. by P. Whitehorne. London, 1905.

Discourses. Trans. by L. J. Walker, S. J. 2 vols. London, 1950.

The Prince. Trans. by N. H. Thomson. Oxford, 1897.

History of Florence. Trans. by H. Morley. London, 1891.

2. Commentaries

E. Cassirer: *The Myth of the State.* London.

P. Villari: *The Life and Times of Niccolo Machiavelli,* trans. L. Villari. London, 1892.

F. Meinecke: *Machiavellianism.* Trans. D. Scott. London, 1957.

L. Strauss: *Thoughts on Machiavelli.* Glencoe, 1958.

J. R. Hale: *Machiavelli and Renaissance Italy.* London, 1961.

F. Chabod: *Machiavelli and the Renaissance.* Trans. D. Moore. London, 1958.

D. E. Muir: *Machiavelli and his Times.* London, 1936.

C. Benoist: *Le Machiavélisme.* 3 vols. Paris, 1907–36.

J. H. Whitfield: *Machiavelli.* Oxford, 1947.

J. Morley: *Machiavelli.* London, 1884.

De Lamar Jensen (Ed.): *Machiavelli, cynic, patriot or social scientist?* Boston, 1960.

H. Butterfield: *The Statecraft of Machiavelli,* London, 1955.

A. H. Gilbert: *Machiavelli's 'Prince' and its Forerunners,* Durham, N.C., 1938.

LOCKE

1. Works

The Works. Ed. Bishop Law. 4 vols. London, 1777.

The Educational Writings. Ed. J. W. Adamson. Cambridge, 1912.

Treatise of Civil Government and a Letter Concerning Toleration. Ed. J. W. Gough. Oxford, 1946.

Two Treatises of Government. Ed. P. Laslett. Cambridge, 1960.

An Essay Concerning Human Understanding. Ed. A. C. Fraser. Oxford, 1894.

A Letter for Toleration. Ed. Mario Montuori. The Hague, 1963.

Essays on the Law of Nature. Ed. W. von Leyden. Oxford, 1954.

2. Commentaries

H. R. F. Bourne: *The Life of John Locke.* 2 vols. London, 1876.

J. Gibson: *Locke's Theory of Knowledge.* Cambridge, 1917.

S. Lamprecht: *The Moral and Political Philosophy of John Locke.* New York, 1918.

C. R. Morris: *Locke, Berkeley and Hume.* Oxford, 1931.

W. K. Jordan: *The Development of Religious Toleration in England.* London, 1932.

N. K. Smith: *John Locke.* Manchester, 1933.

G. Ryle: *John Locke: Tercentenary addresses.* Oxford, 1933.

R. I. Aaron: *John Locke.* Oxford, 1937.

H. McLachlan: *The Religious Opinions of Milton, Locke, and Newton.* Manchester, 1941.

J. W. Gough: *John Locke's Political Philosophy: Eight studies.* Oxford, 1954.

D. J. O'Connor: *John Locke.* Harmondsworth, 1952.

M. Cranston: *John Locke: A biography.* London, 1957.

R. H. Cox: *Locke on War and Peace.* Oxford, 1960.

C. B. Macpherson: *Possessive Individualism.* Oxford, 1963.

THE THIRD EARL OF SHAFTESBURY

1. Works

Characteristics. Ed. John M. Robertson. London, 1900.

Second Characteristics, or the Language of Form. Ed. B. Rand. Cambridge, 1914.

2. Commentaries

B. Rand: *The Life of Shaftesbury.* London, 1900.

T. Fowler: *Shaftesbury and Hutcheson*. London, 1882.
J. Hunt: *Religious Thought in England*. London, 1884.
J. Bonar: *Moral Sense*. London, 1930.

ROUSSEAU

1. *Works*

Oeuvres complètes. 3 vols. Ed. B. Gagnebin *et al*. Paris, 1959—.
Political Writings. Ed. F. M. Watkins. Edinburgh, 1953.
Political Writings. Ed. C. E. Vaughan. Cambridge, 1915.
The Social Contract. Trans. M. Cranston. Harmondsworth, 1968.
Correspondance génerale. Ed. T. Dufour and P. Plan. 20 vols. Paris, 1924–34.
Correspondance. Ed. R. A. Leigh (in progress). Geneva, 1960—.
Annals de la Société Jean-Jacques Rousseau. Geneva, 1905—.

2. *Commentaries.*

A. Cobban: *Rousseau and the Modern State*. London, 1964.
E. Cassirer: *The Question of J.-J. Rousseau*. Trans. P. Gay. New York, 1954.
F. C. Green: *J.-J. Rousseau*. Cambridge, 1955.
B. de Jouvenel: *Essai sur la politique de Rousseau*. Geneva, 1947.
C. W. Hendel: *J.-J. Rousseau, Moralist*. 2 vols. London, 1934.
G. May: *Rousseau par lui-même*. Paris, 1961.
J. Starobinski: *Jean-Jacques Rousseau*. Paris, 1957.
J. H. Broome: *Rousseau*. London, 1963.
E. H. Wright: *The Meaning of Rousseau*. Oxford, 1929.
R. Derathé: *Le rationalisme de Rousseau*. Paris, 1948.
R. Derathé: *Rousseau et la science politique de son temps*. Paris, 1950.
R. Masters: *Rousseau's Political Philosophy*. Princeton, 1968.

DIDEROT

1. *Works*

Oeuvres complètes. 20 vols. Paris, 1875–7.
Encyclopédie. 23 vols. Geneva, 1754–77.
Lettres à Sophie Volland. Ed. A. Babelon. Paris, 1930.
Correspondance inédite. Ed. A. Babelon. 2 vols. Paris, 1931.

2. *Commentaries*

A. M. Wilson: *Diderot*. London, 1957.

J. Proust: *Diderot et l'Encyclopédie*. Paris, 1962.

L. G. Crocker: *Diderot*. London, 1954.

C. Guyot: *Diderot par lui-même*. Paris, 1960.

Diderot Studies

J. Oestreicher: *La pensée politique et economique de Diderot*. Paris, 1936.

J. Thomas: *L'humanisme de Diderot*. Paris, 1938.

VOLTAIRE

1. Works

Oeuvres complètes. Ed. Louis Moland. Paris, 1877–85.

Notebooks. Ed. T. Besterman. 2 vols. Geneva, 1952.

Correspondance. Ed. T. Besterman. Geneva, 1953—.

2. Commentaries

G. Desnoiresterres: *Voltaire et la société française*. 8 vols. Paris, 1867–76.

P. Gay: *Voltaire's politics*. New York, 1959.

R. Naves: *Voltaire, l'homme et l'oeuvre*. Paris, 1942.

G. Brandes: *Voltaire*. New York, 1930.

R. Pomeau: *La réligion de Voltaire*. Paris, 1956.

J. Churton Collins: *Voltaire in England*. London, 1893.

N. Torrey: *Voltaire and the English Deists*. London, 1930.

P. Chaponière: *Voltaire chez les Calvinistes*. Paris, 1930.

F. Caussy: *Voltaire, seigneur de village*. Paris, 1912.

R. Charbonnaud: *Les idées économiques de Voltaire*. Paris, 1907.

HUME

1. Works

Essays, moral, political and literary. Ed. T. H. Green and T. H. Grose. 2 vols. London, 1912.

History of England. 10 vols. London, 1810–11.

Letters. Ed. J. Y. T. Greig. 2 vols. Oxford, 1932.

New Letters. Ed. R. Klibansky. Oxford, 1954.

Political Discourses. London, 1906.

Treatise of Human Nature. Ed. T. H. Green. London, 1874.

Writings on Economics. Ed. E. Rotwein. Edinburgh, 1955.

Ethical Writings. Ed. A. MacIntyre. New York, 1965.

2. *Commentaries*

N. K. Smith: *The Philosophy of David Hume*. London, 1941.

A.-L. Leroy: *David Hume*. London, 1930.

A. H. Basson: *David Hume*. Harmondsworth, 1958.

J. Y. T. Greig: *David Hume*. London, 1931.

S. R. Letwin: *The Pursuit of Certainty*. Cambridge, 1965.

R. Wollheim (Ed.) *Hume on Religion*. London, 1963.

J. A. Passmore: *Hume's Intentions*. Cambridge, 1952.

F. Zabeeh: *Hume: Precursor of Modern Empiricism*. Hague, 1960.

A. Flew: *Hume's Philosophy of Belief*. London, 1961.

E. C. Mossner: *The Life of David Hume*. Edinburgh, 1954.

D. G. C. MacNabb: *David Hume: His Theory of Knowledge and Morality*. London, 1955.

C. W. Hendel: *Studies in Hume*. Princeton, 1925.

F. M. Watkins, ed.: *Hume: Theory of Politics*. London, 1955.

BURKE

1. *Works*

Works. 4 vols. London, 1925–30.

Reflections on the Revolution in France. Ed. A. J. Grieve. London, 1955.

Correspondence. Ed. T. W. Copeland. 6 vols. Cambridge, 1958–67.

2. *Commentaries*

C. Parkin: *The Moral Basis of Burke's Political Thought*. Cambridge, 1956.

L. I. Bredvold and R. G. Ross: *The Philosophy of Edmund Burke*. London, 1960.

F. P. Canavan: *The Political Reason of Edmund Burke*. Durham, N.C., 1960.

P. J. Stanlis: *Edmund Burke and the Natural Law*. Ann Arbor, 1958.

A. Cobban: *Edmund Burke and the Revolt against the Eighteenth Century*. London, 1929.

C. B. Cone: *Burke and the Nature of Politics*. Lexington, 1957.

J. MacCunn: *The Political Philosophy of Burke*. London, 1913.

T. W. Copeland: *Edmund Burke*. London, 1950.

R. H. Murray: *Edmund Burke*. London, 1931.

B. Newman: *Edmund Burke*. London, 1927.

P. Magnus: *Edmund Burke*. London, 1939.

THOMAS PAINE

1. Works

Common Sense. London, 1776.
Additions to Common Sense. London, 1776.
The Age of Reason. Philadelphia, 1794.
Agrarian Justice. London, 1797.
Theological Works. London, 1819.
Dissertation on Government. London, 1795.
Rights of Man. Dublin, 1791.

2. Commentaries

W. T. Sherwin: *Memoirs of Thomas Paine.* London, 1819.
M. D. Conway: *Life of Paine.* 2 vols. London, 1893.
H. Pearson: *Tom Paine,* London, 1937.

MARY WOLLSTONECRAFT GODWIN

1. Works

The French Revolution. London, 1794.
Vindication of the Rights of Man. London, 1790.
Vindication of the Rights of Woman. London, 1792.
Posthumous Works. 4 vols. London, 1798.

2. Commentaries

William Godwin: *Memoirs of Mary Wollstonecraft Godwin.* London, 1798.
E. R. Pennell: *Mary Wollstonecraft Godwin.* London, 1885.
E. R. Clough: *Mary Wollstonecraft and the Rights of Women.* London, 1898.
G. R. S. Taylor: *Mary Wollstonecraft.* London, 1911.

MARX

1. Works

Capital. Trans. S. Moore and E. Aveling. London, 1949.
Critique of the Gotha Programme. Moscow, 1962.
The Eighteenth Brumaire. Trans. E. and C. Paul. London, 1926.
The Poverty of Philosophy. Moscow, 1956.
Selected Writings. Ed. T. B. Bottomore and M. Rubel. London, 1961.
Communist Manifesto. Ed. H. J. Laski. London, 1948.

The German Ideology. Ed. R. Pascal. London, 1938.

The Russian Menace. Ed. P. W. Blackstock. Glencoe, 1952.

Correspondence. Moscow, 1955.

2. Commentaries

J. P. Plamenatz: *German Marxism and Russian Communism*. London, 1954.

H. A. Acton: *The Illusion of the Epoch*. London, 1962.

I. Berlin: *Karl Marx*. London, 1949.

R. N. Carew-Hunt: *Marxism, Past and Present*. London, 1954.

A. D. Lindsay: *Karl Marx's 'Capital'*. London, 1947.

G. A. Wetter: *Dialectical Materialism*. London, 1958.

M. Raphael: *La théorie marxiste de la connaissance*. Paris, 1937.

G. Caire: *L'aliénation dans les oeuvres de jeunesse de Karl Marx*. Aix-en-Provence, 1957.

E. Fromm: *Marx's Concept of Man*. New York, 1963.

R. C. Tucker: *Philosophy and Myth in Karl Marx*. Cambridge, 1961.

G. Lichtheim: *Marxism*. London, 1961.

A. B. Ulam: *The Unfinished Revolution*. New York, 1960.

A. G. Meyer: *Marxism*. Ann Arbor, 1963.

A. G. Meyer: *Communism*. New York, 1961.

D. N. Jacobs, (ed.): *The new Communist Manifesto and related Documents*. London, 1960.

J. H. Jackson: *Marx, Proudhon, and European Socialism*. London, 1957.

MICHAEL BAKUNIN

1. Works

Oeuvres. 6 vols. Paris, 1895–1913.

Marxism, Freedom and the State. Trans. K. J. Kenafick. London, 1950.

L'organisation de l'Internationale. Geneva, 1914.

La théologie politique de Mazzini. Neuchâtel, 1871.

Writings. Ed. Guy Aldred. Indore City, 1947.

La Commune de Paris. Paris, 1899.

Correspondence. Ed. M. Dragomanoff. Paris, 1896.

2. Commentaries

H. Arvon: *Michel Bakounine*. Paris, 1966.

E. H. Carr: *Michael Bakunin*. London, 1937.

G. P. Maximoff, (ed.): *Political Philosophy of Bakunin*. Glencoe, Ill., 1953.

MILL

1. Works

A System of Logic. 2 vols. London, 1848.

Principles of Political Economy. 2 vols. Ed. J. M. Robson. Toronto, 1965.

On Liberty. Reprinted together with *Representative Government* by R. B. MacCullum, Oxford, 1946.

Dissertations and Discussions. 4 vols. London, 1859–75.

Considerations on Representative Government. London, 1861.

Utilitarianism. Ed. J. Plamenatz. Oxford, 1949.

An Examination of Sir William Hamilton's Philosophy. London, 1865.

The Subjection of Women. Ed. S. Coit. London, 1906.

Autobiography. Ed. Helen Taylor. London, 1873.

Chapters on Socialism. Ed. W. D. F. Bliss. New York, 1891.

The Spirit of the Age. Ed., with an introduction, by F. A. von Hayek. Chicago, 1942.

Essays on Culture and Society. Ed. Gertrude Himmelfarb. New York, 1963.

Essays on Literature and Society. Ed. J. B. Schneewind. New York and London, 1965.

Ethical Writings. Ed. J. B. Schneewind. New York and London, 1965.

The Earlier Letters of John Stuart Mill. Ed. Francis E. Mineka. 2 vols. Toronto, 1964.

Letters. Ed. H. S. R. Elliott. 2 vols. London, 1910.

2. Commentaries

A. Bain: *John Stuart Mill*. London, 1882.

M. St J. Packe: *The Life of John Stuart Mill*. London, 1954.

R. Borchardt: *The Life of John Stuart Mill*. London, 1957.

C. L. Street: *Individualism and Individuality in the Philosophy of John Stuart Mill*. Milwaukee, Wis., 1926.

E. Neff: *Carlyle and Mill*. New York, 1926.

E. Nagel, (ed.): *Mill's Philosophy of Scientific Method*. N.Y., 1950.

K. Britton: *John Stuart Mill*, Harmondsworth, 1953.

R. P. Anschutz: *The Philosophy of J. S. Mill*. Oxford, 1953.

J. C. Rees: *Mill and his Early Critics*. Leicester, 1956.

JAMES FITZJAMES STEPHEN

1. Works

Essays by a Barrister. London, 1862.

A General View of the Criminal Law of England. London, 1863.

Liberty, Equality, Fraternity. London, 1873.

A History of the Criminal Law of England. London, 1883.

Horae Sabbaticae. London, 1892.

2. Commentaries

Leslie Stephen: *Life of Sir James Fitzjames Stephen*. London, 1895.

SIR HENRY MAINE

1. Works

Ancient Law. London, 1861. (Ed. Sir F. Pollock, London, 1906.)

Village Communities in East and West. London, 1871.

Early History of Institutions. London, 1875.

Early Law and Custom. London, 1883.

Popular Government. London, 1885.

Lectures on International Law. (Ed. F. Harrison and Sir F. Pollock.) London, 1888.

2. Commentaries

J. W. Burrow: *Evolution and Society: A Study in Victorian Social Theory*. Cambridge, 1966.

Sir M. E. Grant Duff: *Sir Henry Maine: A brief memoir of his life, with selections from his Indian speeches and minutes, edited by Whitley Stokes*. London, 1892.

Sir W. S. Holdsworth: *Some Makers of English Law*. Cambridge, 1938.

J. B. Oldham: *Analysis of Maine's Ancient Law, with notes*. Oxford, 1913.

P. Pillai: *An Epitome of Maine's Ancient Law and Austin's Jurisprudence*. Madras, 1915.

Sir F. Pollock: *Introduction and Notes to Sir Henry Maine's Ancient Law*. London, 1906.

Sir E. Barker: *Political Thought in England, 1848–1914*. London, 1959.

J. Bowle: *Politics and Opinion in the 19th Century*. London, 1954.

C. Brinton: *English Political Thought in the 19th Century*. London, 1933, pp. 266–81.

W. Graham: *English Political Philosophy from Hobbes to Maine*. London, 1926.

B. Lippincott: *Victorian Critics of Democracy*. Minneapolis, 1938.

R. H. Murray: *English Social and Political Thinkers of the 19th Century*. Cambridge, 1929.

G. A. Feaver: *Sir Henry Maine, a biography*. London, 1968.

MATTHEW ARNOLD

1. Works

Complete Prose Works. Ed. R. H. Super. 3 vols. Ann Arbor, 1960–2.

Poems. Ed. K. Allott. London, 1965.

Popular Education in France. London, 1861.

A French Eton. London, 1864.

Schools and Universities on the Continent. London, 1868.

Essays in Criticism. London, 1865.

Culture and Anarchy. London, 1867.

Literature and Dogma. London, 1875.

Mixed Essays. London, 1879.

Discourses on America. London, 1885.

Irish Essays. London, 1882.

Letters of Matthew Arnold, 1848–1888. Ed. G. W. E. Russell. 2 vols. London, 1895.

Notebooks. Ed. H. F. Lowry. London, 1952.

2. Commentaries

J. M. Robertson: *Modern Humanists*. London, 1891.

A. Galton: *Two Essays on Matthew Arnold*. London, 1897.

G. Tillotson: *Matthew Arnold*. London, 1947.

JOHN MORLEY (VISCOUNT MORLEY OF BLACKBURN)

1. Works

Life of Gladstone. 3 vols. London, 1903.

Indian Speeches. London, 1909.

Edmund Burke. London, 1878.

Voltaire. London, 1872.

Rousseau. London, 1873.

On Compromise. London, 1874.

Diderot. London, 1878.

Notes on Politics and History. London, 1913.

Recollections. 2 vols. London, 1917.

Critical Miscellanies. 3 vols. London, 1886.

2. *Commentaries*

F. W. Hirst: *Early Life and Letters of John Morley.* London, 1927.

A. G. Gardiner: *Life of Sir William Harcourt.* 2 vols. London, 1923.